Moscow in World War II

In October 1941, as the Germans neared Moscow, people laid antitank obstacles and sandbag barricades along the city's streets.

Cathy Porter and Mark Jones

Moscow in World War II

Chatto & Windus · London

BOOKS BY CATHY PORTER

Fathers and Daughters
Alexandra Kollontai: A Biography
Blood and Laughter

Published in 1987 by
Chatto & Windus Ltd
40 William I V Street
London WC2N 4DF

British Library Cataloguing in Publication Data
Porter, Cathy
  Moscow in World War II.
  1. Moscow (R.S.F.S.R.) – History
  I. Title   II. Jones, Mark
  947'.3120842   DK601.2

ISBN 0-7011-3009-1

Designed by Alan Bartram
Maps drawn by John Flower

Photoset by Rowland Phototypesetting Ltd
Bury St Edmunds, Suffolk
Printed in Great Britain by
Redwood Burn Ltd,
Trowbridge, Wilts

Contents

Illustrations

All photographs used by courtesy of the Novosti Press Agency.

Europe in 1939.

FINLAND

NORWAY

SWEDEN

Lenin

ESTONIA

North Sea

DENMARK

LATVIA

Dvina

Baltic Sea

LITHUANIA

Memel

Kaunas

NETHERLANDS

EAST
PRUSSIA

PRUSSIA

Narew

Neman

BYELORUSS

BELGIUM

Rhine

Berlin □

Potsdam ●

Vistula

Bug

Warsaw □

Pripet Marsh

GERMANY

Oder

Terespol ●

POLAND

LUX

SUDETENLAND

□ Prague

Vistula

GALACIA

FRANCE

Nuremberg ●

CZECHOSLOVAKIA

CARPATHIANS

Munich ●

SLOVAKIA

Danube

SWITZERLAND

AUSTRIA

HUNGARY

ITALY

ROMANIA

Adriatic Sea

YUGOSLAVIA

Danube

BULGARIA

Volga

□MOSCOW

Oka

Dniepr

RUSSIA

Desna

Don

UKRAINE

Dniepr

DONBAS

Aksai

Volga

Don

Dniestr

Caspian Sea

CAUCASUS

Black Sea

| 0 miles | 200 |
| 0 kilometres | 300 |

The approach to Moscow.

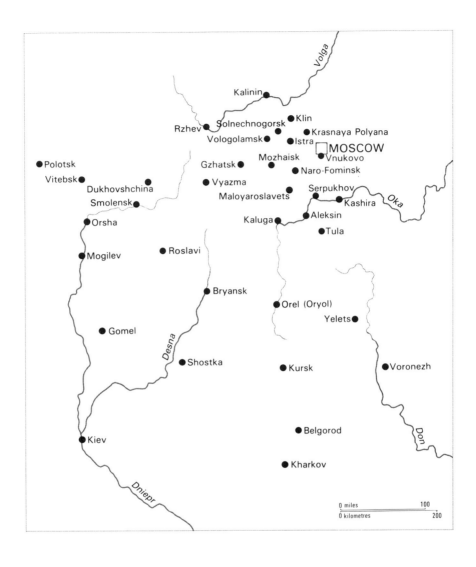

1

Background to War

Mankind has grown great through eternal struggle [said Hitler] and only in eternal peace does it perish. The stronger must dominate, and not sacrifice his own greatness by blending with the weak. Those who want to live must fight. Those who do not wish to fight, in this world of eternal struggle, do not deserve to live. Never yet has a state been founded by peaceful economic means . . . Only terror is capable of smashing terror . . .

Those who had so often been on the receiving end of violence believed readily in the inevitability of this competition to the death, in which only the fittest individuals and states could survive. This experience, and the social desperation it created, gave Hitler his following. For the human wreckage of German society, smashed by the economic hurricanes of the great depression, a society not yet reconciled to the traumatic defeat of 1918 and the ignominy of the Versailles peace treaty, Hitler's ersatz Darwinism had immense appeal.

Through the torchlit processions, the Nordic 'cultural' manifestations and the notorious *Parteitage*, Hitler canalised and expressed all the despair and impotent rage of his two great social constituencies: the dispossessed and downtrodden *Lumpenproletariat* and the once proud *Mittelstand*. These, the burgers, honest farmers and small businessmen who had been the backbone of Bismarck's Second Reich, wanted social and historical vengeance. For them, Germany had not lost the Great War, but had been stabbed in the back by what was, in Nazi demonology, an unholy alliance of Jewish-backed financial trusts and the 'men of November', the social democrats, who had sought an armistice.

Hitler promised to avenge the betrayal of the Fatherland. In the process, justice would also be served on those who had precipitated the country into the economic vortex of 1931, when more than two thirds of German businesses went bankrupt, and the prosperity and savings of the *Mittelstand* went up in smoke. To these people, Adolf Hitler, with his mad dream of *Lebensraum* in the east – and world domination as the payoff – represented a new kind of investment, as well as a new kind of psychological consolation in their present distress. The hard realities of Weimar bankruptcy continually contradicted the old imperial yearnings, and could be overcome only in the imagination, by acts of will whose ultimate rationale lay in the misty regions of Aryan mythology, by reference to the superior will of a master race.

For the German people, and particularly the young, Hitler's personal magnetism combined with a powerfully charismatic vision of Germany's future greatness, based on the solidarity and common purpose of the *Herren-volk* united in the service of one leader, one cause. Of Hitler's extraordinary fascination there is much testimony, beginning with Joseph Goebbels's damascene first encounter with the future Führer, as described in his diary:

I stand by him deeply shaken. He is the creative instrument of fate and Deity . . . He seems like a prophet of old. He spoils me like a child. He singles me out to walk with him, and speaks to me like a father to a son . . . Hitler gives me a bunch of flowers . . . red, red roses . . .

That was in 1925. Later, Goebbels did much to construct the hypnotic apparatus of mass persuasion which was to sweep the Nazis to power in 1933. The bigger the lie, the more persuasive, and no lie was greater than the Nazis' extraordinary fabrication of a new Teutonic mythology. Sitting around their camp fires while seconded on labour service, the *Hitlerjugend* heard the lays of the ancient heroes, and were enraptured. The *Nibelungen-lied* became a metaphor for Germany's predicament. The heroic Siegfried symbolised the Fatherland, and the evil Hagen its enemies, who had fallen on Germany as she lay prostrate on the ground like a wounded hero. Her neighbours had torn great pieces from her territory, like flesh from a living body, and the Nazis' phrase 'the bleeding frontiers' found a popular echo.

And all this time, the Nazis seemed to be visibly restoring Germany, so that Germans could once more lift up their heads. First the Saar was repossessed and foreign occupation forces at last expelled from German soil. Hitler cast aside the 'worthless League of Nations', swept away the remains of the 'Jew-ridden Weimar Republic' and planned to bring back to the national fold the Germans of Austria, the Sudeten and elsewhere. Unemployment fell, and prosperity came to the new Germany being visibly rebuilt from the ruins of the old.

This new Germany could boast a new architecture, solid and gigantic, like Nuremberg's vast *Parteitagsgelande*, overlooked by a granite cliff topped by the medieval Barbarossa castle. It was here that Hitler created his movement, and from here that the first storm-troopers, with shouts of '*Sieg Heil!*' and '*Hoch!*' spewed out onto the streets and narrow alleys. And it was here that Hitler spoke (first practising his gestures before angled mirrors) of his apocalyptic mission: 'Thus did I now believe that I must act in the sense of the Almighty Creator: by defending myself against the Jews I am doing the Lord's

Hitler meeting Youth.

work.' And not just the Jews: gypsies, Russians, Poles, in fact all the Slav peoples and any others deemed to be outside the mystic eugenic borders of Aryanism were to be 'defended against', for they were the polluters of mankind.

The rallies were merely the projection of power in its absence, at a time when the *Wehrmacht* could scarcely have beaten the army of Czechoslovakia. But it was the leaders, more than the led, who succumbed to the mesmeric theatricality of this monstrous edifice of illusion. They forgot that the whole thing was a dream, their armies stage armies, their leader no more a modern Alexander than any operatic major-domo. Hitler called himself 'the sleepwalker', and thought his footing the surer for trusting only his own instincts and intuitions.

The Nazis' popular legitimacy lay in their achievement of full employment and a return to at least a limited prosperity, and this entailed the militarisation of society and of the economy. By 1936, Germany's foreign-exchange reserves were more or less exhausted. By 1939, it was dependent on imports for more than half its raw materials. Only war booty by means of foreign conquest could make up the shortfall. But this too required the creation of a huge standing army, which would lead to the labour shortages which plagued Germany throughout the war. This would necessitate the import of slave labour from defeated countries, a process which in time would serve to alienate their populations (and also result in the economic dislocation of the conquered territories on such a scale that they quickly became liabilities rather than assets). This 'problem' was solved by making a virtue out of necessity: the purpose of the war, it transpired, was not, after all, to fuel the needs of Germany's war economy (absurd enough) but precisely to destroy the economies and eliminate the populations of conquered countries, at least in the east.

This insane policy was justified by Nazi doctrine which had held from the time of *Mein Kampf* (written in 1926) that Germany's racial destiny lay in the conquest, clearance and settlement of lands in the east. 'In speaking of new lands in Europe, we turn our gaze above all to Russia, as well as to its neighbouring and dependent countries . . . We have been chosen by fate to witness a disaster that will provide the weightiest proof of the racial theory . . .'

This was the doctrine of *Lebensraum*: new lands cleared by the German sword, to be tilled by the German plough, in which would be thus forged anew that mystic link between race and earth, *Blut und Boden*, which had driven Friedrich Barbarossa and his Teuton knights to eastern conquests more than 600 years before. Slavs were *Untermenschen*, too backward to be capable of culture, let alone the creation of a state. Recently, true, the semblance of a strong state had been created in Soviet Russia. But by whom? By the Jewish–Bolshevik bacillus, that bringer of chaos and darkness. Such a state, Hitler said, must and would collapse 'as soon as we kick the door'. Once this was uttered, no further discussion of the Soviet state's actual potential was necessary, or indeed possible, without incurring the suspicion of defeatism or treason. Now this crazy logic had somehow to be fleshed out into a strategy, a tactics, a practice; had to be reduced, as far as possible, to a self-acting, even bureaucratic, routine. Its contradictions must be borne, not by the Germans, but by its victims.

The rebirth of German economic power under Hitler's dynamic leadership conflicted with the country's post-Versailles political weakness, creating a strategic vacuum in central Europe. The French and British establishments patronised the new German leaders, with their silly mythology, their passion for uniforms and their boorish and provincial manners. They appeased Hitler's territorial demands, hypocritically claiming to be putting right a wrong done to Germany at Versailles, and they hoped to make Hitler an ally against Soviet Russia.

For Western fear and hatred of Russia was no less keen than in 1917, when Winston Churchill, then navy minister, had said of the Bolshevik Revolution, 'The baby must be strangled in its cradle!' It was Churchill who was the prime mover in the War of Intervention, in which the armies of fourteen countries had invaded Soviet Russia with the aim of complicating and prolonging its post-1917 civil war and bringing down the Bolsheviks. By 1920, the interventionist armies were driven out. Some 15 million Russians had died, factories had been smashed and mines flooded, but the capitalist powers had proved powerless against revolution in Russia, and only with great difficulty did they contain its spread to the rest of Europe.

Traditional Russian ambitions in Asia evolved under Bolshevism into something much more disagreeable – a call to the Indian masses to rise up against their colonial rulers. All this meant that the British could no longer afford to adopt America's policy of nonintervention (which permitted trade with both Hitler and his enemies), and the British and French now planned to channel German aggression away from themselves and towards Russia.

When Joachim von Ribbentrop arrived in London in 1937 as ambassador to the Court of St James, he enjoyed the patronage of many influential establishment figures, including staunch anti-Communists like Lord Halifax, the future British foreign secretary, the Astors, who owned the *Observer* newspaper, and the Marquis of Londonderry, with whom Ribbentrop was on first-name terms and discussed the 'Jewish problem'. He was also a frequent guest at the Astors' house at Cliveden, and it was at Cliveden that British policy towards central Europe developed, as applied by Neville Chamberlain when he became prime minister in May 1937.

The Cliveden set took the view that while the Soviet Union was the main danger to the British Empire, the immediate threat to international stability lay in the Treaty of Versailles, which had imposed such harsh conditions on defeated Germany and had created successor states to the Austro-German Empire which were too weak to serve as an effective *cordon sanitaire* around the Soviet Union. This was the historical conspectus that underlay the political programme of the Chamberlain government and gave the policy its name – appeasement. Hitler was to use the myopic anti-Communism of the Western leaders as a screen for his own grand design. First he would lay hands on the resources of the small countries of central and eastern Europe, in order to strengthen Germany's strategic positions and war machine. Afterwards, when high political quarters in London, Paris and Washington were expecting him to attack the USSR, the Nazis would turn on France. Only then, backed by the military and economic resources of western Europe, would Hitler proceed to his main objective – the conquest and colonisation of the USSR.

When Chamberlain came to power in May 1937, one of his first acts was to send Sir Nevile Henderson to Berlin, as 'our Nazi ambassador' as he soon came to be known, and charge him to draw up a 'Memorandum on British Policy towards Germany'. This called for a comprehensive Anglo-German agreement which would include the demarcation of spheres of influence, world markets, raw materials and colonial possessions. That autumn, Lord Halifax, now foreign secretary, arrived in Berlin and, at his first meeting with Hitler, congratulated the Führer for having turned Germany into a 'bulwark of the West against Bolshevism'.

Within a few months of Halifax's visit, a Nazi-engineered coup overthrew the Austrian government, with the call for union with the Fatherland. Austria appealed for help to Britain, a guarantor of its independence. The appeal went unanswered, and on 12 March, Austria was incorporated into the Reich.

On 22 April 1938, Hitler addressed a secret conference of Party and military staff. Since by Halifax's own account the West had already written off Czechoslovakia, Hitler said, Operation Green, the plan for its liquidation, could go ahead. In Britain, the Foreign Office drew up Plan Z, according to which the prime minister should wait until Nazi Germany had created a tense situation around Czechoslovakia, then 'save the peace' by personally negotiating its dismemberment with Hitler. After all, as Sir Alexander Cadogan, permanent under-secretary at the Foreign Office, wrote in his diary of this scenario for Munich, Czechoslovakia wasn't 'worth the spurs of a single British grenadier'.

Operation Green wasn't a success. The Czech government refused to be cowed by German troop movements on the borders or by Nazi agitation among German-speaking Czechs. Hitler couldn't count on the collapse of mutual assistance undertakings between Czechoslovakia, France and the Soviet Union. The Germans backed down.

But this evidence of the effectiveness of collective security arrangements didn't deter Chamberlain from betraying Czechoslovakia that September, when the crisis in Czech–German relations reached its head. On 15 September, following Hitler's brimstone speech to the Nuremberg Party rally, which seemed to presage quick action against the Czechs, Chamberlain set off, Plan Z in hand, for Hitler's Berghof estate, where he told the Führer, 'From the moment of my appointment as British Prime Minister I have been constantly occupied with the question of Anglo-German rapprochement.'

Hitler, who had hitherto confined himself to expressions of concern for the civil rights of the Czech Germans, announced that the real issue was the surrender of the Sudetenland to the Reich. Chamberlain didn't bat an eyelid. 'As a practical man, I have already thought of how to bring about the possible inclusion of the Sudeten Germans into the Third Reich,' he said, and went on to suggest the abrogation of Czechoslovakia's treaties with France and the USSR. Then, coming to the crux of his position, he asked Hitler:

If German apprehensions could be removed vis-à-vis Czechoslovakia, would it be possible to change the relationship between Czechoslovakia and Russia in such a way that, on the one hand, Czechoslovakia would be free of its obligations to Russia in the event of the latter being attacked, and on the other, Czechoslovakia, like Belgium, would be deprived of the possibility of aid from Russia or any other country?

Chamberlain sought to supply Hitler with a quasi-legal justification for the dismemberment of Czechoslovakia. But he was also seeking to liquidate its role as the linchpin of the European collective security system which connected the Soviet Union with France and, through France, Britain, in the containment of Hitler Germany. The meeting resulted in an Anglo-French statement, handed to the Czech government on 19 September 1938, which called for all Czech territories containing a majority of German-speaking citizens to be ceded to Germany.

The Czech government capitulated, but not at once. Czechoslovakia had a strong army, defensible borders, and repeated offers of Soviet military assistance – a solution which attracted mass support and large demonstrations outside the Soviet embassy in Prague. But the Beneš–Hodza government preferred to put its trust in Anglo-French guarantees of sovereignty, only delaying public acceptance of Hitler's terms, to increase leverage with the British and (given the popular mood of resistance to German demands) to give the Czech government time to manoeuvre the Soviet Union into a repudiation of its treaty commitments to Czechoslovakia.

The crisis dragged on, until Hitler gave Czechoslovakia a final ultimatum, threatening to invade on 1 October.

At this point, President Roosevelt intervened with an appeal to Hitler and

Prime Minister Beneš to 'settle their dispute peacefully', and suggested a conference of Britain, France, Germany, Italy and Czechoslovakia to resolve it. Since the Soviet Union – the only country still to stand by the Czechs – was not invited, there was little doubt how Roosevelt expected the 'dispute' to be resolved. The conference met on 29 September 1938. But the proposals finally adopted had already been worked out – not by the British government, but by Lady Astor's Cliveden set, during a dinner party, with the help of the US ambassador to London, Joseph Kennedy.

After the Munich conference had completed its business – the annulment of Czech sovereignty – Chamberlain asked Hitler for a private meeting to negotiate nonaggression pacts with Britain and France (their price for Czechoslovakia and a free hand for Germany in the east). Chamberlain emerged with his piece of paper, which expressed 'the desire of our two peoples never to go to war with one another again' and 'to continue our efforts to remove possible sources of difference'. A month later, the French also concluded a nonaggression pact with Hitler. The Anglo-French appeasers had thus achieved their old dream of a four-power pact with Fascist Italy and Germany, aimed at isolating the USSR and satisfying German territorial claims at its expense. 'The world can clearly see,' said *Pravda*, 'that behind the smokescreen of fine phrases about Chamberlain having saved the peace at Munich, an act has been committed, which by its shamelessness has surpassed all that has taken place since the first imperialist war.'

The Soviet Union had insistently made known its preparedness to stand by its treaty commitments to Czechoslovakia, and its general commitment to peace as a League of Nations member, and Maxim Litvinov had repeatedly spelled this out from the Geneva rostrum. But now, as the real implications of the Munich agreement began to sink in, the British and French governments and media had one final favour to make to Beneš, who had so obligingly held up the scenery while Hitler carried off the cast. And this was to clear him of the charge of selling out his own people. So, following Goebbels's dictum about big lies being more believable, they decided to foist the responsibility for Czechoslovakia's fate onto the Soviet Union. Soviet support had not been forthcoming, they said; there had been no alternative to capitulation.

Ivan Maisky, an old Bolshevik and from 1932 Soviet ambassador in London, protested in person to Lord Halifax, but the mud stuck, as Chamberlain intended it to, and the USSR was left in a dilemma for the future. The more urgently it criticised the West's appeasement of Hitler, the more its own perceived intransigence encouraged Hitler to solve bilateral problems by fighting rather than diplomacy (exactly as the British wished). Yet to be seen supporting the policy of appeasement, even by silence, was equally impossible. 'An epoch of rampant crude force and the mailed-fist policy is setting in,'

Right: Ivan Maisky (1882–1975), Soviet ambassador to the Court of St James 1932–43. Maisky was an old Bolshevik who'd seen the inside of British jails. He became a popular figure in wartime London.

wrote Maisky. 'A mood of diehard reaction reigns in Britain, and power is in the hands of the most conservative circles, who fear communism most of all . . .'

In France, still formally a Soviet ally, Soviet agents reported a private conversation between Georges Bonnet, the foreign minister, and some intimates in which he had said, 'Sacrifices in the East are inevitable. It is essential to give an outlet to German expansionism.'

In the Soviet Union, it was already a foregone conclusion that Hitler would attack Russia sooner or later, but that he would look for plunder elsewhere before doing so. 'A new imperialist war is already raging over a huge territory stretching from Shanghai to Gibraltar,' Stalin told the 18th Party Congress in Moscow in March 1939, 'involving 500 million people.' The Western powers were still in the grip of economic crisis. The 'aggressive countries', Germany, Italy (which had seized Morocco and Abyssinia) and Japan (which had attacked China), were not, but only because their economies were already on a war footing. If peace were preserved, these countries would soon find themselves on a 'downward path' as a result of the burden of arms spending. The new economic crisis was 'bound to lead, and is actually leading, to a further sharpening of the imperialist struggle'. It was no longer a question of competition in the markets, but of a 'new redivision of spheres of influence and colonies by military action'. The territorial ambitions of the Axis powers, Japan, Germany and Italy, attacked the foundations of the international settlement following the 1914–18 war, which had primarily benefited the victors – France, Britain and the USA, whose global interests were now threatened.

The Axis, founded on the Anti-Comintern Pact, claimed to be directed solely against Soviet Russia. Unfortunately, Stalin said in his speech, Western leaders were only too anxious to take Hitler's and Mussolini's anti-Soviet protestations at face value, and were 'conniving at the redivision of the world'. World war could easily be avoided if they took seriously the need to enter collective security arrangements with Russia. The fact that they hadn't was proof of their bad faith.

Stalin then uttered an ominous warning to the British, French and Americans, who, he said, recognising no human morality, had practised a policy of appeasement of German aggression. But 'the big and dangerous game started by the supporters of this policy of nonintervention may end in serious fiasco for them . . . And we won't pull their chestnuts out of the fire . . .' This was a clear indication to those hoping to channel German aggression towards the East that if all collective security arrangements failed, the USSR would not hesitate as a last resort to seek accommodation with Germany.

With Poland under increasing threat from Hitler's intensified territorial demands, Litvinov proposed renewing the Polish–Soviet pact of 1932. But the Polish 'Government of Colonels', fantasising their role as the West's outermost barrier against Asiatic communism, turned this suggestion down: any Soviet role in 'Europe' was 'needless'. Poland expected to emerge from a future war, in which Germany and the USSR would destroy each other, as Europe's dominant power. Five days later, on 15 March 1939, Hitler's tanks rolled into Prague – 'to clear out a nest of Bolsheviks' – and the world was able to see the fruits of appeasement.

Chamberlain now announced that since Slovakia had declared itself 'independent', the state whose borders Britain had guaranteed did not exist, so that His Majesty's Government could no longer be bound by this commitment. So great was the storm of outrage at this that Chamberlain had at last to renounce publicly his policy of appeasement, and Britain guaranteed unconditionally to enter any war in which Poland became embroiled. This, however, was either an unparalleled abdication of responsibility (giving the Polish rather than the British parliament the right to declare war on Britain's behalf) or an act of calculated cynicism, suggesting that Chamberlain wanted to encourage Polish intransigence in the face of German demands. Chamberlain thought a German attack on Poland would inevitably result in armed conflict

Stalin in the Kremlin, 1938.

spreading to the Soviet Union. Meanwhile Britain and France would honour their 'guarantees' with a *formal* declaration of hostilities, while settling in behind the Royal Navy and the Maginot line with a grandstand view of holocaust in the East. Thus the British anticipated – counted on – a 'phoney war'. They did not count on the possibility that Stalin would settle his diffcrences with Hitler at the last minute. But then neither Chamberlain nor the French premier, Daladier, read Stalin's speeches.

Chamberlain was careful *not* to guarantee Latvia, Estonia and Lithuania, the Soviet Union's small defenceless neighbouring states on the Baltic Sea, whose extreme right-wing governments and social tensions made them perfect targets for indirect Nazi aggression. Guarantees or no, the aim was the same: to channel German aggression eastwards. Chamberlain and his policy were only broken when Hitler made war a reality for him, and British troops had to swim for their lives from the beaches of Dunkirk.

Even as the panzers rolled into Prague, in March 1939, the Federation of British Industry had a delegation in Düsseldorf negotiating an agreement on the division of world markets with its German counterpart, and trade talks between Germany and Britain continued throughout the last spring and summer of peace.

By the end of March 1939, German troops had crossed Czechoslovakia and turned up at the southern borders of Poland, which was still refusing to allow Soviet troops on its territory. Events began to move swiftly. Germany renounced its nonaggression treaty with Poland and its 1935 naval treaty with England, and seized the Lithuanian port of Memel. On 7 April, Fascist Italy attacked and occupied Albania. Britain and France responded with 'guarantees' for Greece and Rumania.

It was then that Germany first put to Russia the idea of a trade pact – and posed the Soviet government with the greatest dilemma it had faced. The unpreparedness of the Soviet army and economy put a premium on its government's diplomatic efforts to avoid a showdown with Hitler Germany. Russia's assessment of German intentions and capabilities suggested anyway that Hitler wouldn't be in a position to attack the USSR before 1942. In fact there was much evidence to support this view. Unlike Hitler, the Soviet government didn't assume an early British capitulation. Stalin said as much on the eve of war, declaring that England, despite her weakness, would wage war 'craftily and stubbornly'.

Stalling Germany's overtures, the Soviet Union approached Britain and France and suggested the one self-evident step which, next to Germany and the USSR becoming allies, the Western powers most feared: the conclusion of a mutual-assistance pact, which in the event of war would have committed them to fighting alongside the Soviet Union from day one. Britain responded by suggesting that the USSR unilaterally promise:

In the event of any act of aggression against any European neighbour of the Soviet Union which resisted such an act, the assistance of the Soviet Union would be available, if desired, and would be afforded in such a manner as would be found most convenient.

Perhaps Downing Street had been encouraged by its success with the Poles into believing that the Russians too could be persuaded to tie a noose around their own necks. But this invitation to make war with Germany at London's behest was turned down.

On 30 March 1939, Germany and Italy rounded off their preparations for war with the formal signing of their 'Pact of Steel'. Two days later, the British cabinet met to discuss the ominous international situation, at which they agreed that their negotiations with Russia could still result in a more 'positive' policy: agreement with Germany. This remained the unchanged goal of British policy, despite Chamberlain's apparent conversion from the indulging of Nazi aggression.

But the machinations of his cabinet were coming under growing criticism, particularly from Winston Churchill – and Churchill deferred to none in his detestation for Soviet Russia and his romantic attachment to the British Empire. As he said to the House of Commons:

I have been quite unable to understand what is the objection to making the agreement with Russia . . . for a triple alliance between England, France and Russia, solely for the purpose of resisting aggression . . . Clearly Russia is not going to enter into agreements unless she is treated as an equal, and has confidence that the methods employed by the Allies would be such as would be likely to lead to success . . . Without an effective Eastern front, there can be no satisfactory defence of our interests in the West . . .

The Soviet government now proposed that the British speed up the start of talks by sending a senior figure with plenipotentiary powers, such as Lord Halifax, who after all had already visited Hitler and the Nazi leader Hermann Göring. But for the Moscow talks that spring, the British government could only find a middle-ranking civil servant called William Strang, with extremely limited powers to negotiate, who was told, 'The draft treaty should be as short and simple in its terms as possible . . . It is realised that this will leave loopholes in the text, and possibly lead to differences in its interpretation at a later date . . .'

Herbert von Dirksen, Reich ambassador to Britain, called the British tactic 'Zwillingspolitik' – twin-track diplomacy, whose primary object was to force Hitler to come to an agreement. It was clear, said the former British prime minister Lloyd George, that 'Chamberlain doesn't want any association with Russia'.

The Moscow talks between the three powers dominated the last months of peace. This was the lull before the storm, a period of intense diplomatic activity. Had the British and French used this time to pursue the creation of a framework for European security, peace could still have been assured.

On 29 June 1939, *Pravda* printed an article by Andrei Zhdanov, chairman of the Politburo Foreign Affairs Committee, complaining bitterly that of 75 days taken for the exchange of views, 16 had been spent by the Soviet government preparing its replies, and 59 had been lost because of delays and procrastination by the Western side.

This shows that, despite their protestations, they don't want a treaty with the USSR based on the principles of equality and reciprocity . . . They want us to play the part of a hired labourer. They don't want a real treaty, they want to talk about a treaty, and, gambling on the alleged intransigence of the Soviet Union for the benefit of public opinion in their own countries, make it easier for themselves to do a deal with the aggressors . . .

In fact, the British government regarded the Moscow talks as the sideshow to the secret negotiations that continued throughout that summer between Hitler and Chamberlain. On 22 July, the London papers were filled with a sensational story, which made headlines around the world, about an offer made by the British government to lend Germany £1000 million. Secretly, Chamberlain offered to abandon the policy of giving 'guarantees' to the eastern European countries and to acknowledge Germany's right to *Lebensraum* there

Hitler didn't respond directly to this latest British offer. His main concern now was that the Soviet Union might still manage to persuade the French and British to negotiate seriously for a mutual-assistance pact. His own overtures to the Soviet government for a nonaggression treaty became more insistent. These overtures were now strengthened by plentiful evidence from Nazi agents that the Allies were not taking the talks seriously, as well as by the tacit assurance of the leaders of France and Britain that he would not be hindered in his attack on Poland.

While the Western powers procrastinated in Moscow, the Polish–German crisis deepened, and it was obvious that a German attack was perhaps only weeks away.

From the start of the Anglo-French talks in Moscow, the Soviet government had set the condition that any political treaty should be supplemented with a military convention, and that both should come into force at the same time and constitute 'one single whole'. They now invited the French and British to send military missions to Moscow, in order to specify force levels, strategy and all the other factors involved in military cooperation between governments. This was just what the French and British were anxious to avoid.

The British put Admiral Drax at the head of their military mission. A semiretired naval officer known for his violently anti-Soviet views, he had no experience of operational planning and no powers to negotiate a treaty. His

French opposite number, General Doumenc, headed a mission that was equally incompetent and undistinguished. Both missions travelled to Russia together. They were supplied by the British Board of Trade with a slow old coastal steamer called the *City of Exeter*, which departed (after many delays) on 5 August and crawled around the coast of Europe at 13 knots while the military played table tennis to pass the time.

In order to avoid the talks taking a serious turn, the delegation's instructions included various draft treaties, hammered together out of general formulas, abstract principles and self-evident platitudes, which could be put to the Russians as material for protracted discussions. Apart from avoiding serious talks, their task was to conduct espionage and gather information about the calibre of Red Army leadership, the specifications of Soviet aviation fuel, Soviet naval policy in the Baltic and White seas, and so on. In the course of their voyage, the missions' senior members evolved a system of secret signals for use during talks. If delicate issues arose on which positions needed to be coordinated, or if someone became indiscreet or compromised, the other members were to scratch, rub or blow their noses.

The French and British intended to drag out the talks for months if need be, either until Hitler pressed them into reaching an agreement, or until Germany attacked Poland. In such a situation, with the *Wehrmacht* on the Soviet borders, the USSR would presumably have the greatest difficulty in remaining outside the conflict, whatever the state of its relations with the Western powers. But the Soviet side was not prepared to be fobbed off by the British and French tactics, and the Moscow talks broke down after a few days over the question of Soviet troop access across Polish or Rumanian territory to make contact with the enemy. At Soviet insistence, the talks were adjourned until the Franco-British missions could get an answer from their governments.

By now, the Soviet side was drawing the obvious conclusion from the French and British refusal to consider its proposals for a tripartite security treaty: that Britain and France wanted to do away with their Bolshevik enemies once and for all by turning Hitler against the Soviet Union in a war that would leave both Germany and Russia so weakened that London and Paris could step in at the last moment to make the peace on their own terms.

The refusal to put pressure on Poland over Soviet troops' right, in the event of war, to cross the Polish frontier to gain access to the front was only a part of Franco-British strategy, but it was a crucial one: to have taken seriously the question of access would have led at once to a discussion of the whole framework of military collaboration between the four countries, who would then be allies bound by common treaty commitments to take definite and prearranged steps in the event of aggression.

Meanwhile, in the course of Chamberlain's semi-secret talks with the Germans that summer, aimed at turning the nonaggression pact with Hitler into a thoroughgoing collaboration, Britain had already agreed to break off talks with the USSR should agreement with Germany be reached. 'Agreement with Germany is still Britain's dearest wish,' said the German ambassador Dirksen in August.

For Russia, such an outcome would have been catastrophic. Still engaged in the attempt to construct a framework for collective security, the Soviet Union would have suddenly found itself isolated, facing single-handed a united front of capitalist countries with Germany armed to the teeth as a strike force. As Churchill later pointed out:

A wholly different policy was required for the safety of Russia ... The Soviet Government was convinced by Munich and much else that neither Britain nor France would fight till they were attacked, and would not be much good then. The gathering storm was about to break. Russia must look after herself ...

Germany now made increasingly persistent overtures to the Soviet Union for a nonaggression pact, an option the Soviet government had until now rejected. On 17 August 1939, Britain's Washington ambassador got word from US intelligence sources that the Soviet Union was about to sign a treaty with Germany. This was what the Chamberlain government most feared, for it meant the collapse of their planned war between Germany and the USSR. The ambassador immediately sent a telegram to the Foreign Office. According to official versions of events, this did not arrive until 22 August, a delay of four days, during which the British had their last chance to save the peace. A successful outcome of the Moscow military mission would abort Hitler's approach to the Soviet government and thus prevent a German attack on Poland, which the German high command would agree to only in the certainty of Soviet nonintervention in Poland. Knowing this, the British could have sent Halifax to Moscow at once, to sign a mutual-assistance pact. This one act would have transformed Soviet–British relations and the chances for achieving collective security. In fact the telegram, it is now known, *was* delivered on time, and the British government was duly alerted to the imminent prospect of a Soviet–German pact. What Chamberlain actually did constitutes a shameful passage in British diplomacy, one which revealed the truth about British intentions.

Determined by any means to foment a war between the Soviet Union and Hitler Germany, Chamberlain sent an intelligence officer, Sydney Cotton, on a secret mission to Germany to try to persuade Göring to accompany him back to London to negotiate face to face with Chamberlain, who would make him a better offer than Stalin could. Göring refused to turn up. Hitler had nothing to fear from the British now, and was concerned only to ensure Soviet nonintervention in his forthcoming attack on Poland. He dispatched Ribbentrop to Moscow, bearing his personal request to Stalin for an agreement. The collapse of the Moscow military mission talks and the obviously imminent attack on Poland forced the Soviet hand.

On 24 August 1939, one week before war began, Germany and the Soviet Union signed their nonaggression treaty, as well as a ten-year commercial treaty, whereby the Soviet Union would supply Germany with raw materials in exchange for German goods. Not to sign would have been seen as evidence of aggressive Soviet intentions, and justification of a forestalling Nazi attack. To sign meant postponing the inevitable attack, cutting the anti-Soviet ground from under the Nazis' feet, and buying time for the Soviet Union to rearm and prepare for war. The Western press immediately claimed that Britain and France had been double-crossed by the USSR in their negotiations for an alliance.

On 1 September 1939, German units crossed the Polish border. Chamberlain and the French premier, Daladier, tried to involve Mussolini in 'mediations'. Within two days, public opinion had forced both governments to declare war on Germany. Two weeks later, the Polish state had ceased to exist, and its government was in exile in London, where they were told that Britain was not in a position to help Poland 'at the present time'. Six million Poles were to die in the war, a higher proportion of its population than any other country lost. This was the real consequence of the London Poles' refusal the previous year to make collective security arrangements with Russia.

At the start of the 'phoney war', Chamberlain broadcast a speech to the German people in which he talked of the perfidy of the Nazis and made a long list of their broken pledges. And here he revealed his attitude to Soviet Russia. 'Hitler has sworn to you for years that he is the enemy of Bolshevism. Now he is its ally. Can you wonder that his word isn't worth the paper it's written on?' This speech marked the start of an intense propaganda campaign in Britain, France and the US, whose purpose was to prepare public opinion, not for the sacrifices and burdens entailed by war, or for any real attempt to discharge British obligations to Poland and the other countries under Nazi occupation – but for a very different goal.

A chorus of voices now called for a war *against Bolshevism*, a creed, according to the *Daily Telegraph*, 'as immoral, as murderous, as antisocial as that of Hitler Germany'. The *Methodist Recorder* said, 'There should now be a war for a "new order" in Europe, a war in which France, Germany, Britain and perhaps Italy would fight side by side in comradeship, in defence of Christian civilisation.' The *Daily Sketch* editorialised, 'Behind the menace of Hitler and Hitlerism, who can say what other dangers, still more frightful and imperilling to civilisation, may be lurking?' The American journalist Walter Lippman wrote:

The question is not what are to be the boundaries of Germany or of Poland, but what shall be the boundaries of Europe against the expanding invasion of Russia and Imperial Bolshevism. The supreme issue of the war is whether Germany is to return to the society of Western nations as the defender of the West . . .

While the Hearst press, more downmarket, wrote:

The time is ripe for Western Europe to stop its senseless war, and prepare the barriers of European civilisation against invasion and destruction by the onrushing hordes of Asiatic Communism . . . The Communist wolfpacks are already circling, waiting for the kill . . .

But what really got them frothing was the war that broke out at the end of November – just weeks after the Germans had completed their brutal and bloody suppression of Poland – between Russia and Finland, a de facto ally of Hitler. This war arose out of a territorial dispute in which the USSR wanted to adjust the border between the two countries to make it possible in the event of war with Germany to defend northern Russia and the strategically crucial city of Leningrad.

Now Western tears poured forth for 'little Finland', the moribund League of Nations was dragooned into expelling the Soviet Union, and a greater uproar was created in Washington, Paris and London than had ever been heard over Spain, Abyssinia, Albania or any of the other states and peoples violated by the fascist powers over the past ten years. An association in people's minds between Nazi Germany and Soviet Russia was deliberately encouraged, and the Soviet Union was increasingly seen as the real enemy.

The *Daily Telegraph* said, 'The object of this war is not to destroy Germany . . . but to save her for Western civilisation against her own leadership, because what has to be destroyed is the "Bolshevik barbarian of the Eastern steppes".' President Roosevelt, according to Walter Lippman, believed that 'the war will continue, since Hitler and Stalin are as yet unprepared to meet the indispensable condition of peace-reparation for the wrongs done to Poland, Finland and Czechoslovakia.'

Before going into recess, the League of Nations secretariat, dominated by the French and British and by US proxies like Argentina (the US itself was not a member of the League), undertook to organise intervention against the USSR in consultation with nonmembers of the League. This could only mean the involvement, not just of the USA, but of the Axis powers – Italy, Germany and Japan. This fact, no less incredible for having been systematically written out of the historical record in the West, meant that the Western powers were *still* trying to create a common front of all the capitalist countries, democratic and fascist alike, to wage war on the world's only socialist state.

Even before the fall of France, in May 1940, Hitler was planning to attack the Soviet Union. Within his general conspectus of the reasons for war in the East, there proved room for considerable debate among the various Nazi ideologists and generals hoping to exploit the anticipated territorial gains in Russia in their own way and for their own purposes. One decision taken at an early stage was that Russia's occupied territory would not be administered by the army. At one level, this reflected the determination of the Gestapo chief, Himmler, that the full benefits of its exploitation should accrue as far as possible to his ss and its related bodies. But Himmler got his way chiefly because Hitler wanted the extermination of the civilian population, a task which could not be safely left to the army. Ultimately, however, all decisions taken about the conduct of the occupation administration were determined by the racist and nihilistic ambitions Hitler had first announced in *Mein Kampf*.

Attack in 1940 proved impossible. Apart from the logistical problems involved in turning his armies from the west European theatre, Hitler was obliged to shore up Italy and deal with the continued British presence in the Mediterranean basin, which meant diversionary forays into North Africa, Crete and Greece. Only by the time France signed an armistice with Germany, on 22 June 1940, could all plans be subordinated to the attack on the Soviet Union.

The great Soviet journalist Ilya Ehrenburg wrote:

France, Poland, Czechoslovakia and Yugoslavia – these were just snacks for the cannibal. He had long been wanting to get his teeth into Russia, and had thought out various methods of exterminating the Russian people. His advisers had presented him with various projects – like driving Russia into Asia, segregating Russian men from their womenfolk, so as to reduce the population to a minimum using Russians to labour outside their own country . . . Hitler wants to free Russia of the Russians.

In July 1940, General Halder, chief of the German general staff, summarising in his diary a meeting of the German Armed Forces Command, wrote, 'Russia must be liquidated. Spring 1941. The sooner Russia is smashed the better.'

The attack on Russia was set for May 1941, an ideal time to start operations, when the ground would have dried out from the spring rains and the *Wehrmacht* would have the whole summer to consolidate its gains.

By October 1940, Rumania and Hungary had been dealt with, and in December, Hitler signed his highly secret Directive 21, or Operation Barbarossa, which began, 'The German armed forces must be prepared to crush the

Soviet Union in a quick campaign before the end of the war with England.'

Operation Barbarossa required an *Ostheer*, or eastern army, of 121 divisions, with a reserve of 20–30 divisions. Of these, only 19 were panzer divisions. The vast bulk of the army would footslog into Russia, like Napoleon's *Grande Armée* before them. There was relatively little motorised transport, and most supplies would be hauled by more than a million horses.

The *Wehrmacht*'s planning assumed the existence of an intact and workable Soviet railway system. But the railways were not intact, and the condition of many of the roads, which were unmetalled, overturned the logistical assumptions on which the campaign rested. Germany had meagre supplies of oil and natural rubber. It was assumed that Soviet oilfields would be taken intact; they were not. Lorry tyres made of Buna, an artificial rubber, lasted for fewer miles in the rugged Soviet terrain than had been anticipated. Engines wore out more quickly than the plans allowed for. The German assault on the USSR was compromised by these difficulties right from the start.

The points of entry of the German thrusts across the Polish–Soviet border were separated by the vast and intractable Pripet Marshes, which created a 200-mile gap in the front. 'Once the battles north and south of these marshes have been fought,' concluded 'Barbarossa', 'the following objectives are to be aimed at: in the south, the early seizure of the Donets coal basin. In the north, the rapid gaining of Moscow.'

The campaign against Moscow, Operation Typhoon, was to be of prime importance. 'The capture of this city will represent a decisive success politically and economically, and will, moreover, mean the elimination of an important rail centre.'

Between 1939 and 1941, a vast programme of military spending got under way in the Soviet Union, involving 125 new Red Army divisions and a large number of new mechanised corps. Staffing them meant training new cadres of thousands of commanders and political instructors. And as the Red Army virtually doubled in size, its personnel requirements grew faster than the number of people graduating from the military educational establishments.

Between January and June 1941, the Soviet armed forces grew from 4.2 million to 5 million. This compared with 8.5 million German soldiers, plus over a million troops drawn from her satellites. The German high command underestimated, by more than half, the number of young men available for conscription into the Soviet armed forces. Since the basic demographic facts were not unknown, the only explanation for an error of this scale was an ideologically coloured view of Soviet potential. The vast mass of Soviet citizens were not just *Untermenschen*, they were illiterate, superstitious peasants who could not be expected to fight a modern war.

Nor, of course, could Soviet industry provide the necessary equipment. According to Hitler:

In terms of weapons, the Russian soldier is as inferior to us as the French. He has few modern field batteries, everything else is old, reconditioned material . . . The bulk of the Russian panzer force is poorly armoured. The Russian human material is inferior. The armies are leaderless . . .

There was little evidence to support these views, which the German generals accepted without question. In fact, the Soviet Union was already beginning to equip its armoured divisions with two tanks, the KV-1 and the T-34, which were superior to anything the Germans possessed. New types of aircraft, better than the existing German ones, were also being produced. And the Red Army was starting delivery of new advanced types of artillery and new and secret weapons, like the fearsome Katyusha rocket mortar.

If the strategic assumptions behind the *Blitzkrieg* were shaky, the operational preparations were not. However inadequate as a vehicle for Hitler's apocalyptic fantasies, the armies poised to invade the Soviet Union were nonetheless the most formidable ever assembled, and equipped with the products of the world's most advanced industrial economy, which, though still not dedicated to full war production, was at least temporarily cushioned by the spoils of previous easy victories. Germany's conquest of France, Belgium, Holland, Norway and Denmark in 1940 effectively doubled its fuel-oil reserves to 16 million tons. Steel production within the German empire amounted to 31 million tons, more than twice that of the USSR. Germany had also accumulated stockpiles of nonferrous metals and rubber, which, together with the oil reserves, were enough to sustain the *Wehrmacht* in its Russian campaign at least for 1941.

German aircraft production in 1939–41 averaged more than 10,000 planes a year. Although less than the British total, it enabled Germany to ensure air supremacy on the eastern front throughout 1941. In that year, more than 6000 tanks were produced, 7000 heavy artillery pieces, 8000 mortars and more than 3 million side arms. The German assault division was a walking arsenal whose submachine guns and automatic pistols alone made it almost impossible to resist for the Red Army infantrymen, who, by comparison, were still hideously ill-equipped.

The German high command assigned 152 divisions, including 19 panzer and 14 motorised divisions, to the Soviet front. These contained 3 million soldiers, with another 1.2 million in the Luftwaffe and 100,000 in the naval forces. The total amounted to 77 per cent of the *Wehrmacht*'s active strength. The satellite countries supplied a further 29 divisions (16 Finnish and 13 Rumanian), totalling 900,000 officers and men. All in all, 181 divisions and

16 brigades were massed along the Soviet frontiers, more than 6 million front-line and support troops, equipped with 50,000 field guns and mortars, over 3000 tanks and almost 5000 aircraft.

By early 1941, the Soviet embassy staff and underground anti-Nazi groups in Berlin were reading the signs – and feeding them back, in coded messages and at enormous risk to their lives, to the Kremlin. That spring, a German–Russian phrase book appeared in Germany in a huge edition, with Roman transliterations of phrases like 'Where's the collective farm chairman?' 'Are you a communist?' 'Put up your hands!' Hitler's gospel *Mein Kampf*, with its talk of *Lebensraum* giving mystical meaning to the Soviet invasion, was suddenly being quoted in all the German newspapers and prominently displayed in the bookshops. Large maps of Russia appeared in the streets. In Poland, the Soviet representative in Warsaw after the invasion spoke of railway lines filled with military trains, and towns swarming with *Wehrmacht* officers. And from the Germans came daily accusations (reported first in the reactionary American press) of 'unprecedented Soviet military build-ups' along the German borders. Meanwhile German troops daily and systematically violated Soviet airspace and borders.

By March 1941, it was widely rumoured in Berlin (and reported back to Moscow) that an attack was imminent, with three dates apparently under consideration: 6 April, 20 April and 22 June. Warnings of the attack were consistently disregarded in Moscow as coming from suspect sources.

By then, there was incontrovertible evidence of German intentions. Not only was this ignored, but the pace of front-line defensive preparations was actually slowed down, so anxious was the Soviet government to avoid a repetition of the circumstances that led to the First World War, when the inexorable timetable of Russian mobilisation created a 'provocation' which the Germans couldn't ignore, and which rendered further diplomacy futile. This time, Germany was not to be provoked, and the Soviet government conscientiously continued to fulfil the terms of its treaty with Germany, supplying millions of tons of grain, rye, mineral oil, cotton and chrome. (Hitler was not so conscientious, and ended up some 239 million marks in debt to Russia.)

The myth of Soviet invincibility and German weakness was a powerful one in Russia, promoted by countless stories and films. A particularly popular film showing in Moscow that year, called *If War Comes Tomorrow*, showed a German attempt to attack thwarted by an uprising of the German proletariat. Yet Russia was preparing for war nonetheless.

In February 1941, the Soviet government took urgent steps to improve the Red Army's combat-readiness, and approved a mobilisation plan which the Defence Commissariat carried out throughout that spring and early summer.

On 26 April, the military soviets of the Transbaikal and Far Eastern military districts were ordered to prepare two airborne brigades and three motorised and six infantry divisions, for dispatch to the western borders.

Throughout that spring and early summer, the German general quartermaster's branch undertook a vast and complex mobilisation of the resources needed to supply its army and to sustain it during an advance of at least 500 miles into the Soviet interior. More than 500,000 lorries were deployed, and over 17,000 trains, to ferry the troops to their jumping-off areas. The Luftwaffe hastily constructed a ramified network of communications facilities and front and rear airfields.

But once again the timetable for invasion slipped, when a popular uprising overthrew the Yugoslav government, a German ally, and panzer divisions already drawn up on the Polish–Soviet frontier had to be rushed over to retrieve the situation.

June 22 became the final deadline for 'Barbarossa'; further delay would make it physically impossible for the German army to achieve its objectives in Russia before the autumn rains prevented further movement. An inexorable momentum of converging timetables swept the *Wehrmacht* forward to B-day.

On May Day 1941, Hitler made a speech on his Balkan campaign, which omitted any reference to the Soviet Union. But tension in Russia was mounting, and May Day in Moscow that year was marked by a particularly impressive military parade, with motorised units, many new tanks and hundreds of planes, which, it was rumoured, were off to Minsk, Leningrad and the Polish border. On 4 May, Stalin addressed a gathering of young officers in Moscow and warned them to be prepared to 'deal with any surprises'. When, the following day, the Supreme Soviet promoted Stalin from Party secretary to head of government, and Molotov to deputy president, many in the Soviet Union interpreted the appointments as further preparations for war.

On 13 May, the 19th, 21st and 22nd Soviet armies were ordered to move up from the deep rear to positions along the western Dvina and the Dniepr, and the 16th Army was redeployed from Transbaikal to the Kiev military district. By the end of May, the Soviet embassy in Berlin had concluded that all practical preparations for 'Barbarossa' were complete, and nearly a million Soviet troops were called up for training from the reserve. This concentration of additional forces in the border districts, the formation of new units and the transfer to professional status of territorial units required more officers. So the defence commissar authorised the preschedule graduation of officer cadets from military schools.

The Soviet gamble that invasion could be forestalled came within a hair's breadth of success. But the consequences of failure were drastically worsened by the wishful thinking which entered the Soviet calculations in the final weeks and days of peace. Extra-large consignments of chrome, oil and grain were rushed over to Germany in those last weeks. And a communiqué of 14 June from TASS (Telegraphic Agency of the Soviet Union, the semi-official news service used by the Soviet government to make its views clear), just a week before the invasion, stated that rumours of German intentions to break off its treaty with the Soviet Union and attack were 'completely unfounded'.

On 12–15 June, the border districts were ordered to move closer to the state frontier all the divisions deployed in depth. Field command posts were installed on the northwestern, western and southwestern fronts, and the combat-readiness of the first-echelon divisions in the border districts was speeded up. But by now, the three vast armies of the *Ostheer* were moving into their final positions on the Soviet borders.

Army Group North, under Field Marshal Ritter, with its two armies, one panzer group and 1000 aircraft, stretched from eastern Prussia to Memel in Lithuania (now under Nazi occupation), and was set to annihilate Soviet forces in the Baltic area, and join with Army Group Centre in the destruction of Kronstadt and Leningrad.

Army Group South, under Field Marshal von Runstedt, its 57 divisions padded out with Rumanian and Hungarian forces, stretched between the Pripet Marshes and the Carpathians, and was to take over Galicia and the Ukraine, secure the Dniepr crossing and take Kiev.

But Army Group Centre, under colonel-generals Guderian and Hoth, with 50 divisions, including 15 panzer and motorised groups, was the most powerful of the three forces. Massed along the 250 miles from Romintener Heide to just south of Brest-Litovsk, and supported by the Second Air Fleet, with 1680 planes, it was set to encircle and destroy Red Army forces in Byelorussia, equipped to tackle the swamps and rivers that separated this from Smolensk, Polotsk and Gomel, and then let loose on Moscow.

Three colossal strikes by the three groups were thus to smash open the Soviet front at its most vulnerable points, before grinding down the Red Army in a series of vast concentric sweeps in its rear. The Germans could then go on to take Moscow and Leningrad, and finally come to rest on the Volga, on a line stretching from Astrakhan to Arkhangel. From there, armoured thrusts and long-range bombing raids could reduce at will the remaining Soviet industrial and population centres in the deep hinterland. That was the theory.

More than 10 million troops were drawn into action on both sides. Eight out of every ten German soldiers marching towards Russia didn't return: the *Ostheer* was a doomed army. Nonetheless the numbers fighting on the eastern front never fell below 10 million throughout the Soviet–German

The Germans, complete with maps and sunglasses, march into Russia.

war's 1418 days and nights. At its height, more than 14 million troops fought in this theatre, more than twice as many as in all the other front-line armies of all the combatant countries put together.

On the afternoon of 17 June 1941, Heinz Guderian arrived at a look-out post near the Western Bug, and through his binoculars watched the Soviet border guards walking up and down. It was his last inspection. By that evening, his *Panzergruppe II* was drawn up along the Warsaw–Moscow road facing the border fortress of Brest-Litovsk. 'Barbarossa' allowed him no more than four hours to seize the fortress, secure the river crossings and burst through Brest to the open Minsk road.

Brest was the door to Moscow which Hitler had said he would kick open. The last tank transporters hauled their burdens through endless encampments up to the starting line. Two hundred and fifty miles to the north, *Panzergruppe III* lay poised to plunge east and south through Soviet Lithuania, to meet up with Guderian's panzers at Minsk, 200 miles in the Soviet rear. In this vast encirclement the *Wehrmacht* meant to bag the bulk of the Red Army deployed on the Central Front. Timing was crucial; the

Germans meant at all costs to prevent a Soviet withdrawal to positions beyond the Dniepr where they could regroup and counterattack. Guderian was confident. The following day – 18 June – the Führer signed Directive No. 32 setting out strategic objectives to follow the destruction of Soviet Russia, which was to take no more than four months. Then the *Wehrmacht* would have new assignments in the Mediterranean, Africa and the Middle East. With the planned reduction of Great Britain and long-range bombing of the US mainland from bases in the Azores, Directive No. 32 took the Axis war for global domination to its logical conclusion.

Many living in Brest were refugees. Now September 1939 had returned to haunt them. People whose business took them over the border saw German troops massing with no attempt at concealment. Hoarding had begun; salt and matches suddenly disappeared from the shops. Yet the authorities continued to emphasise the prospects for peace, and Brest's marshalling yards were full of grain and iron-ore trains destined for Germany. But many frontier units were put on alert while airmen had their leave cancelled.

On the night of Thursday to Friday, 19–20 June 1941, while Moscow lay dreaming of summer holidays and Sunday excursions, 3 million Nazi troops lay hidden in the forests and fields of Russia. Three miles from the river Bug, troops from Army Group Centre moved into the Pratulin forest, and there, in a silence broken only by the croaking of frogs, they assembled to hear their officers read the Führer's Order of the Day:

160 Russian divisions are lined up on the frontiers of Germany and Rumania. A build-up is in progress which has no equal in world history. In Rumania, on the Prut, on the Danube, down to the Black Sea, German and Rumanian troops stand side by side – the greatest front in world history, destined to save the whole of European civilisation and culture . . . Have neither pity nor nerves – they are not needed in war. Stamp out whatever pity and compassion you may feel, and kill every Russian, every Soviet person. Do not hesitate – if there is an old man, a woman or a child before you – kill, and you will thereby save yourself, ensure a future for your family and cover yourself with eternal glory . . .

By the end of that day, Nazi troops were stretching along a 1000-mile front from the Baltic to the Black Sea.

Behind the panzer line on 21 June, the shortest night of the year, an army of traffic police were marshalling a vast mass of motorised and infantry units. More than a million troops had their movements choreographed with clockwork precision, keyed to a master assault timetable. As the minutes ticked away to B-hour a hush fell on the front; for the first time for weeks sentries on duty in Brest fortress saw no activity on the far bank of the Bug. But they captured two German soldiers dressed in special camouflage. These

were men of the *Brandenburger*, commando units which had already infiltrated behind Soviet lines to cut communications and destroy ammunition
dumps and supply depots.

Up and down the Western Bug, for many miles in each direction, Red Army
soldiers slept in flimsy tents, after a day spent digging the foundations of the
new border fortifications. Dozens of miles in the rear, other units were out on
summer manoeuvres. Further still to the east lay the fortified line of the 1939
frontier. Its deep defensive layers were dark and abandoned.

At 2am Berlin time (3.15 Moscow time) on 22 June, a goods train chugged
across the Koden bridge over the Bug – Russia's last wheat train to Hitler. The
train moved slowly on towards Terespol on the German side; the driver
waved.

In Brest marshalling yards German commandos emerged from concealment in gravel trains and began putting Soviet railwaymen to death; *Wehrmacht* engineers were already commandeering Soviet broad-gauge rolling
stock.

At 3am Germans approached the Soviet guards on the Bug bridges
shouting about 'important news', then shot them as they drew near.

As dawn came, spangling the horizon as far as the eye could see were whole
constellations of red and green stars, drifting slowly towards the Soviet
border. There was a growing rumble of aeroplane engines. As the rumble
turned to thunder hundreds of German heavy bombers passed overhead. Star
shells began to burst, followed at once by pinpoint artillery bombardment of
the frontier posts and, a mile or so down the road, the Brest fortress itself.

As it grew light the bombardment stopped and retreating border guards
appeared in the marshalling yards, closely followed by German motorcycle
troops and infantry. Stuka dive bombers could be seen making their run-ins,
sirens howling, then circling slowly through the smoke. Huge columns of
smoke rose from the station buildings, from the fortress and from fires all over
the town itself.

Within hours of the first artillery barrage across the river Bug, communications had been so seriously damaged that Moscow had lost touch with the
front, and the Soviet high command had little idea of the chaos piling up on
the borders. In Berlin, at 4am local time on 22 June 1941, Ribbentrop
summoned Dekanozov, the Soviet ambassador, to inform him that in view of
the Soviet government's constant frontier violations and invasion threats, at a
time when Germany was involved in a life-and-death struggle with Britain,
German troops had crossed the Russian frontier. The Soviet embassy lines
were cut, and staff tried to get a coded message back to Moscow. The message
never arrived, but reports of the invasion were now pouring into the Kremlin.
Yet, because the bulk of the Russian forces were deployed far behind the

frontiers, the seriousness of the German attack was at first taken there as merely another, larger-scale, border skirmish, and before ordering any military counteraction, Stalin demanded a meeting with the German ambassador, Schulenburg.

2

Moscow Prepares

It was not until 5.30am, Moscow time, on 22 June 1941, as Moscow Radio came on the air with its usual physical-fitness and children's programmes, that Stalin and Molotov received a visit from Ambassador Schulenburg, who informed them that Germany had attacked Russia.

By 6am, as Moscow News was broadcasting its regular reports on industry and agriculture, German troops were advancing over the frontiers, towns and bases were being bombed, airfields were littered with burning planes, and Russian dead were piling up in their thousands. Only at 7.15 did the Moscow high command meet in the Kremlin, and order 'active offensive operations against the enemy'.

On the morning of Sunday 22 June, the streets of Moscow were deserted. Workers of the Hammer and Sickle metallurgical factory had been up late the night before, celebrating the opening of their new sports club, which was to hold a cross-country race that day in the Izmailovskii Park. Many people had already set off on their summer holidays, or were out of town for the weekend, staying with relatives. Tyulenev, commander of the Moscow Military District, had left for his dacha on summer leave the night before.

Moscow slept, little dreaming of the gigantic battle now unfolding from east Prussia to the Ukraine. It promised to be a beautiful summer day. As the sun rose over the city, people switched on their radios to the usual Sunday-morning popular-music programme.

By eleven, Moscow's broad streets and boulevards were crowded, the shops were full (Sunday was the main shopping day; on Monday the shops were closed). Restaurants were packed. Cheerful folk music blasted out of the loudspeakers on street corners. Smartly dressed people were queuing for tickets outside Moscow's fourteen theatres, with an especially large queue for the Vakhtangovo's production of *Field Marshal Kutuzov*, a patriotic play about the 1812 war, which started with the words, 'War, gentlemen, is a parade.'

By now hundreds of Soviet frontier guards had been gunned down. Ammunition depots, airports and vehicle parks had been flattened by

German bombers. The roads were filled with death, destruction and disintegration. The situation on the frontiers was desperate.

In Moscow, a dazed sense of dread lurked beneath all the cheerful appearance of normality. 'It seemed everyone had been expecting war for a long time,' wrote Konstantin Simonov in his novel *The Living and the Dead*, published in 1958. 'And yet, at the last moment, it came as a bolt from the blue. It was apparently impossible to prepare oneself in advance for such a calamity.'

For a long time now, people had refused to accept the possibility of a German invasion. But when, at twelve o'clock, the folk music was abruptly interrupted and Molotov's halting voice came over the radio, they already knew its stark inevitability. 'Men and women, citizens of the Soviet Union,' he said. 'The Soviet government and its head, Comrade Stalin, have instructed me to make the following statement.'

People gathered silently around the loudspeakers, as Molotov continued, stammering slightly:

Today, at 4am, without making any claim on the Soviet Union and without any declaration of war, German troops attacked our frontiers at many points, bombing Zhitomir, Kiev, Sevastopol, Kaunas and other places. This unheard-of attack is an unparalleled act of perfidy in the history of civilised nations. The whole responsibility for this act of robbery falls not on the German workers, peasants or intellectuals, of whose sufferings we are fully aware, but on Germany's bloodthirsty rulers . . . The greatest discipline, organising ability and selflessness worthy of a Soviet patriot must now be demanded of everybody, to meet the needs of the Army, Navy and Airforce and to secure victory. The Government calls upon you, men and women of the Soviet Union, to rally around the glorious Bolshevik Party and its great leader, Comrade Stalin. Our cause is just. The enemy will be beaten. We shall be victorious!

Shortly after noon at the Vakhtangovo Theatre, the familiar hush was suddenly broken by a flustered voice over the loudspeaker, 'Colonel Astakhov to the lobby, please!' The actors on stage, momentarily thrown off their stride, went on with the play. In the dressing room, Yurii Ryzhakin and Vasilii Kuza, who were playing Mikhail Kutuzov and Sir Robert Wilson, were waiting for their cue at the end of the dialogue between Loriston and Napoleon. Another name was called, then another. Kuza and Ryzhakin, by now completely bemused, ran to the lobby, and from the pale face and trembling lips of the ticket woman, they realised something terrible had happened. 'War has started,' she whispered, barely audibly. 'The fascists have attacked!' Ryzhakin said:

I returned to the wings. Everyone knew. No one spoke. 'What now?' I asked Kuza. 'Act!' he said. 'Act well!' And Kutuzov's iron will, the Russian soldier's heroic

Noon, Sunday 22 June. People in a Moscow street listening to Foreign
Commissar Vyacheslav Molotov announcing over radio loudspeakers the
outbreak of war with Germany.

strength, Bagration's fiery speeches to the troops to sacrifice their lives, but not their country or their honour, rang out, both to the audience and to those already giving their lives in battle, like a direct response to the enemy.

So the mortal anguish of war had come, with its separations, its unremitting toil, its daily toll of dead and injured. Everything was suddenly new and menacing. The air was filled with rumours, confusion and fear.

By the end of the first day, with German troops already penetrating deep into Soviet territory, the catastrophe at the front was compounded by the chaos in the Defence Commissariat. One of the Red Army's few battle-tested leaders was Stalin's chief of staff, Marshal Georgii Zhukov, victor of Khalkin-Gol in the Soviet–Japanese border conflict of 1939. And it was Zhukov whom Stalin now sent to Kiev to find out what was going on, since 'our Front commanders don't have enough experience in leading troops in combat, and are somewhat lost'.

In Kiev, Zhukov was met by the Ukrainian Party's first secretary, Nikita Khrushchev, who could tell him little, but advised him to proceed by car, rather than risk flying. Consumed with anxiety, Zhukov rang Vatutin, his deputy at the high command in Moscow, who could say only that 'despite energetic efforts' they had still extracted no information from 'the headquarters of the fronts, armies and air forces' on either the scale of the losses or the depth of German penetration. 'We know only that our aviation on the Western Front has suffered very great losses' and that the high command had lost touch with Kuznetsov and Pavlov, commanders of the Northern and Western fronts, who 'have gone off somewhere, without reporting to the defence commissar . . .' Vatutin then told Zhukov that despite all this, Stalin had called for an immediate counteroffensive and wanted Zhukov's signature on the directive ordering it. Stunned, Zhukov protested at the idea of calling an attack rather than organising an orderly retreat, but after a heated discussion, he agreed.

Nonetheless the Red Army was in no condition to fight the Germans then or for many weeks to come, and those first months were an unmitigated disaster for Russia. Within three weeks, the Germans had seized Byelorussia and the Ukraine; the Red Army was routed, the Red Airforce incapacitated. In three months, the Germans had seized territory greater than that of France. Towns and villages were blown up, set on fire and razed to the ground, with special attention given to the destruction of schools, hospitals, churches, museums and other monuments of Russian history and culture. Nazi policy was to wipe even Leningrad off the face of the earth. German soldiers fired revolvers at portraits of Pushkin. Tolstoy's and Tchaikovsky's estates, near

Moscow, were vandalised, as were those of Chekhov, Korolenko, Rimsky-Korsakov and Gogol. And all these were no mere casual excesses, but part of Nazi policy aimed at the systematic destruction of Russia's past and civilisation.

Hitler wanted, for a start, the 'liquidation of the Jewish–Bolshevik intelligentsia' as well as 'Bolshevik commissars and bosses'. He seriously expected the cooperation of Russia's citizens in the process, and Russian-language leaflets were printed calling on people to identify, or themselves kill, not merely Communist Party functionaries, nor just rank-and-file Party members, but even members of the Komsomol, the Young Communist League.

'It will be a war of extermination,' said Hitler. 'In the east, cruelty is a boon.' 'I am not interested in the slightest if 10,000 Russian females die digging an anti-tank ditch for us,' said Himmler to his ss troops in Poznan, 'provided the ditch is dug.' 'The correctness of our race theory is proved by its application to Russia,' said Baron Rosenberg, Administrator of the Eastern Territories and Kaiser of Russia. 'The existence of Russia constitutes a mortal danger to the Nordic, that is the German, race. It is necessary to keep in check a people who have been corrupted by Tolstoy.'

The practice of the *Untermensch* doctrine was spelled out in a mass of directives, orders and instructions to the troops. There was the Commissar Order, whereby any commissar, communist or Jew (or anyone else) was to be shot on the spot without trial. Another directive, signed by Field Marshal Wilhelm Keitel, absolved officers and men of the *Wehrmacht* of responsibility for crimes committed on Soviet territory, demanded that no mercy be shown to Soviet citizens, and called for the shooting without trial of all who offered the slightest resistance or sympathised with the partisans. Mass public executions were held in countless towns and villages. Special ss teams hunted out Jews, communists and other species of *Untermenschen*, and over 3 million Russians, Byelorussians and Ukrainians were rounded up for deportation to Germany, where they worked as slaves. One slogan summarised the entire campaign: 'The Russians must die so that we can live.'

Russia's war against Germany was a total war, a war that made all previous battles in World War II seem like dress rehearsals. It was also, more than any other, a people's war, a war of total social mobilisation, known in the Soviet Union then and now as the Great Patriotic War. Popular Western histories which say that the war was won because of Russia's limitless manpower resources ignore the fact that these resources had to be mobilised and then organised into large well-equipped armies – providing for which also required a massive mobilisation of the home front. In planning 'Barbarossa', Hitler's general staff were well aware of basic facts like the size of the population and its available manpower reserves. But they based their strategy on the assumption that much of this population consisted of ignorant and apathetic peasants. Soviet power, they reasoned, was largely a myth. The Communist Party would never succeed in organising these vast masses, let alone in inspiring them to the degree of collective heroism and self-sacrifice needed to win the war.

As Army Group Centre hurtled forward, with eyes fixed on Moscow, the June mailbag of one s s regiment revealed high hopes for a victory parade on Red Square. For these ardent young Nazis, reared on fascism and knowing no other life than slaughter and war, the destruction of Moscow, the economic and political nerve centre of the Soviet Union, meant the destruction not only of Germany's traditional enemy and Nazism's bitterest ideological foe, but of Moscow's international prestige as the symbolic heart of the international workers' movement. And Moscow, they were convinced, lay wide open to them. 'It will all be over very soon,' wrote Company Commander Herman Kurzberg to his mother. 'I hope to be in Moscow before long,' wrote C. C. Wegner. 'We'll settle Russia just as quickly as we settled the other countries,' wrote s s man Schweitzer. 'We've just reckoned that we'll be in Moscow in a week's time!' wrote s s man Mukker.

But Moscow did not submit to its sentence of doom.

Hitler is bringing us degradation and the yoke of serfdom, and that means life as animals, life on all fours [wrote Ilya Ehrenburg]. We're being invaded by savages of the s s, Pomeranian landowners, beer-bloated sergeant-majors, executioners whose methods are the last word in torture . . . They want their thugs to control our towns, where they'll shout in German at the crossroads.

People enlisted or were conscripted in their thousands into the army, and they worked as never before, often to the point of utter exhaustion and in conditions of near slavery. Yet they did so voluntarily, and this gave it a dignity that transcended suffering. They had no choice – the alternative was slavery to the Nazis.

When Roman Karmen, a young cameraman on the Moscow Film Chronicle, heard Molotov's broadcast on the street, he made straight for the three-storey house on Bryansk Street which housed the Chronicle's studios. Cameramen and journalists who were out of town caught the next train back, and within a couple of hours the entire Moscow Chronicle newsreel team had divided into front-line groups.

The Red Army Ensemble met and applied to the Defence Commissariat to be sent to the front, 'to inspire our soldiers to victory'. The composer A. V. Aleksandrov, on hearing the declaration of war, immediately sat down and wrote for them 'in one great burst' the music for a new song, 'Sacred War', to words by the poet V. I. Lebedev-Kumach. 'I was never a military person,' said Aleksandrov, 'yet here I had a mighty weapon in my hands – song. And that song could wound the enemy as much as any weapon.'

That Sunday morning, as people recoiled from the shock, they flocked to their factories and workplaces and there, amid a score of questions, discussed how best to put the capital onto a war footing and prepare for the inevitable air raids.

The president of the Moscow City Soviet, V. P. Pronin, hastily called district soviet members to his office in the red Soviet Building on Manezh Square. During their long and often emotional meeting, scores of questions were asked, as soviet members discussed the practical everyday implications of the threat to Moscow, and tried to work out precisely how people should behave in air raids. Members of the Soviet executive committee were allotted their tasks: Korolev, the transport chief, was to guarantee uninterrupted transport during raids; Yasnov, the construction chief, was to draw up reconstruction plans for bomb-damaged buildings; Fadin was responsible for food supply, and Mairov for bomb shelters.

Yulia Polyakova and N. V. Popova, soviet presidents of the October and Krasnopresnya districts, where there were no underground stations, were especially worried about the safety of children in raids (they both had young children), and proposed evacuating from Moscow as many children as possible and all the capital's children's homes.

A. S. Shcherbakov, chairman of the Moscow City Party (and a member of the Politburo), called a meeting of all the capital's leading Party workers. Although it wasn't yet clear exactly where the enemy was, he said, the situation was desperately serious. All available manpower must be mobilised into the Red Army, all workers at strategically important factories must consider themselves mobilised and attached to their workplaces, and children must be put into creches so their parents could work. District parties were to form defence committees, responsible for checking the general command's orders for defence supplies, and Party offices were to be turned into army mobilisation depots.

The soviet presidents went back to their town halls, which over the next three years they would rarely leave. Now, in addition to their usual responsibilities for local housing, education and transport, members of the local soviets had to work out plans for evacuation, local air-raid precautions and anti-aircraft defences, to prepare underground stations and all available basements and cellars as shelters, and build new ones where necessary. All local ARP wardens were put on readiness to fight chemical and incendiary bombs and give first aid.

At the factories, Party workers called mass recruitment meetings, at which thousands of workers enlisted on the spot, while those remaining vowed to fill their places.

'We know our cause is just. The enemy will be beaten!' said workers at the Moscow Car factory. 'To achieve this, each of us will work unstintingly at our post, prepared at any moment to replace our workbench for a rifle, and to enter the ranks of the heroic Red Army!'

'We'll give our beloved motherland tons of metal over the plan,' said workers at the Hammer and Sickle factory, 'so as to help our splendid soldiers defeat the enemy!'

'We promise to work as selflessly as the army, to feed and clothe our beloved army,' promised the mainly female work force at the Trekhgorka cotton mill. 'We promise the Party and government to work faster, to mobilise our energy and increase by 100 per cent our vigilance, so as to defeat the enemy.'

And although it was a Sunday, workers stayed on after meetings to work a whole shift for the front. From then on, Sunday was regarded as an ordinary working day.

At the end of that first terrible day, general-command officials visiting the border areas were aghast at what they saw, as Red Army officers struggled, amid raging fires and mounds of dead, to reorganise their depleted forces and distribute scanty food and ammunition supplies. In Moscow, couriers brought in the Foreign Ministry TASS bulletins from the telegraphic agencies with communiqués from the Soviet–German fronts. And as domestic radios were confiscated and replaced by loudspeakers in streets, dwellings and workplaces, people gathered around the large black trumpets, holding their breath for the majestic voice of the veteran broadcaster Yurii Levitan, reading the latest news of German encirclements.

As the world followed the titanic struggle unfolding all the way from the Barents to the Black Sea, many in the Western embassies in Moscow were openly declaring Russia's position to be hopeless, and giving the Germans two to eight weeks to bring the USSR to its knees. The British ambassador in Moscow, Sir Stafford Cripps, who was on the left wing of the Labour Party and supposedly a Soviet sympathiser, reported to the war cabinet, 'Russia cannot hold out against Germany for more than three or four weeks, by which time the enemy might be in Leningrad, Moscow or Kiev.' The chief of the British Imperial General Staff, John Dill, stated that the Germans would go through Russia 'like a hot knife through butter'. The US secretary for war, Henry Stimson, told President Roosevelt that the Germans would take 'a minimum of one month, and a possible maximum of three months' to quell the Red Army. It was this expectation of an early Soviet collapse that conditioned official British and American attitudes.

Yurii Levitan (born 1914), veteran radio broadcaster, whose powerful,
expressive voice read the daily war communiqués, Orders of the Day and
important political documents, as well as reporting on major events from Red
Square and the Kremlin.

A US State Department memorandum issued just the day before the
Germans invaded had dismissed any commitment to Russia other than
material support, since the US might later 'refuse to recognise a refugee Soviet
government, or cease to recognise the Soviet ambassador in Washington . . .
in case the Soviet Union should be defeated and the Soviet government
obliged to leave the country'. And although two days later the US government
was describing the Nazi invasion as 'fresh proof of Germany's ambition to
win world supremacy', any defence against which would 'redound to the
benefit of our own defence . . .', many American politicians did not disguise
their delight at the prospect of a mutually exhausting war between Germany
and the USSR. As Harry Truman, then a senator from Missouri, said, 'If we
see that Germany is winning we should help Russia, and if Russia is winning
we ought to help Germany, and that way we let them kill as many as possible.'

Though historians in the West tend nowadays to minimise the importance
of the eastern front, many at the time felt that events there would predeter-
mine the whole course and outcome of the Second World War, and as the
gigantic scale of the campaign was revealed, this conviction grew. After just
the first week of the war, even Alexander Cadogan at the Foreign Office was
writing in his diary that Russia was now 'the only hopeful sign'.

Nonetheless the idea that Britain, with its long history of anti-Sovietism and appeasement, should be an ally of Russia was still something few Russians dared dream of. So that on the evening of 22 June 1941, less than twenty-four hours after the German invasion, it was with a sense of utter astonishment that they heard Winston Churchill, architect of the War of Intervention against the Bolshevik revolution, make his historic broadcast to the Russian people, in which he denied that Britain was about to make a deal with Hitler and pledged British support for Russia.

'Nobody has been a more consistent opponent of communism than I in the last twenty-five years,' he began, 'and I will unsay no word I've spoken about it . . .' But, he said:

I see the Russian soldiers standing on the threshold of their native land . . . I see them guarding their homes where their wives and mothers pray – ah yes, for there are times when all pray – for the safety of their loved ones . . . I see the 10,000 Russian villages . . . where there are still primordial joys, where maidens laugh, and children play. I see advancing on all this in hideous onslaught, the Nazi war machine . . . I see the dull, drilled, docile brutish masses of the Hun soldiery plodding like a swarm of crawling locusts . . . [Hitler could not be allowed to destroy his enemies one by one, for] the Russian danger is our danger, and the danger of the United States . . . Let us learn the lessons already taught by such cruel experiences. Let us redouble our exertions, and strike with united strength . . .

So at least it was clear from the start that the British would not be making deals with Hitler. Although Churchill was not proposing a political or military alliance, and at this stage was limiting himself to the offer of munitions, hardware and technical support to the Soviet Union, his speech made an immense impression, and that first day ended in a note of new and unexpected hope. But Moscow was still preparing for the worst.

By the end of that day, thousands of Muscovites, most of them with no previous fighting experience, had enlisted into the Red Army; after receiving a basic military training in drilling, marching and shooting, they would set straight off for the fronts. About a quarter of those enlisting were from Moscow's Komsomol organisation, which had become a legend in the 1930s for its labours on building the Moscow underground, and over the next few months 100,000 Komsomol members joined the ranks of the army.

Women, fired by memories of those who had fought twenty years before to defend the Bolshevik revolution, enlisted in their thousands. More traditional soldiers were initially uncomfortable about working and fighting with women. ('We don't need women to fight the Germans for us, we can do that ourselves,' one officer told the British journalist Charlotte Haldane.) But they had no choice. By the end of the year, some 8 per cent of all those in the army

Muscovites enrolling in the Red Army at a local enlistment centre, probably a
district Party office.

were women, fighting at the fronts as tank-crew members, machine-gunners
and snipers, signallers, dispatch riders, telegraphists and reconnaissance
workers. Virtually all those who attached themselves to Red Army units as
nurses, cooks, typists, medical orderlies and stretcher bearers were women
(many of them teenage girls), as were about half the front-line doctors and
surgeons.

Almost all Moscow's pilots who had been in civil aviation before the war
enlisted into the Red Airforce, to fly communications planes, air ambulances
and war planes, and to train as fighter and bomber pilots. But many new
recruits had no previous flying experience, like the fourteen women students
from Moscow's Lomonosov University who trained and qualified as bomber
navigators, and went on to distinguish themselves at the front.

Behind the courage and enthusiasm of this vast collective mobilisation lay
all the anguish and hardships of changing to a military life at such short
notice. As Ehrenburg wrote:

When a man puts on a soldier's uniform, he leaves behind his former snug and
complex life for ever. All that filled his life yesterday becomes like shadows in a dream.

It hardly seems possible that yesterday he was wondering what sort of cover to put on the armchair, or shaking his head over a broken cup.

At the factories, workers were exhorted to show the same fortitude at the workbench as at the front. 'All for the front!' 'Don't leave the factory if the demands of the front haven't been fulfilled!' Men brought their wives to the factories and taught them their jobs before leaving for the battlefield. And as men enlisted for the army, their families, Komsomol organisations, even entire school classes, still on their summer holidays, turned up to replace them.

'Let's take over the men's professions!' appealed women at the Vladimir Ilich factory in their paper *Ilichevets*.

Let our soldiers go calmly to the front, knowing that they'll be replaced at the rear by an army of women and girls, who'll take over the instruments, sit at the wheel of a car or tractor, or stand at the machine . . . We're sure all girls and women of the capital will quickly take over the men's jobs!

While their mothers worked, children were looked after by older brothers and sisters. Children's canteens were hastily converted to creches and kindergartens, and existing ones at factories and offices made as cheerful as possible for the infants and toddlers who now spent most of the week there. For the older children, talks and exhibitions were organised, and in the first days of the war a new children's reading room was opened in the hall of the Lenin Library. All children were deeply involved in the war effort, visiting soldiers in hospitals, writing to the front and working in the factories.

People gathered anxiously around the loudspeakers blaring out the latest communiqués, with their nightmarish news of new Russian losses.

Thousands of casualties of bombing and mechanised warfare were treated at front-line stations by the Red Army medical corps, augmented by Red Cross–trained volunteers, mostly women. These volunteers helped to develop a system of removing casualties from the battlefield immediately, under enemy fire if necessary, for blood transfusions and treatment. Casualties too badly injured to be moved were nursed on the spot, at rudimentary front-line hospitals, eventually to be evacuated to hospitals in the deep rear. But most of the injured were flown from the front by the air ambulance fleet to the major cities, which served as base hospital centres.

Perhaps it was partly because Soviet public health campaigns against epidemics and disease had since the Civil War been conducted as battles that Moscow's hospital system was able to cope so swiftly with this sudden influx of wounded soldiers flown in from the battlefields. Nurses away at the front were replaced by Red Cross volunteers, and internists, obstetricians,

The 1918, 1925 and 1939 statutes on military service in the new Red Army had limited conscription to men. But between 1941 and 1945 about 800,000 Soviet women joined the Red Army, as volunteers and draftees, in special female formations or in mixed units, including bomber regiments.

Over 400,000 women and girls were trained by the Red Cross and Red Crescent, and sent to the battlefields as nurses, orderlies and stretcher bearers.

gynaecologists and paediatricians were trained to replace surgeons and perform operations. Many of Moscow's more modern hospitals were converted to specialise in injuries of the spine, skull, nerves and face, and at the existing Institute of Nerve and Brain Surgery, Professor Grashchenkov was to make major surgical advances in restoring to brain-damaged soldiers their speech centres.

New sanitary-control centres and bathhouses were opened, and health stations in factories. The Red Cross and Red Crescent trained new nurses. Hospitals opened blood-donation centres and campaigned for new donors, and Moscow's large modern Botkin hospital was soon receiving some 200 donors a day. Because of the extra risk of infections and epidemics in wartime, anyone suspected of having an infectious illness was immediately hospitalised – resulting in a marked drop in common children's diseases like whooping cough, measles and scarlet fever.

But the immense difficulties of putting the capital on a war footing at such short notice also produced confusion, anger and mistakes. At 3 am on 24 June

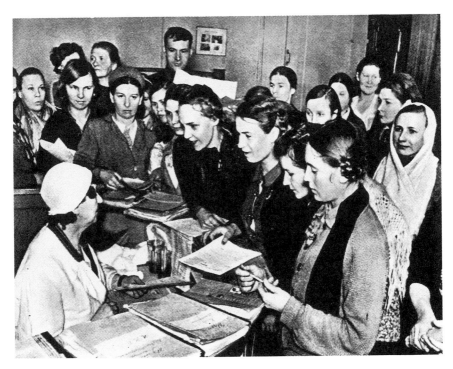

Women donating blood at a Moscow hospital. Most major hospitals opened donation centres. People donating over 700 litres of blood were awarded the title Honorary Blood Donor of the Soviet Union.

1941, Major-General Gromadin, commander of the Moscow-zone air defences, informed the Soviet executive that a group of enemy aircraft was flying towards Moscow. The siren (shorter and more high-pitched than in London) was sounded for the first time, a silvery soothing voice announced, '*Trevoga! Alarm! Citizens of Moscow take cover!*' and people trooped towards the underground stations and cellars of their houses. Anti-aircraft guns and first-aid posts were manned, and ARP wardens prepared to fight chemical and incendiary bombs. There was an explosion of anti-aircraft guns, and many mistook their smoke for parachutes descending on the city. Gromadin then announced that he had been mistaken and that Moscow's guns had been firing at their own planes returning from a bombing mission.

That 'night of the mistakes' revealed some serious defects in Moscow's air-raid precautions – including the fact that ARP wardens had taken thirty minutes to get to their posts. And henceforth Red Airforce planes were forbidden to fly over Moscow.

On 26 June, Moscow Radio broadcast Order MO 1, on local anti-aircraft defence and air-raid precautions, and next day, local soviets set about preparing in earnest for bombing.

From that night, a midnight curfew was imposed and anyone with urgent business outside their home after then needed a permit. All factories, homes, streets, buses, trains and trams were blacked out. Since Moscow's many wooden buildings (especially in the Sadovoe Koltso district) made it especially vulnerable to incendiaries and destruction bombs, all wooden sheds, warehouses and fences surrounding the main factories were dismantled, and all essential remaining wooden structures were covered in fireproof paint. Meanwhile Moscow's leading architects worked on plans to camouflage the city's central squares, some roads and most of the larger buildings, including the Kremlin. Over the next few months, 875 new water reservoirs were constructed, in case the capital's water mains were hit, and new polyclinics and dispensaries were set up to administer first aid to air-raid victims.

The city's air-raid defence was strengthened and reorganised. Now, instead of the old ARP teams, dispersed around the capital, the local soviets organised six paid full-time ARP regiments, under the command of Colonel Lapirov. These consisted of 27 battalions, from Moscow's 27 districts, and contained professional fire brigades and engineering and technical specialists, organised into rescue, repair and demolition squads equipped with transport and equipment, as well as a first-aid corps, composed mainly of women Red Cross volunteers. All full-time ARP staff were put under barrack conditions.

Firefighting was also taken extremely seriously. House, factory and office committees, normally responsible for maintenance, plumbing and rent collection, appointed rotas for firewatching, first aid and the extinguishing of incendiary bombs. At the factories, offices and theatres, 24-hour watches were set up and beds brought in, and all free time was devoted to mastering basic techniques in first aid, air-raid drill and firefighting. On every vacant plot, park and garden of Moscow, thousands of men, women and children gathered after working hours to be given demonstrations in how to pick up firebombs with asbestos gloves, and carry them with tongs to buckets of water or sand.

On the dot of midnight, Moscow's street lights were turned off, and anyone on the street after that, particularly a foreigner, was regarded with extreme suspicion. There was a mania about spies. Several times at night, people would be stopped by patrols checking documents, and pounced on by militia men and women ordering them to put out cigarettes and torches for fear they might be signalling to enemy aircraft. It was suddenly impossible to buy a map of Moscow or get street directions, so thoroughly trained were people to guard against fifth columnists.

By the third day of the war, according to the army paper *Red Star*, more

Issuing arms to Moscow's Home Guards at a training camp outside the city.
Many volunteers had to fight the Germans on the approaches to Moscow with
nothing but spades, pickaxes and petrol bombs.

than 70,000 Muscovites had enlisted for the defence of their country. Tanks moved slowly down the streets. Columns of soldiers, accompanied by weeping women and young children, and led by young women army doctors and nurses in army greatcoats, marched grimly through the streets shouting songs of defiance. The stations filled with troops on their way to the fronts, and with schoolchildren setting off with their teachers to work on the farms around Moscow.

At the Byelorusskii station on the evening of 26 June, troops leaving for the front were sent off by the Red Army Ensemble, under their conductor, V. S. Lyubimov, giving the first performance of 'Sacred War'.

It's a people's war we're fighting,
It is a sacred war!
Arise, vast Soviet land,
Arise to mortal battle,
To rout the cursed Nazi band
Its evil force to smash.
Let wrath and righteous anger
Mount higher evermore,
It's a people's war we're fighting,
It is a sacred war!

'Sacred War'

Music by A. Aleksandrov, words by V. Lebedev-Kumach

'Anthem of the USSR'

Music by A. Aleksandrov, words by S. Mikhalkov and G. El-Registan

The sun of freedom shone through the storms
And our great Lenin showed us the way
He raised us up to a cause that was just
And inspired us to toil and courage!

Broadcast the glory etc.

After two encores, the composer himself conducted, and the audience spontaneously rose to their feet and listened in silence, with tears of emotion. From then on it became the custom to stand while 'Sacred War' was being performed. The song, usually performed after the 'Anthem of the USSR' (music by Aleksandrov, words by S. Mikhalkov and G. El-Registan), became the theme song for Moscow Radio when it came on the air in the morning, and the anthem of the Great Patriotic War. 'It was like a military oath,' said the singer A. F. Lanin, 'a holy vow to fight to the last drop of our blood, to our last breath . . .'

By the end of that fourth day, the German infantry were struggling to keep up with the panzers as they raced eastwards, and the thinly spread Soviet border defences, outnumbered two to one overall and as much as ten to one on the axes of the German advance, were in shreds. Two days later, Hoth and Guderian's panzer pincers met at Minsk, the capital of Byelorussia.

'The situation on the Western Front has deteriorated,' Stalin told Zhukov on the phone. 'The enemy is near Minsk. It is unclear what has happened to Pavlov.'

But the 'Barbarossa' timetable was already beginning to falter. Hitler was nervous about the fierce resistance of Soviet forces encircled in the German rear. The *Wehrmacht* had advanced more than 200 miles, their lines were extended, and to Guderian's fury, the panzers had to sit tight while large Red Army formations in the Minsk–Bialystock pocket were eliminated. During the delay, Zhukov and Marshal Timoshenko, commander of the Central Front, were able to rush new forces to the Smolensk area. It was here, on the banks of the Dniepr, that the Red Army planned to stop Hitler's *Blitzkrieg* on the capital.

Three special 'destruction detachments' were rushed from Moscow to the new defence lines, and the general command started to discuss the idea of setting up Home Guard detachments capable of giving substantial help to the Red Army in the defence of the capital.

On that day, Sir Stafford Cripps returned to Moscow from a visit to London at the head of a special military and economic mission, and met Molotov.

During the first week of the Soviet–German war, the British government had been increasingly preoccupied with the question of opening a second front in Europe. Aneurin Bevan, addressing the House of Commons on 24 June, had spoken of the need to 'effect a second land front as an urgent necessity'. He was supported by Lord Beaverbrook, a member of the war cabinet, who stressed that if the Soviet Union proved unable to hold out, then Britain's fate too would be sealed. In discussions with Maisky, the Soviet ambassador, Beaverbrook suggested several military actions the British could take on the northern coast of France, which might, however temporarily, take pressure off the Soviet front. But the British continued to redeploy their troops away from the European theatre altogether and into British bases and possessions in the Middle East, the Far East and India. The events of 22 June had made no major change to British grand strategy – which was never openly discussed with the Soviet government. And when Cripps met Molotov, he had little more to offer than vague promises of help.

By the end of June 1941, evidence of Moscow's vigilance was already visible. Shops and buildings were sandbagged and boarded over, the windows of many of the larger ones 'blinded' with wooden frames or hung with heavy black paper. House and office fronts were painted in green and brown camouflage, and windows were crisscrossed with strips of white or black paper or cloth as air-raid protection. Many of Moscow's larger buildings were screened or tarnished by the crude colours of camouflage. The façade of the Great Palace was concealed behind a net festooned with green branches. The Bolshoi Theatre was hung with canvas painted with false entrance doorways to make it unrecognisable from the air. The new glassed Le Corbusier offices of the Commissariat for Light Industries were coated in thick rust-red paint. The gold onion domes of the Kremlin had disappeared under battleship grey, its walls under a camouflage of yellow, terracotta, black, cream and orange. Although some road widening and building work still went on, most new building projects of the ambitious 'Moscow Plan' had had to be postponed, and many buildings remained unpainted. The framework of the new Palace of Soviets loomed on the horizon until the end of the war as a half-built steel skeleton.

Yet, in many ways, life in the capital continued much as before. Most of the older children had been mobilised into a children's land army and were now out of town with their teachers, bringing in the harvest. But there were the usual crowds of people on the streets, enjoying the summer sun. People from all over the Soviet Union continued to pack the grounds of the agricultural exhibition, looking at the displays and eating ice creams. And the theatres were invariably packed.

Many waiters, maids, porters and taxi drivers had been able to converse with foreigners in German, but the moment war broke out they suddenly forgot they knew it, and German disappeared off restaurant menus, to be replaced by English. But restaurants continued to do good business. Moscow was still well supplied by provincial and suburban collectives, there were no food shortages, and street stalls were bright with onions, tomatoes, mushrooms, small apples and fresh and pickled cucumbers. The larger shops, although sandbagged and boarded up, were well stocked with tinned vegetables, buns, cakes, ice creams and enormous mounds of sweets, and were packed with shoppers. And although only a very limited supply of clothes and luxuries were displayed, people would be queuing long before the shops opened at ten for cosmetics and perfumes, cameras, gramophone records and dress materials. But now all the results of peacetime were withering away. 'Before the war we had masses of food in Moscow, and we were beginning to have plenty of everything else as well – clothes, perfumes, powder and lipstick. And now these brutes are destroying everything we've built up,' the receptionist at the Hotel Internationale told Charlotte Haldane.

Right up to the invasion the hotel was overflowing with Germans. They ate like pigs, and raided all the food shops in Moscow. Every week they'd send home parcels of food to Germany – kilos and kilos of butter, sugar, coffee, chocolate, caviar, tinned foods, even white bread. When they heard of the invasion they were dumbfounded. They threw all they could into suitcases and tried to sneak out of the hotel, but they didn't get far . . .

Since neither the anti-Nazi coalition nor the European liberation movements yet existed, and Russia was still fighting the bulk of Germany's armies without military or economic support from abroad, the Soviet state budget had to be drastically revised to meet the vast cost of raising production and tipping the scales in the Soviet Union's favour. On 29 June 1941, Stalin took over the Defence Commissariat from Marshal Voroshilov and formed a State Defence Committee, the *Stavka*, of five men (L. Beria, K. Voroshilov, G. Malenkov, Molotov and Stalin), responsible for the military conduct of the war, the rapid mobilisation of all the country's resources and the reorganisation of the Red Army. The next day, the government announced the replacement of the Third Five-Year Plan, for 1938–42, by a new economic mobilisation plan, focusing entirely on meeting the needs of war.

All enterprises of European Russia that might be important to the war were to be moved to the Volga region, eastern Siberia and the Urals, which would become the country's main arsenal. In the factories, the working day was lengthened to eleven hours, and annual leave was replaced by money compensation, credited to workers at savings banks. Workers at factories previously producing strictly peaceful goods like furniture, crockery, clothes and textiles, now started producing grenades, submachine-gun components, engineering goods and uniforms, while those in the food industry produced biscuits and tinned and concentrated foods for the front.

Skilled workers who had left for the front were replaced by young untrained novices, most of them women. Indeed, by the end of the summer, some 70 to 80 per cent of all factory workers were women. Women were everywhere. They drove buses, trams and trains, they worked on the railways as platelayers, signallers and firewomen, mending lines and checking cargo.

And after long hours at work, they joined firefighting teams or brought their children along to fill fibre and textile sacks with sand for fortifying shelters and buildings. Skills that normally took years to learn had to be acquired in weeks, and the output in many factories initially fell. But within a few months productivity was at its prewar level again.

'For success at the front, work twice, three times as hard!' workers were exhorted, and soon red flags were appearing beside the benches of factory workers, especially at the textile mills, who worked two or three shifts or 'deaths') to fill in for absent workmates. Enormous importance was attached to these '200- and 300-percenters', and books, articles and radio broadcasts assured lasting fame to those like '500-percenter' V. E. Zagvozdin, at the Red Proletarian factory, who worked four extra machines, and metalworker G. N. Voropaev, who had two comrades at the front and worked for three. And there were many more examples of heroism on the labour front.

In the Hammer and Sickle factory, where half the workers had gone to the front, women worked in the open-hearth workshops, the rolling mills and the steel-melting ovens. 'They gave the warmth of their good hearts to the common cause,' wrote I. V. Turtanov, a veteran Hammer and Sickle worker and Party organiser. 'We men, I won't deny, were unhappy to accept women's demands to work in the hot parts. There's no such word as "foundress" or "rolleress". How can a woman be a founder, when it's a job for which only the strongest men are taken?' But with no choice but to train women and young girls for these jobs, the men found all their old assumptions about male and female skills breaking down. Output leaped, as the Hammer and Sickle laboured to replace the metal of the south. But quality fell. Then a new higher-quality metal, named SIM, was developed, and output leaped again. And even experienced workers were at a loss to explain how it had happened, when most of the work was being done by inexperienced women.

A small frail girl of eighteen called Anastasia Savicheva was apprenticed to a founder at one of the open-hearth workshops, and there she worked throughout the entire war. Evdokia Vinogradova, Agrippina Boborova and Anastasia Anikienko all worked in the rolling mill. Seventeen-year-old Galina Pikulina, who had dreamed of fighting with the men at the front but was persuaded to learn a male skill instead, turned up at the Hammer and Sickle factory with her mother, and soon became one of the factory's fastest steel rollers. Maria Khachevnikova, who had remained alone in Moscow after her large family was scattered by war, worked a twelve-hour day in the hot ovens of the steel-melting workshop. And at the end of long days at the open-hearth workshop, '200-percenter' Anna Tsypliankova and the beautiful Ukrainian Maria Belash gave hundreds of litres of blood – for which they were later awarded the title of Honourable Blood Donor of the Soviet Union.

Hundreds of letters from wounded soldiers at the front arrived to their 'little sisters', who had helped to save their lives.

But everyone's minds were on the front, and they measured their time from one communiqué to another, each of which concealed countless personal tragedies and acts of courage.

A woman called Aslanova, from the Trekhgorka textile mill, had gone to visit relatives in her native village near Smolensk just before war broke out. As the Germans rolled on, she tried in vain to persuade her relatives to escape, then herself left by train for Moscow with some other women and their children. The train was bombed, several mothers and babies were killed, and the rest, guided by peasants, walked through forests and swamps by night, crossing streams and wading through marshes until, starving and unable to feed their babies, most of them had lain down to die. The small band of survivors struggled on, and eventually met rearguard patrols of the Red Army, who put them on the train for Moscow. Aslanova returned to her factory, but so aged was she that her friends didn't at first recognise her, and when they did, they voted her a month's paid holiday.

In people's eyes appeared the watchful look that comes to those who have known much tragedy but have no time to mourn. Perhaps it was this dazed uncertainty that made people cling to their everyday routines and pleasures in those days. 'Home is the illusion of security,' wrote the Moscow poet Vera Inber, 'and illusions help one to survive the minefields in the mind, the places you daren't think about, the absent family and friends.'

Many people still found it hard to take in what was happening. The eminent Slavonic scholar Pyotr Bogatyryov, more at home with ancient Czech folklore than with military maps or communiqués, was under the impression that Guderian was an Armenian general coming to the defence of Moscow. 'I was on my way here, and someone, not just anyone but a military chap, said that Guderian's army was approaching,' he announced cheerfully to Ehrenburg one day. 'Lots of tanks. So they'll soon be driven off!'

But each day was bringing fresh losses. On 24 June 1941, Kaunas and Vilno fell to the Germans. On 27 June, the Nazis seized Minsk and started bombing Leningrad. On 30 June, the Germans encircled large Russian forces at Bialystock. On 1 July, the Germans seized Riga and advanced towards Pskov. This string of successes fired the Germans with fresh hopes, and even generals previously apprehensive about invading Russia were now convinced that Moscow would be theirs in a few weeks.

Behind the German lines bitter fighting continued in many centres of resistance. Large numbers of Red Army soldiers managed to fight their way out of encirclement. Others eluded capture and were soon to form partisan nuclei. In the Brest fortress the handful of defenders hung grimly on for more than a month, tying up thousands of German soldiers and causing a major logistical headache on the Warsaw–Minsk artery. Their defiance, unknown at the time, became legendary after the war.

With the first shock of the invasion turning into the multiple catastrophes of July, the rush was on to defend the approaches to Moscow – which it now seemed unlikely that the Red Army could hold on its own. It was then that the capital's Party organisation was told to supplement the army units around Moscow with Home Guard detachments, which all Muscovites (except those working in defence factories or carrying out urgent orders) were exhorted to join. An extraordinary commission in charge of recruitment was established under the command of General Artemev, commander of the Moscow district, and twelve district registration centres were set up at schools and clubs around the city.

On 2 July, schools, factories and local parties organised recruitment meetings. 'We'll send our best people to the Home Guards!' said workers of the Moscow Rubber factory, where 200 joined. At the Kuibyshev transformer factory loud applause greeted the announcement that 320 had volunteered. After a three-hour meeting at the Red Heroes factory, over a thousand joined. Another thousand joined after a two-hour meeting at the Sergo Ordjokonidze factory. Thousands enlisted from the Moscow Car factory. There were collective applications: the entire meeting at a woodworking factory in the October district, and at the Paris Commune factory in Kirov district. The next day, workers from the Vladimir Ilich, Dynamo, Calibre, Machine-Tool and Red Proletarian factories marched into the military registration centres.

Civil War veterans dug out old uniforms or borrowed them from their sons. I. I. Reznichenko, from the Apakovskii tram depot, a former Civil War partisan in the Far East, volunteered at the Leningrad district recruitment station. Fyodor Orlov, who had commanded units in the Russo-Japanese war and the First World War, and was invalided out of active service in the Civil War, volunteered at the Dzherzhinskii district, and was put in command of a Home Guard division. Many women volunteered, also with memories of the earlier war against Western interventionists. K. S. Ivanova, a nurse, had been a sister on a medical train in 1920. 'I ask you to send me to the front as an army nurse,' she wrote in her application. 'I have higher education, and could be useful in political work too. My health is good.'

But for most volunteers, this was to be their first experience of war. And it was this last-minute mobilisation, joined so eagerly, which spoke most eloquently of Moscow's desperate unpreparedness that July. Untrained, most of them, often chronically unfit or anxious to disguise their age or inexperience (practically all those applying were accepted), Moscow's Home Guards would be sent to the major approaches to the capital, at Volokolamsk, Mozhaisk, Maloyaroslavets and Kaluga, to hold up the enemy, at devastating cost of life, until Red Army reinforcements arrived.

Throughout the next four days, columns of men and women in civilian dress could be seen marching and shuffling down the streets from their factories and plants into the military registration centres. But in those days it wasn't bearing that people noticed, it was a more ordinary kind of dignity. The Home Guards were to be Moscow's last hope.

One of the first applicants to arrive at the Leningrad district Military Commissariat was P. N. Kravchenko, who had four sons at the front (one a twice decorated hero of the Soviet Union), and one in intelligence. 'The enemy will know no pity,' he wrote in his application. 'But my old hand will not shake. I shall do my duty to my motherland.' 'Although I'm over sixty-two, I don't want to stand aside from life and want to do all I can to defend the Soviet Union,' wrote E. V. Chechevitskii, of the Moscow car factory, to his local party. 'I ask to be enrolled in the Home Guard. I could be useful with the infantry, as I know a bit about hunting.' N. I. Bolotin, one of the oldest workers at the First Moscow Printworks, applied with his two sons and his daughter, leaving his wife to replace him at the factory.

B. A. Keller, the elderly and distinguished botanist, volunteered at the Lenin district recruitment station. 'Put me in a cart and take me off,' he wrote, 'then drive my car to the front.' Professors Golovenchenko, Blagoi and Zhorov (later surgeon of the 33rd Army) joined, along with the sculptor Vuchetich and seventy-eight senior scientists from the Academy of Sciences. The philosopher Mikhail Kedrov, son of Old Bolsheviks, applied with his wife T. N. Chentsova, a biochemist. Members of the Institute of Philosophy formed the nucleus of a complete battery of 76-mm field artillery.

On 3 July, Guderian's leading troops had reached the Dniepr, 320 miles into Russia and halfway to Moscow. On that day, General Halder, chief of the German general staff, wrote in his diary, 'It is probably no exaggeration to say that the campaign against Russia has been won in fourteen days.'

For Moscow, the battle had only just begun.

3

Home Guards and Firefighters

At 6.30 on the morning of Thursday 3 July 1941, before the start of the long working day, everyone in the capital was within earshot of a radio or loudspeaker to hear Stalin speak on Moscow Radio, the first time he had spoken since 1938. Red Square and the surrounding streets, usually deserted at that hour, filled with people and resounded with his words, which were carried by amplifiers to every corner of the capital. 'Brothers and sisters, friends,' he began. He was clearly very moved. The German attack continued, he said, the Nazis had taken Lithuania, Latvia, Western Byelorussia and much of the eastern Ukraine. But the German army was not invincible,

... and only on our territory has it for the first time met with any serious resistance ... This war has been inflicted on us, and our country has entered into a life and death struggle with its most wicked enemy, German fascism ... Our people must be fearless in their struggle, and selflessly fight our patriotic war of liberation against the fascist enslavers. We must immediately put our whole production on a war footing.

He then issued his famous scorched-earth and partisan orders, which were to have an immense impact on the nascent liberation movements elsewhere in Europe, and which in Russia signalled the revival of the old guerrilla warfare from the Civil War days:

We must not leave a single kilogramme of grain, or a single litre of petrol to the enemy ... Partisan units must be formed in the occupied areas, to spread the partisan war, blow up and destroy roads, bridges and telephones and telegraph wires, set fire to forests, enemy stores and road convoys. It is necessary to create in invaded areas conditions unbearable to the enemy, which must be persecuted and destroyed at every step.

Stalin's 3 July broadcast, with its enunciation of the rules of war conduct, and its appeal to people's pride, courage and patriotism, had a galvanising effect on people for whom the war was still a tragic and bewildering shock. Konstantin Simonov describes the impression his speech made in his novel *The Living and the Dead*, where it is heard over the radio in a field hospital.

Stalin spoke in a slow toneless voice, with a strong Georgian accent. Once or twice you could hear a glass clink as he drank water. His voice was low and soft, and might have seemed perfectly calm, but for his heavy tired breathing and that water he kept drinking . . . There was a discrepancy between that even voice and the tragic situation he spoke of. And in that discrepancy was his strength. It was what people expected of him. They loved him in different ways, wholeheartedly or with reservations; admiring him and yet fearing him; and some didn't like him at all. But nobody doubted his courage and his iron will. Stalin didn't describe the situation as tragic. But the things of which he spoke – Home Guards, partisans, occupied territories, meant the end of illusions . . . The truth he uttered was a bitter truth, but at last it was uttered, and people felt they stood more firmly on the ground . . . 'My friends,' he said, 'brothers and sisters' . . . Was it only a tragedy like the war that could give birth to these words and these feelings? Above all, what was left in the heart after Stalin's speech was a tense expectation of a change for the better . . .

For most people, he had been a distant and frightening figure. Now, as many of them heard him speak for the first time, he became simply the boss, the one who knew what was happening. (The writer Alexander Werth recalled people cheering in the cinemas whenever Stalin appeared in the newsreels.) And having heard the worst, people began more and more to talk of victory.

While people living in the towns and villages under German occupation were trained to establish secret bases from which to fight the enemy, some 310,000 people from the capital and its outlying districts joined the Home Guard. On 6 July 1941, the volunteers assembled at their recruitment centres, most of them in civilian dress and bearing spades, shovels and whatever weapons they could find. Thousands of men, women and children lined the streets in respectful silence as they marched past to the accompaniment of brass bands, shouting 'Death to the invaders!' 'Defend our capital!' 'Victory will be ours!' all the way to the assembly point in the Mosfilm district. Workers from the Rusakov tram depot and the Moscow Metalware factory solemnly presented them with mess tins, mugs, field kitchens and uniforms, the roll call was taken, and they set off for training camps 20 to 30 miles outside the city.

There, at Krasnogorsk, Tolstopaltsevo and Vnukovo, Red Army officers gave them a hasty training in the arts of advance, reconnaissance, encounter and tank battle. A newly formed volunteer sappers' division, composed of engineers from Moscow's Institute of Engineering Transport, taught them to mine fields and construct dugouts, wire traps and antitank obstacles, while Party organisers had the hard task of explaining the seriousness of the situation, raising morale and generally setting an example. Everything was done at breakneck speed. 'Mum, there's no time!' wrote seventeen-year-old Mitrofan Merkulov, of the Second Stalin Home Guard division, from his camp at Planernaya. 'We're busy all the time. We get up at four and go to bed at eleven. I'm writing this on the rifle box. They're giving us rifles now, and we've all got uniforms.' He was one of the lucky ones. Factories restored tanks and armoured cars, but weapons remained for many weeks in acutely short supply.

Out on the Leningrad Highway, amid the sweet smell of clover and the sound of the larks, cars slowed down for marching groups of Home Guards. The entire side of one building by the roadside was filled with Toidze's poster of a stern-faced woman holding in her raised hand the military oath, with below an inscription that read, 'Your Motherland Calls You!' In Moscow, buildings were plastered with exhortations: 'Women, go and work on the collective farms! Replace the men in the army!' Walls blazed with posters of bursting shells, exploding bombs and rodent-faced Hitlers; of a Russian tank crushing a giant crab with a Hitler moustache; a Red Army soldier ramming a bayonet down the throat of a Hitler-faced rat; a huge red shell hitting Hitler in the stomach with the words, 'We'll wipe the fascist invaders off the face of the earth!'; and a Red Army soldier shouting 'Death to the fascist rattlesnake!' as he bayonets a swastika-shaped snake.

Russian antifascist art was superb. The tragedy of those early days found emotional expression in countless paintings of women and children, murdered or dying, pleading or defiant. There was the powerful understatement of Koretskii's 'Death to the Child Murderers!', the more direct emotive power of his 'Soldier, Save me from Slavery!' and the savage defiance of his 'Shoot the Murderers of our Wives and Children!' Then there were exhortatory calls to struggle and sacrifice, like Moore's 'What are you doing for the Front?', Kokorekin's 'Death to the Nazi Scum' and 'We've Fought, We're Fighting, and We'll Fight On!' And there was a mass of satirical anti-Nazi posters, turned out every day at desperate speed.

Early each morning the editorial boards of Moscow's poster workshops would meet to plan the subject matter for that day's pictorial sheets – often with the help of suggestions from passers-by. Artists would then sketch in the designs (mainly of Hitler, Göring and company) and block in the slogans to accompany them, and by noon people would be crowding round shop windows and the sides of buildings to read the day's fresh crop of posters. Poets like Bedny, Marshak and others seized on the Nazi high command's every word and flung it back at them daily in poems and verses for the TASS news agency. These were then handed over to artists like the famous 'Kukriniksy' trio (Mikhail Kuprianov, Porfirii Krylov and Nikolai Sokolov), to be attached to savagely satirical drawings and paintings of Nazi hideous-

'Death to the Child Murderers' by Koretskii.   'Your Motherland Calls You!' by Toidze.

ness. The daily posters displayed in the TASS windows on the Kuznetskii Most gathered especially huge crowds, even from passing trolley buses, whose drivers would be ordered to stop and let passengers get a good look. Many sober peacetime artists and poets were turned by the war into satirical snipers, and Russia's centuries-old tradition of revolutionary satire, with its character assassination, its sting of contempt for the enemy, and its grotesque humour wrenched from the heart of tragedy, was now given perhaps its most potent expression. It was not surprising that so many satirists appeared on the Nazi death list, with Hitler's personal inscription, 'Find and kill!'

Attached to every German army were special 'propaganda companies', known as RK, instructed by Goebbels to 'portray with the aid of portable easels the insignificance of the enemy and the inspired faces of the German soldier. RK must engage in active propaganda, breaking the enemy's will to resist by spreading false and demoralising rumours,' he said, and by 'dressing up' facts ('Better a German lie than a human truth,' said Baldur von Schirach, leader of the Nazi youth movement). And interspersed with Berlin Radio's regular reports of Red Army officers murdering their own men and Russian babies being taken from their mothers at birth to be reared by the state were war broadcasts filled with roars and hysterical shrieks of 'We've done it again!' Nazi soldiers in Russia were still convinced by Goebbels's 'big lie' – or

'Our Strength is Incalculable' by V. Koretskii, 1941. 'Glory to the Defenders of Moscow' by N. Solovyov, 1944.

wanted to be. 'Today they told us on the wireless that 30,000 Russians were encircled,' wrote a Corporal Stampe in his diary. 'Maybe it's all lies, but it's good to hear it anyway.'

Meanwhile, within the marbled halls of Moscow's Broadcasting Station, Ehrenburg and others allowed access to captured Nazi diaries and letters were able to hit directly at German weaknesses and fears with anti-Nazi propaganda broadcast directly to workers and soldiers' wives in Germany and the occupied countries. In Russia itself, people heard stories, rather like those of the BBC, of individual heroism at the front and at sea, and of factory workers exceeding their norms.

Never had so many beautiful and powerful songs been written in Moscow as in those early days of the war. There were light lyrical songs, like 'Vasya Kryuchkin', 'The Dark Girl' and 'In the Dugout'. And there were patriotic songs, like Blanter's 'Goodbye, Towns and Villages' (lyrics by Isaakovskii), Fradkin's 'Song of the Dniepr' (lyrics by Dolmatovskii), Prokofiev's 'Forward! Forward!' and Aleksandrov's 'For the Great Soviet Land', 'Poem of the Ukraine' (words by Koluchev) and of course 'Sacred War', which was taken to all the war fronts, performed at the garrisons, stations and hospitals of Moscow, and sung on Moscow Radio. 'I think if song can express some political slogan necessary to people, that's a colossal thing,' said its lyricist,

'Song of the Dniepr'

Music by M. Fradkin, words by E. Dolmatovskii

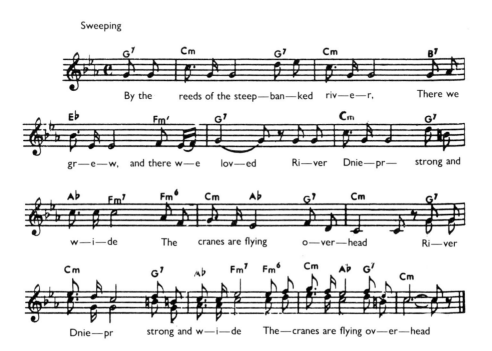

(three verses)

Our river will flow with the fascists' blood,
They won't take our Soviet land.
Like the Dniepr in spring, they'll be washed away
By our people and by our Army.

Lebedev-Kumach, in 1944. 'We must respect the power of music's influence and ascendancy . . . and approach its creation with beating heart and burning soul. Only thus can song be created, for song is speech in emotion . . .'

Moscow's filmmakers went off to the front to film the battles around Moscow. In June 1941, some 200 cameramen and reporters from the Moscow Chronicle went off – some eventually joining active service with the partisans. Everyone had seen the Chronicle's historic films of the steps of Smolny in 1917, the battles of the Civil War, the first tractors on the state farms and the building of Dniepostroi, Turksib and Magnitogorsk. By the end of 1941, Moscow Chronicle front-line teams had filmed (and fought in) every battle on the approaches to Moscow.

Moscow's journalists and writers too put their talents to the service of the army, in booklets for Russian and German soldiers, and in articles and stories for the regional and national press which made them the envy of many a Western journalist. J. B. Priestley said in his introduction to a popular English translation of Ehrenburg's war articles:

I wish we were slamming it across as these Russians are. You're made to feel that he's writing in a hurry, with his typewriter on a packing case, and the world about him in blazing ruins, but that he succeeds, where so many of our own propagandists fail, because he communicates the terrible urgency of the moment in lively and witty phrases.

From the first days of war, some 900 writers, including Ehrenburg, Surkov, Korneichuk, Simonov, Krymov, Jalil, Gudzenko, Tvardovskii and Sholokhov, worked behind enemy lines and at the fronts, often writing their articles with rifles and grenades on their knee. Many writers joined the active fighting, and more than 400 of them were killed at the front. By July, most of Moscow's writers were writing for the Red Army paper *Red Star*, and had settled into a pattern of prodigious activity. Ehrenburg recalls turning out three articles a day, reading German documents, intercepting German radio messages, editing translations, writing photo captions – and finding arguments to prove inevitable victory, 'for there was no alternative'.

In Moscow's streets, squares and doorfronts, people stood around in the blazing sun talking of war, crowding around housefronts where the morning's edition of *Pravda* or *Izvestia* was pasted up, and gathering glumly around the large map of Russia in the windows of the *Izvestia* newspaper offices.

By 4 July, the Germans had captured Ostrov, south of Pskov. On 9 July, Vitebsk was taken. By 10 July, Guderian's panzers had forced the river Dniepr, and on that day, the Nazi command announced the start of its 'decisive' attack on Moscow, aimed at splitting the troops of the western front, encircling and destroying its main forces in the Smolensk area and opening the way to the capital. On 11 July 80,000 women and children were hurriedly ordered to leave Moscow for the east.

That week the Kursk and Kazan stations were packed with crowds of people, jostling for tickets, clutching sobbing loved ones, and weeping for fear they might never see them again. The best carriages on the trains were reserved for children leaving in the care of committees of parents, teachers and nurses for children's homes in the east, and parents staying on in the capital without them hurriedly wrote names and addresses on their hands in indelible pencil, and said goodbye to them – many for the last time.

A council for evacuation was set up, and local bureaus and committees helped find work and accommodation for the massive influx of people swelling the population of the east. Children were settled in creches, kinder-gartens and children's homes, while women laboured until they dropped, building new settlements, working in the mines and on the farms – where they often stood in not just for the men who'd gone to war, but for horses and tractors too. A central enquiry office was set up at Boguruslan, on the Volga, to help locate lost relatives. But many people lost touch with them for ever. Children arriving without their parents were given baths when they arrived at their new homes, and their names and addresses were washed off their hands, so that mothers had to be summoned out to identify them. But many remained unidentified. Others were only reunited years after they had lost hope of seeing them again. Maria Khachevnikova, who worked at the Hammer and Sickle factory throughout the war, had given up her family for dead, and it was only in 1966 that she eventually tracked down her younger sister Galina in Siberia and settled there with her.

Every day Moscow became a more depressing sight. The once crowded and cheerful streets and squares were now filled with tanks, artillery and Home Guards. In the parks and squares, thousands of people in government jobs or at important war work gathered every evening for military exercises and shooting practice. Special trucks began to run along the tram lines distributing piles of sand in preparation for air raids, and short films were shown in the cinemas and factories instructing people how to put out incendiaries and disable tanks.

In the two years before the war, Moscow had become a city of quick lunch counters and cafeterias, some with automatic vending machines. There had been plenty of meat, milk, fish and eggs, though not always in the same shop. Queues had been disappearing, and people were even able to make telephone orders. Now, although sumptuous meals could still be had at the Metropol and Moskva hotels and the Aragvi restaurant, and the Cocktail Hall in Gorkii Street was still packed, there was less conviviality and less vodka being drunk,

By early July, all Muscovites not already in the army (except those fulfilling military contracts) had to do military training.

as the potatoes and grain from which it was made were needed for food. Before, Moscow had been a night city, and the streets had been wide awake until two in the morning. Now, as the combined effects of bombing threats and physical exhaustion drove everyone home early, Moscow's night life stopped at nine, and dance orchestras played to half-empty halls. There was still a big demand for afternoon concerts in the parks, though, and on weekends and in the long summer evenings after work and before blackout, people would crowd the parks to eat sandwiches, drink fruit juice and ride on the merry-go-rounds, or lie in the grass listening to music on the loud-speakers. All Moscow's theatres were still open, and its cinemas and circuses were packed (although performances now started two hours earlier). For out-ings like these, people still dressed as smartly as before. But in general, since no clothes were being made and clothes rationing was strict, people looked more shabby now – and would remain so for the rest of the war, wearing only their old work clothes and putting aside their best until the war was over.

By the second week in July, Moscow's food kiosks and stalls were emptying, goods were becoming more expensive, and there was even a certain amount of hoarding. On 18 July, stringent rationing was brought in for meat, fish, bread, sugar, butter and cereals, and prices were stabilised. Everyone had a ration book, as in England, and people were divided into four categories. Heavy manual workers in war factories, shipping and mining were allowed one and a half pounds of bread a day, and a monthly allowance of four and a half pounds of meat, one and a half pounds of sugar, two pounds of fish and four pounds of cereals. Writers, artists, scientists, office and shop-workers were allowed over one pound of bread a day, plus a monthly allowance of two and a half pounds of meat, three quarters of a pound of sugar, one and a half pounds of fish, and two and a half pounds of cereals. The third category – dependants, housewives and the elderly – were allowed over one pound of bread a day, and a monthly allowance of two pounds of meat, two pounds of sugar, half a pound of butter, one pound of fish and two pounds of cereals. Children under fourteen received less meat but more butter and sugar and all available milk, and pregnant and breastfeeding women were also given an extra milk ration. In most of Moscow's large factories, which were supplied directly from the Ministry of Food, canteens provided cheap three-course meals of soup, meat, vegetables and cake, in return for coupons, while at the creches and kindergartens, children would exchange their ration cards for meals of oatmeal soup, cottage-cheese pancakes and cocoa.

There were two kinds of shops: the cheaper ones, which applied their own rationing system according to supplies, and the more expensive ones, which sold foods produced by small farms, collectives and state farms. The govern-ment, rather than suppressing this potential black market of goods surplus to basic rationing, decided instead to exploit it. Unlike people in England, Russians were not made to register in one shop, so that at the beginning of the month the cheaper shops would be crowded with people using up their coupons on basic foodstuffs. But since they were not able to buy there everything to which their coupons entitled them, they would then use these later in the month in the more expensive shops, where prices were roughly double, and they could buy luxuries like chocolate, tea, sweets and coffee, fresh and smoked fish, and caviar, black, red, fresh and pressed. Sometimes the most outlandish luxuries appeared in these shops, and people would form instantaneous queues, wondering whether they were queuing for crabs, champagne or chocolate. But despite the sporadic availability of these luxuries, shopping became an increasingly fraught business, and rationing brought back long queues, especially at the bread shops, where shoppers and assistants became increasingly short-tempered.

In mid-July 1941, British ARP and shelter experts arrived in Moscow to share some British experiences of bombing, which were suddenly of urgent interest, and a short film of the Blitz was shown. Crowds of people gathered anxiously around the loudspeakers on every street corner blaring out the latest war communiqué, with their laconic words of defeat 'in the direction of . . .'

At Kiev, three doomed Soviet armies were sucked into a vortex as Army Group South swept around them. Leeb's Army Group North had descended on Leningrad – and the city's population was dumbfounded by the sudden threat, which caught the civilian and military authorities in disarray. Meanwhile on the central front, Guderian's panzers were advancing on Smolensk, just 100 miles from Moscow, and the Germans estimated that the 'mass of the operationally effective Russian Army has now been destroyed'.

But this wasn't the case at all, as the battle for Smolensk soon revealed.

Racing into Smolensk on 16 July, Guderian ordered his panzers quickly on to the Desna River, convinced by his experiences in France that by keeping the Russians on the move he could reach Moscow and paralyse Russian resistance. Hitler disagreed. The German offensive on Moscow, launched on 10 July, although at first successful, had been halted at Yelnya, and the attempt to complete the encirclement of the 16th and 20th armies was frustrated by a Soviet counterattack. Army Group Centre should wheel north to Leningrad and south to the Ukraine, Hitler insisted, before seizing Moscow. Several weeks slipped by in arguments between Hitler and his generals, while from July to early September massive tank and infantry battles raged at Smolensk. The carnage spilled north and south, as the Germans tried to find a way round fierce Russian resistance, and Zhukov's counterattacks meant that the *Wehrmacht* was in effect fighting defensive battles. More than 90 per cent of Soviet

Russian prisoners from encircled troops at Priluki.

men aged between eighteen and twenty-one at the start of the war died during it, and the inferno at Smolensk consumed 100,000 of them – three Soviet armies – before burning itself out under the clear skies of a glorious autumn.

The Red Army had by now suffered disastrous losses of men and material, and the consequences of its prewar strategy, which had only envisaged offensive operations on enemy territory, were becoming increasingly apparent. At Stalin's instigation, the bulk of fuel, ammunition and other stores had been kept on or near the borders, and were now lost. Compounding the critical shortage of ammunition and weapons, and the extreme muddle and confusion both on the fronts and in the Defence Commissariat, was the absence of any prearranged defensive strategy. Tactics were improvised, and the high command, making a virtue of necessity, took advantage of the decimation of its forces to remodel huge and unmanageable prewar force structures into smaller, more mobile armies.

People in Moscow derived what hope they could from official reports which put German losses at one million dead – three times heavier than Soviet losses – and from the first newsreel clips of the war, in which the Soviet infantry and air force made a heartening impression of competence and courage. But perhaps the firmest grounds for hope in Moscow that summer – indeed for many a forecast of Hitler's full and utter defeat – was the Anglo-Soviet agreement, signed on 12 July 1941 by Molotov and Cripps in the Kremlin, in which both sides pledged mutual action against Hitler, and agreed not to conclude a separate peace.

This agreement, which consisted of only two sentences, nonetheless formed the basis of future cooperation between Britain and the Soviet Union, and was of profound significance. In addition to its provision of mutual military assistance it stated, 'During this war, neither Britain nor the USSR will negotiate an armistice or treaty of peace except by mutual agreement.' This was an epochal step in ending the Soviet Union's diplomatic isolation and capping the schemes of the Munich dealers. It also meant that the framework of the postwar peace would be one created out of mutual cooperation between the Allies. This initiative later led to the Big Three meetings at Tehran, Yalta and Potsdam, where the wartime Allies created the basis for the postwar international settlement and the United Nations Organisation.

By 20 July, *Panzergruppen* II and III had taken Orsha, Krichev, Velnya and Smolensk. Nonetheless, what General Halder called 'the fierce and dogged resistance' of the Soviet troops was now slowly beginning to weld the desperate, fragmented battles of the first weeks into a continuous resistance, which here and there enabled them to take the initiative. Two armies, encircled west of the Dniepr, managed to extricate themselves and withdraw to the eastern bank, and a flurry of fierce Soviet counterattacks were later to drive in the German bridgehead over the Dniepr at Smolensk.

The Germans, pushing on south to Roslavl, managed to encircle and maul the Soviet 28th Army. But time was passing, the lightning rapidity of the German advance on Moscow, for all its ferocity, was already slowing down, and the Red Army, at immense cost, was absorbing the first shock of the *Blitzkrieg*. 'Barbarossa's' apocalyptic timetable was beginning to slip. At Smolensk, 'Barbarossa' had become a dead letter. Deprived of food and water in many occupied areas, the *Wehrmacht* had to wait for all supplies to be transported from Germany, by air or along an immensely long front, so that many soldiers were more interested in finding food than in fighting. Strong clothing was also wearing out – and the spectre of the Russian winter was already looming.

'In occupied Russian territories it is necessary by all means to seize all leather articles, such as Russian boots, bags and belts, to use for our own supply,' said a German general HQ order of 13 July. 'Take away all footwear from captured Russians.' German boots, superbly constructed of soft leather, with a special box for the great toe, were marching boots, with which socks couldn't be worn. The thirty-two nails in each sole were rods which could conduct the 20, 30 or 40 degrees of Russian frost into the feet of the German soldiers as winter deepened. But, more importantly, the advancing German army was increasingly impressed by Soviet courage, and it was becoming apparent that the Russians were prepared to sacrifice far more in their country's defence than most countries would have done.

The Red Airforce ('Stalin's falcons') had also begun to fight back, and the skies were black with dogfights, with several instances of Soviet pilots suicidally ramming enemy aircraft. (One of the first and most famous of these, known to every Soviet schoolchild as an example of courage and daring, and the subject of countless songs and poems, was a former Moscow factory worker called Captain Gastello, who died crashing his plane into a column of German oil trucks.)

But already in the villages west of Moscow, people were living as slaves to the Germans. And Army Group Centre ploughed on towards its number-one target – Moscow. By now, twenty-eight Soviet divisions had been destroyed and another seventy had been half destroyed. And still more terrible losses were in store.

The fascists were now only some 100 miles southwest of the capital, but they had been stopped, making it possible to mobilise troops and move supplies to the front, and to strengthen Moscow's air-raid defences. Three circles of air defences were constructed around Moscow, and anti-aircraft batteries, screened by leaves, were moved to the woods outside the city. Moscow's chief architect, D. M. Chechulin, designed plywood camouflage screens for many of Moscow's central squares and some roads, as well as for the Obvodnoi Canal and the Moscow River (whose bends were reported by Soviet pilots to provide good orientation for enemy planes). In the unpopulated outlying areas, lighted structures were built to give the appearance of working factories. The district soviets converted basements into shelters, and mobilised people to strengthen them with heavy supporting timbers and to sandbag all outlets other than exits. Teenagers patrolled the streets, checking sandbags and water buckets, and warning of faulty blackouts.

On 20 July, the Germans started the systematic bombing of Leningrad, and the following night, Moscow endured its first raid, from German planes carrying 110 tons of bombs.

At 10pm, the siren sounded from Moscow's Mozhaisk district, warning of the approach of large groups of enemy bombers, and over the radio came the familiar soothing voice announcing, '*Trevoga!* Alarm! Citizens, take cover!' Since there had already been three false alarms, not everyone was inclined to take this one seriously. But people nonetheless dutifully trooped off to the shelters and underground stations, which within twenty-five minutes were full. Police and firefighters stood in doorways and on rooftops. The streets were empty. The blackout was total. Then a deafening explosion spread a bloody orange fan across the village of Kutuzovskaya, reared up to the Khoroshevskii Highway and leaped on to the Vagankovo cemetery. There was a loud crack, and flames roared at Mokhovoi.

Some 200 aircraft tried to break through the outer defence rings of the

Actors raided the prop box for their firefighting costumes. (The sign above
them says 'Air-raid shelters'.)

city that night, roaring, reversing course and stabbing again and again at
Moscow's powerful air defences. Scores of searchlights wheeled around the
sky, occasionally finding a plane and sending it down to its destruction. Soon
the whole horizon from the Moscow River to the Lenino district was ablaze
with the summer lightning of anti-aircraft guns, and shrapnel from their shells
clattered onto the streets like a hailstorm.

The Byelorusskii station was hit, its cisterns smashed by a demolition
bomb. As water poured towards the nearby underground station, a break-

down repair team rushed over and, in a chaos of smoke, fire and anti-aircraft guns, firefighters extinguished the blazing cistern while engineers repaired the pipe before the water reached the underground station, where several thousand women and children were sheltering. The Vagankovo Viaduct was hit, and a large apartment house in the Mokhovoi was destroyed, killing several people in its basement. A small crater was made by a bursting bomb at the exact spot marked out by workmen about to excavate a water main – so that in the morning they found their work done for them.

As each new fire started, intelligence teams dashed off on motorbikes to the spot, to inform ARP and first-aid workers on the place and nature of the destruction. On the roofs of houses, in doorways, in the squares, people (many disobeying orders to take shelter, and many of them teenagers and young children, still theoretically on their summer holidays) stood vigil for firebombs, which rained down like small cucumbers.

At the Vakhtangovo Theatre, actors put on their firefighting costumes. Mikhail Sidorkin created much merriment by appearing in the pointed kaiser officer's helmet he had worn in *The Soldier Left for the Front*. Vasilii Kuza couldn't find any costume big enough, and kept his old brown suit on. The others wore the German boots, French helmets and summer overalls left over from their recent performance of *Intervention*. They were kept busy that night. A number of incendiaries hit the roof and went through to the attic, but were easily dealt with. More serious was the large bomb that exploded over the roof over the stage and set fire to its acoustic padding, so that they were battling with it all night.

The city's underground stations overflowed with people, mostly the elderly or mothers with young children. All stations provided first-aid posts and rudimentary brick-enclosed latrines, with shallow trenches flushed by running water. The more luxurious stations had little libraries, with benches, books and magazines, which had to be signed for and returned after the all clear. Some even organised concerts and film shows. Stationary trains were reserved for mothers and babies, and equipped with folding wooden cots. Bunks were laid down for the women, children and old people with sacks and bundles who packed the platforms and corridors – and sometimes even the rails. After gazing anxiously up at the ceiling for a while, most people went straight to sleep, exhausted after their long day's work. Others read newspapers and books, wrote letters, talked quietly or rummaged through their belongings. (Smoking was forbidden.) Some three hours after the alarm, when the same friendly voice announced 'All clear', people stumbled out of the shelters to learn the worst, or discover undamaged houses with a new affection. Mothers and babies were allowed to sleep on till morning.

Of 200 German planes appearing over Moscow that night, 21 July, only

The Mayakovskii underground station during the Moscow blitz. All the
capital's underground stations were used as shelters, and this was one of the
better-appointed ones. The moment the sirens sounded, the trains stopped
running, the arcade shops were shuttered up, and people poured in from the
streets to spend the night on the platform.

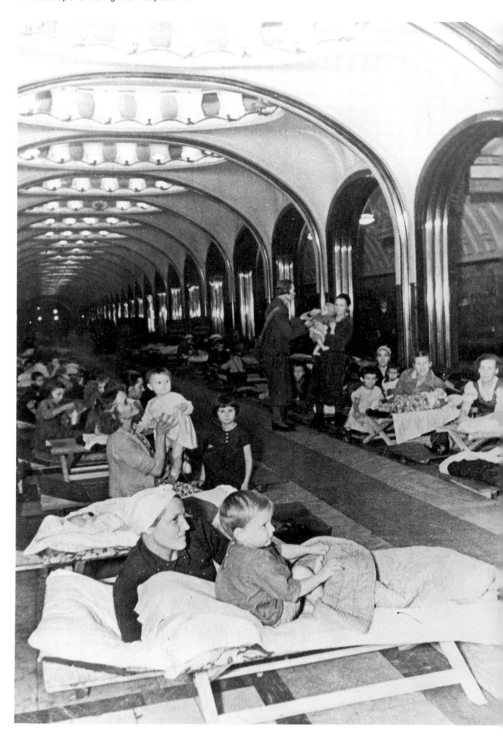

some ten or fifteen got through, dropping several high-explosive bombs and a number of incendiaries. There were a small number of people killed, a few buildings damaged, a number of broken windows, a few bomb craters, including one in Red Square, and a few fires. But in general, the damage was not too serious, and can have given the Germans little satisfaction.

Next night, the siren went again at ten, again crowds of people hurried to the shelters, and the bombing, longer this time, resumed. Firebombs and demolition bombs rained down over the city without any apparent targets, many of them falling on streets and parks or on the outlying countryside. Again, only a small number of planes got through, and many of those that did were shot down by Soviet fighter aircraft. The damage was more serious this night, and over a hundred people were killed when a large shelter off the Arbat Square received a direct hit.

At 2am at the Vakhtangovo Theatre, just as things seemed quiet, Yurii Ryzhakin came out of the theatre onto the Arbat and heard a plane droning ominously in the sky. There was a dull crash, he heard people screaming and saw the entire right-hand corner of the theatre, the foyer and part of the auditorium collapsing under the impact of a demolition bomb. Through the smashed windows he saw flames licking the building. Thirty-seven Vakhtangovites were killed that night, including the Party organiser Vasilii Kuza, who had been helping people to get into shelters. A marble plaque on the rebuilt theatre now records their names.

On the night of 24 July, some 150 German planes appeared over Moscow. After trying unsuccessfully for half an hour to penetrate the city's outer defence rings, they loosed some of their bombs onto the surrounding country-side, then climbed higher and tried again, before giving up and returning to base. Fifteen minutes later, a small group of planes appeared and tried for three hours to penetrate the city's southern air defences – with even less success – then started randomly dropping incendiaries and parachute flares.

Every night the sirens wailed, people trooped to the shelters, explosions were heard in the roofs and floors of houses, doors burst open, glass crashed from windows. Several hours later, at three or four in the morning after the 'All clear', people would stagger out to blazing fires and dead bodies hauled from buildings, and go straight to work. Yet, despite all the deaths and the damage, terrible though this was, one witness, the American writer Erskine Caldwell, considered that the German bombing produced 'less wear and tear on lives and property in Moscow than in the course of a normal day in Los Angeles'. Given the ineptness of the German bombing tactics, it would appear that their main intention was to exhaust and demoralise the population of the capital. But here too they were to be disappointed. The first air raids on Moscow came when morale was exceptionally high, and weeks of air-raid and firefighting preparations showed impressive results.

Firefighting was organised on a vast scale, which was why the Germans found it so difficult to get their incendiaries to catch fire. Every Moscow rooftop, doorway and street corner had two to ten firewatchers. More than 200,000 people worked as firefighters (some 577 of them later awarded medals for bravery), and volunteers alone put out more than 44,000 fires. Behaviour during raids was governed by draconian new laws – three men were shot for negligence when a large warehouse worth 3 million rubles was bombed. Everyone but police and firefighters was banned from the streets, as were all cars, except those with official passes, and children under sixteen were not allowed on rooftops. Citizens were required to obey police orders unquestioningly and to help old people and children into the shelters.

But many children refused to go, putting on gas masks and wiling their way into firefighting teams by lying about their ages. Many mounted guard on the roofs and attics, to be forcibly dragged down by their parents, or kept watch on their own, with reckless courage and frequently tragic consequences, often picking up bombs with their bare hands. Three thirteen-year-olds called Tolya, Maya and Seryozha staked out the roof of their tall narrow house into three sections, and argued about whose section the bombs fell on. Five small boys guarding the roof of the Tretyakov Gallery used spades to toss off the bombs raining onto it. Pronin, the president of the Moscow Soviet, recalled returning during a raid one night from Krasnokholmskii Bridge into Red Square, where hundreds of firebombs were falling. Suddenly, amid the din of anti-aircraft guns, he saw three little figures tearing out of the entrance of the GUM department store, their hands covered in wet capes, to extinguish the incendiaries.

Thousands of women volunteered for the barrage-balloon section, and for firefighting, antichemical and first-aid teams. Maria Nesterova, in her sixties, organised a firefighting team in her apartment block and helped to extinguish 150 fires, even after being twice wounded. Maria Semyonova organised a first-aid team, and continued bandaging even after her leg was hit by a mine. (Her leg was later amputated.) Yulia Borisova gave her life dragging twenty people out of the ruins of the house on Mashkova Street of which she was janitor.

Women party and soviet workers too distinguished themselves, and N. M. Shakhova, secretary of the Kuibyshev district party, was later decorated for her organisational abilities. Many men on the Soviet executive had had their initial anxieties about the women presidents of Moscow's October and Krasnopresnya district soviets. 'I won't tell a lie, we did have our doubts about the behaviour during air raids of the women,' wrote Pronin afterwards. 'What if their female souls suddenly can't take the strain, we wondered? And women represented Soviet power in all the largest areas of the city, too.'

Yulia Polyakova, who before the war had spent ten years in a factory, developing and organising the production of a new metal alloy she had created, had already shown herself a competent and popular organiser since her election in 1940 as president of the October district soviet. The moment war broke out her husband left for the army, and when in July 1941 her daughter was evacuated, she made her home in her soviet building, from which, since there was no underground in her district, she organised the digging of new shelters and the conversion of existing basements, as well as supervising the construction of several large new water reservoirs.

Anti-aircraft gunners outside the Red Army Theatre. Moscow's air defences were so efficient that German planes spent much time dodging the guns and searchlights in the clouds, before releasing their bombs.

Bottom: Barrage balloon on Sverdlov Square.

Pronin readily admitted that his fears had been groundless:

From the first enemy raids, the women behaved excellently. In neither of these areas did the fascists destroy one factory or large house. Polyakova's district became a model for air defence, in fact, and suffered not a single fire, though thousands of incendiaries were to fall on it.

Yulia Polyakova's ARP work earned her a medal 'for meritorious service', which she wore pinned to her military uniform.

The bombing continued over the next eight months, with some eighty raids, thousands of tons of demolition bombs and more than 10,000 fire-bombs. But such were Moscow's air defences that evidence of bomb damage was scarcely noticeable, and every night, only a few German planes managed to get through. Anti-aircraft guns, previously confined to the outer defence zones, moved into the city, and the strengthened anti-aircraft flak inspired tremendous confidence. Several bombs fell on the artificial factories outside the city, and soon journalists and filmmakers were being proudly shown the wrecks of downed Junkers and Heinkel bombers littering the surrounding countryside.

So ineffectual were the Germans' attempts to break through that in a desperate attempt to terrorise the population of Moscow, they resorted to hurling from the skies imitation bombs in the form of plastic phosphorus-coated balls and perforated tin cans, which people collected along with firebombs as trophies, and turned into vases and flowerpots.

By the end of July, Hitler was having to rethink his plans for a quick victory in Russia and the 'decisive' attack on Moscow. Yet Nazi troops were still being told that Moscow was theirs for the taking, and a middle-aged German soldier captured at Smolensk that July told interrogators that he had been practising triumphal music on his trombone to accompany Nazi tank detachments entering Moscow.

On 27 July, after the fifth night of bombing, in which no more than seven of the hundred planes seen over Moscow got through, Goebbels announced in Berlin, 'After yesterday's bombing Moscow is on fire. Eight hundred houses are destroyed. The Kremlin is a heap of smoking ruins. Moscow's power station is demolished. Moscow is without electricity and the trams aren't running.'

Mailbags taken, a month into the war, from Army Group Centre soldiers advancing on Moscow reveal a different story.

We thought the war in the east would be completely different [wrote Corporal Ruhsam on 31 July]. We knew the Russians would fight, but nobody thought they'd fight so desperately. We hope to see the Russian capital soon, then this dreadful war will be over.

By late July, Soviet newspapers were carrying pictures of wrecked Heinkels and Junkers bombers shot down in the thick birch and conifer woods outside Moscow.

Our only hope is to see the end of this dreadful war as soon as possible [he wrote a few days later]. If Moscow falls, Russia will realise that their position is hopeless. But I think it would have been better not to start this war . . .

[And the next day:] You want to know when we'll be in Moscow at last. We are having some delay, as the Russians are putting up a desperate defence.

'It looks as though it will be a year before the war is over,' wrote ss man Mathias Haas. 'We're only now beginning to see what war is really like,' wrote ss man Willi Kurt.

The situation in Moscow was rather different from Goebbels's 'dressed-up' version.

As the light fell, ARP teams appeared with gas masks in bags. Hundreds of barrage balloons were driven along in lorries, escorted by young women in ARP uniform, and at sunset, 'as if a mastermind were in charge of the whole operation,' recalls Vera Inber, the women would hoist the balloons up on their powerful steel cables and steer them aloft. 'There was something so hopeful about those balloons' calm presence,' wrote I. Grekova, in her story 'Ship of Widows'. ' "Go to sleep, people," they said.'

At night, Moscow was plunged into deep darkness. Trams and buses

By night, Muscovites were out on the roofs, watching for incendiary bombs, and early each morning, ARP repair teams could be seen mending the night's damage.

moved slowly down the dark streets. District soviet presidents and party secretaries were now living in their town halls and offices, and the offices of the Kremlin, which had moved underground, were fiercely busy. Behind the blacked-out windows of the factories, men, women and schoolchildren toiled eleven and twelve hours a day, while others stood by their anti-aircraft guns or did firefighting duty. Early each morning, after the night's bombing, Home Guard and ARP detachments would be seen marching briskly down the centre of the streets, shouldering long-handled shovels with which to repair the damage.

Boxes of sand and barrels of water stood on every corner, and children would play with them in the back streets, but most of Moscow's children were now bringing in the harvest in the surrounding countryside, or had been evacuated to the east. Thousands of people had left for the front over the past month. Others were labouring in central Asia. Teachers were out of the city, driving trucks for the army. There were few private cars on the streets. The pace of life quickened. Mealtimes, which often used to last several hours, were now taken in snatches. Conversations became briefer, the hours of sleep shorter, leisure almost a thing of the past. The blackout was very strict and at night, because there wasn't enough blackout material, lights had to be depressingly dim. But according to Ehrenburg (not one to idealise), people who before had squabbled over a crust of bread or a saucepan became kinder, sharing food and caring for one another's children. People became more disciplined. The crime rate went down by half. Queues were more orderly.

The raids didn't stop, and the Germans moved further east, seizing more and more towns and villages on the road to Moscow. But in those weeks the city was learning to cope.

By day, despite the intermittent thunder showers which now broke the sunshine, the usual Sunday crowds filled the Hermitage Park for concerts, patriotic plays and satirical sketches about Hitler and Goebbels. The Moscow Arts Theatre was showing *Three Sisters*, *Anna Karenina* and *The School for Scandal*. The Bolshoi Ballet was continuing its usual season at its Pushkin Street theatre. In the *Red Star*'s new offices in the basement of the Red Army Theatre, surrounded by potholes and ditches, writers worked through the raids to pound out their daily articles.

At night, people now went automatically to the shelters rather than waiting for the sirens. Vera Inber took her typewriter to the basement under her flat, and wrote during bombings. Some people tried to lug bags, bedding, possessions – even sewing machines – into the shelters. Others became demented with anxiety. In one shelter, Inber met a woman on the stairs, half-mad, looking for her husband. 'He was with me all the time. Then he lagged behind. How is he managing without his coat?' (In fact he was still in the flat.) In another, she met a woman rushing to and fro in a frenzy, looking for her baby, who was wrapped in a shawl in her arms. Most people endured the bombing stoically, though – or were just exhausted, having come straight from the factory to the shelter, and many in the underground stations managed to sleep on the rails without bedding.

In Britain and America, it had always been widely felt that the Germans wouldn't have an easy time of it in Russia, and that their governments should negotiate with the Soviet Union. Now Moscow's resilience under bombing was producing a great wave of support for Russia. In London, banners appeared on the streets saying 'Quiet Nights, Thanks to Russia', and Ambassador Maisky was greeted with spontaneous applause whenever he appeared in public. In the United States, a Gallup poll showed that nearly 90 per cent of Americans wanted cooperation with Soviet Russia, and the Roosevelt administration, as it reassessed the dangers presented to it by German and Japanese global ambitions, began to move the US stance from neutrality to a more active opposition to the Axis. More than anyone else, it was Harry Hopkins, the lend-lease administrator and Roosevelt's close personal friend and emissary, who forged the links between the USA and the USSR which grew from these grim days of the war to become a powerful alliance. And at the end of July, Soviet newspapers were filled for a week with the cheering news of his visit to Moscow.

Hopkins flew into Moscow's Central Airport on 28 July, via Scotland and Murmansk, to form an independent assessment of the situation on the Soviet front. With him he carried a letter from Roosevelt to Stalin which read, 'May I express the great admiration of all in the United States for the superb bravery displayed by the Russian people in the defence of their liberty and their fight for the independence of Russia . . .'

Hopkins went on to tell Stalin of the president's conviction that 'the most important thing is to defeat Hitler and Hitlerism'. Stalin talked of the need for 'a minimum moral standard between all nations', saying that without such a standard, nations could not exist. Germany's present leaders 'know no such minimum standard, and therefore represent an antisocial force in the present world'. Talking of the progress of the battles on the fronts, he was guardedly optimistic but, more importantly, in Hopkins's view, Stalin expressed that implacable will to victory which he and his team found everywhere among soldiers and civilians alike. Stalin thought the Germans could mobilise as many as 300 divisions, but that the Red Army would have 350 divisions by the spring of 1942. In their assault on the USSR, the Germans had met with unprecedented resistance, and had found that 'moving mechanised forces through Russia is very different from moving them over the boulevards of Belgium and France'. Stalin hoped to be able to stabilise the front during the autumn campaign, and though Hopkins thought (rightly) that this was too optimistic, he came away convinced that the Soviet Union would hold out. 'I feel ever so confident about this front,' he reported to Roosevelt. 'The morale of the population is exceptionally good. There is unbounded determination to win.'

But the very day after Hopkins's arrival a fierce row on the strategy for this victory had broken out between Stalin and Zhukov. Surveying the status of each sector of the front, Zhukov concluded that in the Moscow and Leningrad areas the Germans had sustained too serious a level of losses to resume the offensive in the immediate future. He proposed withdrawing behind the Dniepr and strengthening the fronts to the south of Moscow. This meant weakening the Moscow defences at least until reinforcements could be brought in from the Far East. 'So then, you want us to give the Far East to Japan,' Stalin said.

Undeterred, Zhukov made plain it would also be necessary to abandon

Kiev. At the same time he wanted to counterattack in the Yelnya–Smolensk direction, to relieve the potential pressure on Moscow. 'What counterattacks?' Stalin exploded. 'What nonsense!' 'If you think the chief of the general staff is only able to talk nonsense,' Zhukov snapped, 'then he has no business here.' And Zhukov asked to be relieved of his duties forthwith and sent to the front, 'where I shall be of more use to the motherland'. 'Don't get heated,' Stalin said, 'but now you mention it, we can manage without you.' Zhukov was sent to organise the counterattack at Yelnya which he himself had proposed.

Within days, as Zhukov predicted, Guderian swung south on the exposed central front.

On 9 August 1941, Churchill and Roosevelt met in Argentia Bay, Newfoundland, to coordinate their plans. Germany's attack on Russia had changed the balance of world forces, and now neutrality did not constrain Roosevelt from signing with Churchill what came to be known as the Atlantic Charter. This set out the principles of respect for national territory and the sovereign independence of states, the right to self-determination and the creation of international structures to guarantee peace in the postwar world – all of which arrangements would be made, according to Roosevelt, in the context of an 'international police force' composed of America and Britain. Thus, for the first time, the three were publicly united in the declaration of their common goals.

By then, such was Moscow's confidence in its air defences that workers in many factories were disobeying instructions to leave their benches for the shelters, and there was an unwritten rule to work as normal during raids. Early in August, a demolition bomb fell on the Hammer and Sickle factory and destroyed the roof. Reconstruction brigades worked for three days and nights to repair the damage, while work continued as usual. Discipline eased. More blackout material arrived, and lights were turned up. When there was no raid, street lighting was sometimes allowed.

On the night of 3 August, a large demolition bomb fell by the Nikitin gates. A tram was thrown several metres aside and its passengers killed, while beside the 10-metre-deep crater the monument to the scientist Timiryazev was thrown off its pedestal. First thing next morning, an engineering team, led by Moscow's chief architect Chechulin, arrived with a repair team and soon had the crater filled in, the tram lines reconnected and the monument back on its pedestal.

On 5 August, Berlin Radio announced:

Strong units of German aviation are each night subjecting this major industrial centre of the country to devastating bombardment. Factories and plants on the outskirts of

Moscow are destroyed, the Kremlin is destroyed, Red Square is destroyed . . . Moscow has entered into the final phase of ruination . . .

'Moscow is an empty city,' said Berlin Radio on 8 August. 'Half the government offices have left for Gorkii. The other half will be sent to Nizhnii Novgorod.' The Germans apparently didn't know that the two places were the same.

'We have destroyed the Soviet air force,' said Goebbels.

Meanwhile, in Moscow, people gathered around the underground station on Revolution Square, where a shot-down German Junkers bomber, festooned with sinister black crosses, had been put on display, along with several large defused bombs. In the pocket of a crew member of one Heinkel 111 bomber, shot down over Moscow on 10 August, was found a diary for Nazi soldiers, published in Paris. Along with information for soldiers in occupied France, such as which wines to drink with fish, were useful phrases in French: 'Mademoiselle, are you free this evening? I can treat you to ice cream.'

'The German command chooses experienced ss men for their raids on Moscow,' wrote Ehrenburg. 'Alfred Kerrle had learned what wine to drink with turkey, and how to insult women in unhappy subjugated France. From his dive bomber he killed miners' children in Swansea. Then he ventured to appear over Moscow . . .'

By late August intense battles raged along the entire front, with the fighting especially severe around Novgorod, Kingisepp and Gomel. The Germans had overrun large parts of the Ukraine. Krivoi Rog and Dniepropetrovsk were already lost, and the situation at Leningrad was critical.

On 23 August, the newspaper *Pravda* concluded its editorial thus: 'The day of payment will come. The Soviet people have entered into a fight to the death with the robbers' horde. Blood for blood! Death for death!'

4

Moscow on the Front Line

On 6 September 1941, Hitler signed Order No. 35, authorising Operation Typhoon – the capture of Moscow. An enormous shock group of more than a million soldiers from army groups North, South and Centre, were to attack from three points – Roslavl, Dukhovshchina and Shostka – and encircle the troops on the three fronts surrounding Moscow. This would be followed by an infantry assault on the capital from the east, with pincer movements north and south. Army Group Centre was to be reinforced by nearly 2000 tanks and assault guns and 950 planes, and the whole operation was to be a guaranteed success.

Shortly after signing the order, Hitler addressed a conference of Army Group Centre: Moscow was to be surrounded, so that 'not one Russian soldier, nor a single inhabitant – man, woman or child – will be able to escape, and any attempt to do so will be suppressed by force'.

The Battle of Moscow was one of the greatest events of the Soviet–German war – and indeed of World War II itself. Throughout that autumn and winter, over 2 million soldiers, supported by 2500 tanks, 1800 aircraft and 25,000 guns and mortars, were to fight a succession of intense battles over hundreds of miles. Here both sides concentrated their forces, and here the outcome of the Soviet–German war was decided.

For Stalin, there seemed at this stage of the war few grounds for hope. Crushed by omnipresent defeat and fears of German superiority, he had little confidence in the loyalty and capability of the Red Army and its leaders, or in their ability to conduct orderly retreats or wage defensive battles. (Visitors to the Kremlin were shocked by the aged, crumpled figure who greeted them, almost unrecognisable from the ubiquitous posters and portraits.) For the Germans, the destruction of the Soviet capital, the 'centre of Bolshevist resistance', was a foregone conclusion.

Yet it was in the bloody battles of that autumn and winter that Moscow's resistance was born – and a new hatred for the enemy, eclipsing every other emotion, which numbed the soul and drove countless people to vote with their blood.

That hatred didn't come easily. Soviet education had taught that cultural standards were measurable in terms of technical advance and industrial production, so that, months after the Nazis had invaded, many Russians hesitated to attack people they felt to be so 'cultured', and would examine in awe German kitbags containing patent safety razors and fancy cigarette lighters. Many were also waiting for German workers to come to their senses and rise up against their leaders. 'Who are we shooting?' Ehrenburg recalled a group of young artillery officers saying, as Nazi troops advanced on their village. 'They're just workers and peasants like us!'

But in the terrible autumn and winter of 1941, the most tragic months of the entire Soviet–German war, it was a just and necessary hatred. 'We hate the Germans for murdering our children, but we also hate them because we're obliged to kill them,' wrote Ehrenburg. 'Because out of the whole treasury of words in our possession we've been left with only one: "Kill!" We hate the Germans for despoiling life.'

Strategically, too, the Battle of Moscow was to be a turning point. Stalin's early policy of static defence, which had led to one army after another being encircled and annihilated, had been immensely costly in lives and material. Yet it was from these catastrophic beginnings that there developed a synthesis between Stalin's strategic preoccupations and Zhukov's operational genius. And it was in the Battle of Moscow that this synthesis was first to see the light of day. But before that, the crisis of Leningrad had to be dealt with.

Hitler had planned to take Leningrad, raze it to the ground and exterminate its inhabitants. German gunners were given special maps of the city with orders to 'destroy housing and exterminate people', and special 'objectives', like the Hermitage gallery, the Kirov Theatre and the zoo, were singled out for intensive shelling.

As the front neared, people in Leningrad had begun frantic preparations for a siege. Nearly a third of the city's 3 million inhabitants, ninety-two of its factories and hundreds of art treasures from the Hermitage and other museums were loaded onto trains and evacuated east beyond the Urals, along with offices, theatres and whole research institutions, down to the doorman. The remaining population, as in Moscow, volunteered for Home Guard detachments, and worked round the clock digging trenches and bomb shelters. Strict rationing was introduced. Military installations, architectural masterpieces, hospitals and schools were hidden and camouflaged. And the city itself turned into an armed camp, with its own arsenals, shipyards and factories turning out a stream of tanks, artillery, ammunition and small arms. There, in factories within spitting distance of the German lines, cold and hungry workers achieved feats of production foreshadowing those in the great new armaments centres beyond the Urals the following year, and guns

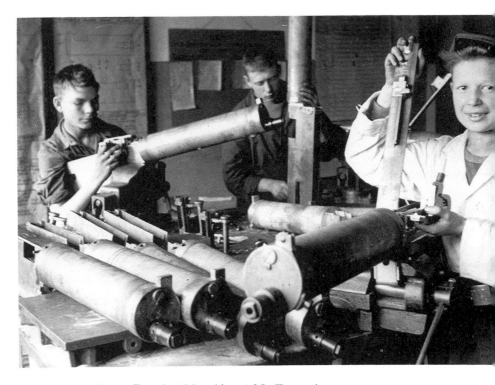

Boys in a Leningrad factory. Throughout July and August, 2.5 million people
(including 400,000 children) were evacuated from Leningrad. As the Germans
closed in and the blockade started, the remaining adults and children endured
bombing and starvation rations to dig defences, work the factories, and fight the
Germans on the city's outskirts. 'They knew everything depended on them,' wrote
Daniil Granin, survivor and historian of the 900-day siege. 'With Stukas howling
overhead, and the rye fields and villages burning all around; the heat, the choking
smoke, the sour smell of explosives and the rattle of German machine guns
everywhere – and we, who were no soldiers at all, had to fire back and let the tanks
come in close . . .'

and ammunition were airlifted to Moscow in such quantities that a disbeliev-
ing *Stavka* called for special reports.

In the early hours of 25 August, the last evacuation trains had slipped
through Mga station. By noon, the Germans had already arrived there. By 8
September, they had taken Schlusselberg, on the shores of Lake Ladoga, thus
cutting off the last land route. The blockade had begun.

On that day, Stalin called Zhukov to the Kremlin. The Northern Front was
collapsing, he said, and 'if the Germans seize Leningrad and link up with the
Finns, they could strike Moscow from the northeast'. Next day, Zhukov flew
from Moscow's Vnukovo airport to the besieged city. There he found chaos,

demoralisation and disintegration. Within a few days of his arrival, 700,000 German and Finnish troops had completely encircled the city.

But these were stopped on Leningrad's last defensive perimeter by remnants of the Red Army and by tens of thousands of Home Guard volunteers, untrained and ill-equipped, but determined.

On 14 September Zhukov reported to the *Stavka*, 'To hold back the enemy offensive and his attempt to widen the gap, we now have to move in hastily organised units, separate regiments, and newly formed workers' divisions'; to the commander of the 54th Army, trying to break through the blockade from outside, 'I have to send people straight from the factory floor to meet the advancing enemy.' But in the last week of September, equilibrium was reached; unable to storm the city, the Germans were in any case already draining panzers off for 'Typhoon'. This equilibrium was to last for nearly three years; the city suffered a slow torment of hunger, shelling and bombing in which almost one million died before the blockade was finally lifted.

On 17 September 1941, Kiev fell and the *Wehrmacht* crashed on to Kharkov and the Crimea. By now, vast areas of European Russia had been overrun, and territory containing nearly half the prewar population of the USSR was under Nazi domination. These were the most industrially developed and agriculturally rich parts of the country. Their loss meant the loss of one third of Soviet food production and two thirds of its basic industries. The energy resources of the coal-rich Donbas had also fallen to the Germans, opening up to the Nazis the dizzying possibility of turning Russia into a vast labour camp of slaves to work for them.

'I don't care who rules Russia,' Hitler said. 'Tsars or Bolsheviks, the Russians are our enemy.'

Had these losses been the result of a natural catastrophe, the outlook would have been bleak enough. As it was, reconstruction had to wait another four years, in which the Soviet people endured a nightmare of dark, cold, hunger, constant danger and unremitting labour.

The loss of the industrialised areas of the country had an immediate effect on arms production. The output of tanks, aircraft, guns and ammunition collapsed, at a moment when all were in short supply. The situation at the front grew increasingly desperate, and the immediate question became one of mere survival. The moment of supreme danger had arrived with terrifying suddenness. By the beginning of October, the fall of Moscow seemed imminent, and with it the inevitable destruction of the Soviet state.

At this moment, when there seemed few resources left but blind resistance and the will to resist, there was a resurgence of the national spirit, and, bracing themselves for what lay ahead, people rallied to the leadership.

True, the *Blitzkrieg* had faltered, and the Germans had also suffered heavy losses – more than half a million officers and soldiers on their own count. The knights of the skull and crossbones hadn't reckoned on Russian resistance. 'The Russians' behaviour in action is simply incomprehensible,' said a letter found on the corpse of Guderian's adjutant in September 1941.

They are incredibly stubborn, and refuse to budge even under the most powerful gunfire. And then the gap will be immediately closed with fresh ranks. It is the result of their Bolshevik training and Bolshevik outlook. The life of the individual means nothing to them. They despise it.

For all that, Hitler considered the war against the Soviet Union effectively won; now its 'economic suppression' could begin. Only one postscript to 'Barbarossa' remained to write, and that was the capture of Moscow and the destruction of the city and its inhabitants.

Seventy-seven divisions, containing the *Wehrmacht*'s best officers, soldiers and infantry, were assembled, tank divisions were transferred from elsewhere in Europe – even from Africa – and the newly appointed Commandant of Moscow, counting on a quick victory, ordered invitations to be printed and new uniforms made for a victory parade, to be held in Moscow's Red Square on 7 November 1941 – the twenty-fourth anniversary of the Russian Revolution.

On 30 September, Army Group South received their orders: 'Forward! To the east!'

Defending the capital, on two lines running 400 miles north–south and 200 miles east–west of Moscow, were 800,000 soldiers, fighting on three fronts, the Western, the Reserve and the Bryansk. In the capital itself, now the intersection of front-line traffic, the trolley buses were still running, but just a few miles from their terminus on the Leningrad Highway people would soon be fighting and dying.

With many children out of town, most teachers away at the front or seconded to other work, and school buildings requisitioned as hospitals, all infants' schools remained closed that September, when the new term was due to start, and turned into overcrowded creches, where children often stayed throughout the week, seeing their parents only at weekends. Secondary schools had also been requisitioned, but most moved into other buildings, where they reintroduced the shift system from the Civil War days, with one building being used day and night for three schools. Classes became larger (though seldom larger than forty-five), but even so, there were not enough places for everyone, so that teachers had to find time from other work to organise classes, and even examinations, in their own homes.

On 29 September 1941, as the Germans were preparing for their onslaught on Moscow, an Anglo-American mission, headed by Lord Beaverbrook and Averell Harriman, both firm supporters of cooperation with Russia and determined to make amends for their governments' failings in 1939 and 1940, flew into the capital to discuss Allied aid to the Soviet war effort.

By this time thc US government, realising that war with Germany was sooner or later inevitable, had concluded that aid to the USSR was therefore an investment in the future, and Beaverbrook and Harriman brought with them firm promises from their governments to increase future supplies of military equipment and other necessities. This was the first conference of representatives of the Big Three powers in the war, and that week Stalin and Molotov sat closeted for hours on end in the Kremlin in discussions with Beaverbrook and Harriman, whose ambassadors sat in the next room waiting to be called if need be. Every evening after the talks finished, the two envoys were treated to a feast of opera, theatre and ballet – *Ruslan and Lyudmila*, *The Forest*, *Othello*, *The School for Scandal* (at the Moscow Arts Theatre), *Evgenii Onegin*, *Romeo and Juliet*, and a gala performance of *Swan Lake* at the Bolshoi, with Ulanova.

One immediate benefit of their visit was that Moscow's central heating (still off, as the Germans ploughed towards the coal mines around Moscow) was turned on by order of the district soviets (and turned off again the moment they left). The longer-term benefits, in terms of promised British and US aid, were small in relation to the demands either of the front or of Soviet war production – and the amounts actually delivered smaller still. But this aid did come to play a role in the Soviet war effort. More importantly, cooperation between the Allies was now beginning to be a practical reality, at a time when it was critically needed.

On 2 October, Hitler addressed the troops of army groups Centre and North. 'The way has at last been paved for crushing the enemy with a powerful blow before the winter. All preparations, so far as humanly possible, have been completed. Today is the start of the final, decisive battle of the year.'

Hitler's 'final offensive' speech was omitted from the Soviet press, and that Wednesday, as the entire Moscow front was being battered by artillery bombardments and tank assaults, life in the capital was continuing much as usual, with the usual crowds of soldiers and civilians at the Hermitage Park, and queues for tickets outside the Moscow Arts Theatre.

In just a few days of fighting, Soviet units and whole divisions of the defensive ring had been ground down and destroyed. By the end of the first day the Germans had broken through the central Rzhev–Vyazma defence line. The following day, German panzers raced into Oryol, an important rail junction and administrative centre 25 miles south of Moscow, shooting and imprisoning its citizens and looting the famous Turgenev Museum. By 5 October, according to the German press, Nazi troops were already in the suburbs of Moscow. These 'suburbs' were to prove unexpectedly resistant.

On the same day, 5 October, as Nazi tanks hurtled towards Moscow, a *Pravda* editorial warned the people of Moscow not to be 'carelessly complacent' about the terrible danger facing them. The atmosphere in the capital grew terribly tense then, and there was much talk of evacuation.

Less than four months into the German invasion, the Red Army had lost over 21,000 tanks, over 32,000 guns and 10,000 planes – and also, as arms production collapsed, the means to replace them. The first gust of 'Typhoon' swept away some 750,000 Soviet soldiers, and less than a week after its start, Moscow's defences were shattered and the city lay wide open to the Germans.

By 6 October, the 16th, 19th, 20th, 24th and 32nd armies on the Western and Reserve fronts had been encircled, and the 22nd, 21st and 29th had been forced to retreat. Although the encircled Russians fought on, and in Vyazma managed to pin down twenty-eight German divisions, thousands of Russians died in the ensuing bloodbath and Vyazma was lost. Zhukov, who had fought Army Group North to a bloody standstill on the outskirts of Leningrad, was recalled by the *Stavka* to Moscow, where the deepest crisis of the war had so suddenly and unexpectedly arrived, and told to do the same thing to Army Group Centre at Moscow, with fewer than 90,000 soldiers – all that was left from Vyazma.

On 7 October, Zhukov arrived in Moscow from Leningrad to find Stalin alone in his Kremlin office, ill with influenza and beside himself with worry. 'Look at this!' He pointed to a map. 'A very difficult situation has developed, and I can't get a proper report from our Western Front headquarters.' Zhukov set off at once to find out what was going on – a familiar problem, as fronts collapsed and the *Stavka* groped in the dark.

At 2.30 the next morning, Zhukov rang Stalin from the western front headquarters and told him of the catastrophe at Vyazma. The State Defence Committee would have to order the western front to fall back, Zhukov said, and regroup on the half-prepared defensive line drawn north–south through Mozhaisk, less than 50 miles from the Kremlin. 'What do you intend to do?' asked Stalin. 'Find Budyonny,' Zhukov replied. (Marshal Budyonny, hero of the War of Intervention and a close colleague of Stalin's, was commander of the Reserve Front, supposedly now shoring up the Mozhaisk line.) Zhukov then set off in the pouring rain for Budyonny's headquarters in Maloyaroslavets. No one there knew of the front commander's whereabouts, or indeed that of their own troops, let alone the Germans, who were at that moment racing towards them down the Mozhaisk Highway. Zhukov eventually came across Budyonny, who had got lost in a forested area, and gave him directions back to his own headquarters.

Mozhaisk was then chosen as the main resistance line, and defences were organised and reinforcements brought in (mainly from the Far East) to the reorganised Moscow Reserve Front, under General Artemev.

In an energetic life, the days that followed were, by Zhukov's own account, the most arduous. His staff worked as if possessed to carry through at breakneck speed an immense labour of defensive preparations. Gradually the soldiers and Home Guards hauled themselves into place.

A change in the weather gave them some respite, and for a few vital days 'Typhoon' flagged, as rain turned unmetalled roads into bogs and the Germans' narrow-tracked armour began to flounder. But more important than the weather was the fact that, for all its cruel losses, the Red Army was still fighting. The Germans did eventually crash through the ill-prepared Mozhaisk defence line, but only at a heavy price. As Guderian said later:

Reports of the quality and, above all, the new tactical handling of the Russian tanks were very worrying . . . The Russian infantry attacked us frontally, while they sent their tanks against our flanks in mass formations . . . The bitterness of the fighting was gradually telling both on our officers and our men. You could see that this was not physical fatigue but nervous shock. It was disturbing to note that the recent battles were affecting even our best officers.

And he went on to note a growing difference in mood between combat units no longer confident of easy success, and a headquarters still drunk with the scent of victory.

The morale of Hitler's soldiers wasn't improved either by the constant compulsion to shoot, kill and destroy every Russian in sight. And they were further demoralised by the activities of Russians fighting behind the German lines. For 'Barbarossa', although the largest military operation in history, was particularly vulnerable to guerrilla tactics.

By August, partisan training centres were instructing people in the towns and villages in the rear of the advancing enemy to gather arms from retreating Red Army units and establish secret bases from which to fight the Germans. As the German front advanced, it became longer, thinner and harder to control, its rear swarming with leaderless soldiers and abandoned military equipment. By the autumn, the guerrilla movement, from its spontaneous, ill-organised beginnings, was already becoming a formidable force operating in the rear of enemy lines, destroying roads, bridges and railway lines, ambushing German detachments and providing intelligence to the Red Army. Partisans had an important political role, too, in representing Soviet rule in places free of German control, and encouraging resistance in the occupied areas. And in the Battle of Moscow, in which some 10,000 partisans fought behind enemy lines, the guerrilla movement came into its own.

By the second week of October, the fighting had reached a critical stage. Mozhaisk was lost, and Nazi soldiers were already plundering the holiday homes on the Leningrad Highway. To the west, German troops were nearing the outskirts of Moscow, and to north and south the flanks of the German armies were enveloping the city like the claws of a crab. In Berlin, cinemas were already advertising their forthcoming documentary, *The Germans Enter Moscow*.

Along the highways outside Moscow, tanks, guns and columns of lorries moved forward under cover of night. In Moscow itself, now almost within gunfire range from the front line, the atmosphere was grim and tense. Bombing continued, with less ferocity now than in July, but by night the city still shook with the roar of the cannons and anti-aircraft guns posted on every rooftop, square and boulevard. And as raid followed raid, the atmosphere became grimmer, the losses heavier, and the jokes fewer. People began to lose dangerous amounts of sleep, ambulances were in short supply, and with hospitals filled with invalids from the front, there were only local first-aid teams to deal with the casualties of bombing. It was an exceptionally cold autumn. Buildings would not be heated until 15 October, and in unheated schools, homes and factories people shivered in their padded cotton jackets and felt boots (only the comparatively rich wore fur). In the factories, as more and more people left for the front, skeletal work forces laboured under increasingly barracklike conditions.

Many of them now stopped going home at night, moving in beds and blankets from home, working double and treble shifts, and eating at their benches. Children who now spent whole days and nights at creches, schools and kindergartens grew solemn and watchful. There was little time for play. Most were enlisted to visit soldiers in the hospitals, and in their spare time at school sewed hospital sheets and made spare gun parts. Teams of women knitted and collected warm clothes to send to workers away fighting, and factory theatre groups took plays and songs to the front, where they were reunited with their colleagues. Letters from the front were seized on, read collectively and treasured. Outside, anti-aircraft guns stood on every rooftop and street corner. The skies were dark with barrage balloons, carried on lorries to be steered aloft by young men and women in uniforms. There were few others on the streets now, as the capital prepared itself for battle.

Early on the morning of 12 October, the high command telephoned the Moscow Soviet asking for 1000 lorries to be sent to the Kalinin front, 100 miles northwest of the capital. Later that day, the Germans captured Kaluga, some 60 miles to the southwest. On that day *Pravda* warned of the 'terrible danger' threatening the capital. Pronin and Shcherbakov were summoned to the Kremlin, and told to mobilise all the available population for battle and organise the building of defences outside and within the city. Moscow was to be turned into an 'unassailable fortress'.

The lorries never returned. The next day, Kalinin fell to the Germans, and a large German force, released from the week-long encirclement at Vyazma, were now ready for the final attack.

On that day the front became almost tangibly close. It was then that the State Defence Committee started to plan the evacuation of half a million children and a million adults, including workers (plus plant and equipment) from crucial arms factories, scientific research and cultural institutions, the foreign diplomatic community and some government departments, including the Ministry of Foreign Affairs. The Politburo of the Communist Party Central Committee, the State Defence Committee and the general headquarters of the high command, together with other government departments essential to the war effort, remained in the capital, along with all the major newspapers. On that day, the Moscow Party organisation ordered factories to increase the production of war supplies. In a few short days each Moscow district party had to mobilise the remaining male population into volunteer Communist and Death battalions, in a desperate effort to supplement the Home Guards closing the gaps in the defence lines around Moscow.

All district party buildings were turned into enlistment centres, and within two days some 12,000 (most of them Party members) had been formed into platoons and battalions, most of them without any military experience or training.

Whole families enlisted. The Lebedevs, father and son, enrolled as machine-gunners. A. N. Zakharina, who had fought in the Civil War, enlisted with her daughter, Oktyabrina, to avenge the death of her husband, who had died at the front. (Several women joined the Communist Battalions — including twenty-six in the Kirovsk district and seventy-six in the Krasnogvardeisk.) A huge battalion was formed from students of the N. E. Bauman Technical College, and by the end of the year half the members of Moscow's Komsomol organisation had enlisted.

The remaining population of Moscow and the suburbs were mobilised by the Soviet into the Labour Front, to increase production in the factories of supplementary war supplies, to dig three massive defence zones ringing the city and antitank ditches along the highways into Moscow, and to lay sandbags, dragon's teeth, 'hedgehogs' and other antitank devices along the city's streets. Iron discipline was to be maintained, and 'a merciless struggle

The German bombing continued into the winter, but with less ferocity, thanks to Moscow's air defences.

Factory workers previously making clothing and household goods now turned out
mines . . .

against even the slightest manifestations of panic from cowards, deserters and
rumour-mongers'. Moscow was fighting for its life.

Meanwhile the Moscow Soviet issued their orders: all women with children under fourteen were to register at evacuation centres and prepare for
immediate departure to the east.

Monday 13 October was freezing cold, with flurries of melting snow filling
the streets with slush. The new menace to Moscow could be felt in the terrible
tension in the air. That day the shops were crowded with women buying food
for the journey or selling unwanted household goods. Queues formed at tram
stops. In the Western embassies, 'friends' of the Soviet Union talked of the
'end' and spread stories to Western correspondents of food shortages in
Moscow, of imminent civil revolt, and of the Germans' 40-kilometre-a-day
advance. (Not all Western correspondents were convinced, especially since
embassy staff, while loading their own petrol tanks to capacity, made no
provision for the evacuation of their own citizens.)

. . . and improvised new weapons. These women from a lemonade-bottling factory filled their half-litre bottles with inflammable liquid for Molotov cocktails to be hurled at enemy tanks.

On 13 October, *Pravda* exhorted people to work as never before, and soldiers to fight with the utmost heroism. And on that day, teams of people, three quarters of them women, turned out into the snow to dig defence lines around the city.

Workers at haberdashery and crockery factories started turning out mines, grenades and mortars. Workers at Moscow's concrete and metallurgical factories were ordered to produce 'hedgehogs', barbed wire for entanglements, and reinforced concrete for pillboxes and gun emplacements. Emergency measures were taken to produce desperately needed weapons for the new volunteer fighters. I. E. Kozlov, the manufacturer of a highly popular soft drink, who had brought his secret ingredient from the Caucasian republic of Abkhazia to Moscow, was called to the Kremlin and told to adapt his factory to the production of half-litre bottles of inflammable liquid, or 'Molotov cocktails', to be thrown at tanks.

Moscow was now a front-line town. Every man, woman and child in the capital was a soldier. 'We've ceased to live by the minute-hand from the morning communiqué to the evening one,' wrote Ehrenburg. 'We've regulated our breath to a different tempo. We boldly look ahead, to where grief is, and victory.'

That evening, the Moscow Radio Symphony Orchestra, remaining in the capital with its conductor, Nikolai Golovanov, gave a concert in the Trade Union Building's Hall of Columns for soldiers and volunteers going to the front. There was such an extraordinarily charged emotion in their performance of Tchaikovsky's 1812 Overture that night that uniformed soldiers wept and applauded and demanded five encores. The concert ended with everyone rising to their feet and singing Mokrousov's song 'The Defenders of Moscow' to words by Surkov:

We won't flinch in battle for our capital
Mother Moscow is dear to us
We'll build a defence of steel
An unassailable wall
And rout and smash the enemy!

The soldiers marched off to training camps in the outskirts of the city. The Communist Battalions were hurriedly given a rudimentary training in shooting, mining, grenade-throwing and tank-fighting, then sent off, under the command of generals Zhukov, Konev and Sokolovskii, to fill in the gaps on the western front, many of them ultimately to merge with active units. Within three days some 12,000 volunteers had left for the front, where, armed often with nothing more than spades and pickaxes, they fought, at devastating cost of life, against vastly superior enemy forces.

Pasternak's poem 'Conqueror', published in 1944, vividly expressed the exhaustion, rage and helplessness of those days:

Do you remember that dryness in your throat
When rattling their naked power of evil
They barged ahead and bellowed,
And autumn advanced in steps of calamity?

On the morning of 15 October 1941, foreign journalists and diplomats were ordered to leave Moscow for Kuibyshev, on the Volga. On that day streams of women and children, bundled up against the snow, trudged with their luggage to the Kazan station. The station waiting rooms, decorated with ominously cheerful posters of holiday scenes and folk dancers, were packed with people sitting wearily on their bundles, unsure of where they were going or whether they would ever return.

An endless stream of limousines brought in the entire foreign diplomatic corps, who proceeded to storm the buffet, and a special train was set aside for foreigners, with diplomats in one sleeper and Comintern officials – including the famous Spanish Communist, Dolores Ibarruri ('La Pasionaria') – in another.

It took five days to travel from the war zones deep into the Russian interior. All along the route, women worked day and night to repair the lines, station loudspeakers broadcast the latest communiqués from the front, and crowds of refugees besieged the trains for news of Moscow. Over 100 food-distribution centres and infants' milk kitchens had been set up along the route (mainly by local Komsomols), each providing 3000 free meals a day.

But people went hungry nonetheless. This large-scale evacuation into the heart of Russia involved millions of frightened, cold, hungry people carrying their children and bundled-up possessions along muddy roads, or sitting with stoical patience for long hours in the cold. There were huge bottlenecks at rail junctions like Cheliabinsk, and people suffered terrible hardships in that mass exodus to the east. Many lost relatives, many children lost their parents for ever.

The evacuees swelled the population of the east, and for many critical months, there was a desperate shortage of housing, food, transport and schools. Yet countless men and women, living in tents and on minimal rations in subzero temperatures, worked till they dropped to build new settlements. Women worked in the mines and on the farms, where they often stood in not just for men but for horses and tractors too.

On 16 October, the general staff was evacuated to Kuibyshev, along with most of Moscow's main museums, orchestras and theatres. Skeletal front-line teams from the Bolshoi, the Vakhtangovo and the Moscow Philharmonic remained to prepare performances to take to the troops, dig defences, work in the factories and help with the evacuation.

Many people just refused to leave. Eighteen-year-old Tamara Lisitsin, from Tbilisi in Georgia, was a student at the Moscow Theatre School. On 16 October, when students received their evacuation orders and assembled with their rucksacks at the station ready to leave, she reported to the Komsomol Central Committee, told them she could ride a motorbike and was a champion rifle shot, and applied to join the army. After three months of daily military exercises at the Izmailovskii Park, she was given a new name and was assigned to the intelligence section of the Fifth Army, on the Mozhaisk front. From there, she was sent into the rear of the German army, where she led a partisan detachment. She was captured, sentenced to death, escaped, fought again – and, she said later, 'The war ended for me in 1945.' Tamara Lisitsin is now a well-known actor and film director.

In those days, when every day brought news of the death of a loved one, the young grew up quickly. People who came to enjoy the sideshows and gardens of the Izmailovskii Park that October saw many young volunteers (a large number of them women) learning to attack and disarm sentries and demolish tanks.

Before the war, Sonia Butseva, the Komsomol secretary at her factory, had dreamed of love affairs and weekend outings. Now that more than half her friends from the factory had left for the front, the 'Red board' in the hall displayed letters from absent friends and portraits of those who had died, and she was working eleven or twelve hours a day, producing mines and grenades. Olga Sapozhnikova, a weaver at the Trekhgorka cotton mill, had three brothers at the front, two wounded and one 'missing'. For them and countless other women, Konstantin Simonov's poem 'Wait for Me', written in that terrible winter to his wife, became like a sort of prayer:

Wait for me, and I'll return, only wait very hard
Wait, when you're filled with sorrow as you watch the yellow rain
Wait when the winds sweep the snowdrifts, wait in the sweltering heat
Wait when others have stopped waiting, forgetting their yesterdays
Wait, for I'll return, defying death
And let those who did not return say I was lucky.
They will never know that in the midst of death
You with your waiting saved me.
Only you and I will know how I survived
It's because you waited, as no one else did.

On 16 October, Moscow's major factories received their evacuation orders – along with highly secret instructions, entrusted to leading Party workers, to blow up the crucial operating parts should they fall into enemy hands.

Opposite top: Members of the Komsomol (Communist Youth Organisation) collect money for tanks. (The posters on the wall read 'Komsomol member, be a hero of the Great Patriotic War!' 'Fascism is the cruellest enemy of women!') Thousands of Moscow's Komsomol members enrolled in the Red Army, joined the partisans, and organised production of war goods in the factories.

Opposite bottom: A factory relocated in the Urals. Every time an industrial town was threatened, a new one was built to replace it in the barren areas of the Urals, western Siberia and central Asia, which became the country's main arsenal. In the autumn of 1941, as the Germans approached Moscow, entire factories and masses of machinery were transplanted to the east, along with their workers. The factories were reconstructed in record time, communities were built, and people laboured to bring production up to its pre-1941 level. On the wall is V. Koretskii's famous poster 'Soldier of the Red Army, Save Us!'

'Everything was mined, it was just a question of pushing the button,' said Olga Sapozhnikova. 'I felt as though a stone was on my heart,' said I. I. Turtanov, of the Hammer and Sickle factory, 'when I took my heavy load of bombs and looked at the machines. The secret got out, and dozens of bleary eyes reproachfully followed my every step, begging me to wait till the last moment.'

Many of the older workers, who'd worked at the same factory all their lives, refused to budge. Others lovingly packed every nut and bolt, as though it were part of themselves. 'Who knows,' said one worker, 'maybe we'll need to screw them back on the same bolt before too long.'

Thousands of Russia's key factories were moved east in a massive industrial evacuation and resettlement programme which must count as one of the most extraordinary achievements of the whole war. Of Moscow's factories, 498 were dissassembled, loaded onto 710 railway vans and set off, covered with birch branches, for Magnitogorsk, Cheliabinsk, Omutninsk and other points east. Flywheels, cogs, lathes and machine parts, greased and wrapped in parchment, were packed separately. Behind them went vans, heated by stoves, carrying 210,000 workers and their families. Alongside them, often in the same trucks, were loaded canvases and art treasures from Moscow's major museums and art galleries.

Many of Moscow's factories merged with local enterprises in the east, while some of its industrial giants, like the Electrosteel plant, were split up into smaller units. The men and women who moved east displayed an almost incredible fortitude and endurance, working at the height of winter, with inadequate food and housing, to rebuild factories, and within less than a year they had increased production.

In Moscow, at the now deserted factory sites, even the oldest workers couldn't remember such a bitter October. Workshops grew cold where once hearths had blazed, molten metal had raged and steel had been forged. Years of proud work had gone.

5

The Battle for Moscow

For the people of Moscow the speed of the evacuation had come as a blow. Three million Russians were already prisoners of the Nazis. In the fields around the capital, the corn was still unreaped. The Germans were breaking through Soviet defences south and east of Moscow. 'Don't panic,' said the authorities, then left, without ever properly explaining why. No one was sure whether Stalin was in Moscow or not. Even the bravest and most determined could not be sure that Moscow could be saved if the Germans broke through. There was a rapid succession of air raids, during which defending Russian airmen suicidally rammed enemy planes. At the factories, exhausted people sleepwalked through working days that seemed endless. On the streets, Home Guards and Communist Battalions shuffled along sullenly. A pall of black smoke from the Kremlin's chimneys filled the air with the acrid smell of burning documents.

A particularly ominous communiqué on 16 October 1941 referred to a 'breakthrough on the Volokolamsk sector', but there was a general feeling that the Germans had advanced even further towards Moscow than the communiqués would admit. Suddenly the uncertainty and depression reached their limit and raced through the city, setting off an acute collective panic. There was a stampede for the railway stations. Lorries that brought food to the capital loaded up for the return journey with whole families, plus their bedding, mattresses and saucepans. Officials rushed around town in search of petrol, trying to leave without permits. All the highways east out of Moscow were lined with trucks and cars filled with people trying to escape. Rumours proliferated that surrender was imminent. Many offices and factories stopped working. There were several cases of looting. Olga Sapozhnikova, the Trekhgorka cotton-mill weaver, told Alexander Werth:

On the 16th, when the Germans had broken through, I went to the factory. My heart grew cold when I saw that it was closed. A lot of the directors had fled. The factory people suggested I could evacuate Mother and Father to Cheliabinsk. But whatever happened to the old people, there was only one thing I could do, and that was to follow the Red Army. I went and talked with Mother. 'God will protect us here,' she said, 'and Moscow won't fall.' So we went down to the cellar and buried our sugar and flour, and also Father's Party card. We thought we'd live in the cellar if the Germans came, for we knew they couldn't stay in Moscow long. There was a feeling the Germans might appear in the street at any moment, and Krasnaya Presnya was the district through which they'd come . . . But they didn't come . . .

Konstantin Simonov recalled the panic and despair of the 'big skedaddle' of 16 October in *The Living and the Dead*:

Later, when all this belonged to the past, and somebody recalled that October 16 with sorrow or bitterness, he would say nothing. The memory of Moscow that day was unbearable to him – like the face of a person you love distorted by fear. And yet, at the front that day the war seemed to have taken a fatal turn, and there were people in Moscow that same day who, in their despair, were ready to believe that the Germans would enter tomorrow. As always in tragic moments, the deep faith and inconspicuous work of those who carry on was not yet known to all, and had not yet come to bear fruit, while the bewilderment, terror and despair of the others hit you between the eyes. That day, tens of thousands getting away from the Germans rolled like an avalanche towards the railway stations and towards the eastern exits of Moscow. And yet out of these tens of thousands there were perhaps only a few thousand whom history could rightly condemn.

Most people were just bewildered. On Friday 17 October, workers at a big clock factory in Moscow's Leningrad district refused to let cars loaded with machinery out of the gates, and crowds of people on the Chaussée of Enthusiasts mobbed a cargo of lorries and prevented them from going east. The leaders of the Moscow Soviet were called to explain. The government was staying, they said, along with Moscow's city services, its bakeries and its hospitals. All the approaches to Moscow were fortified. No one would surrender her to the Germans.

Meanwhile people continued to dig defences around the city. For the next one and a half months, in snow and frost, under bombardment and fire, and on normal rations, hundreds of thousands of people, most of them women, turned out from early in the morning until late at night, to dig the hard earth with spades, shovels, crowbars, bare hands. Even Zhukov was impressed when he visited the digging operations:

I saw with my own eyes how thousands of Moscow women left their homes to do heavy navvy work for which they are altogether unsuited, digging ditches and trenches, erecting barricades and obstacles, lugging heavy sandbags. The raw mud stuck to their feet, to the wheelbarrows in which they carted the earth, to their spades, making the digging – which is really a man's work anyway – incomparably more difficult.

October–November 1941. Teachers, students, housewives, pensioners and schoolchildren turned out in rain, mud and snow to dig three huge defence lines around Moscow. Many slept beside their trenches at night, like sappers, to save strength and time.

Ehrenburg wrote:

The Germans thought Russian women would do their washing for them in the morning and dance for them in the evening. Those gross insolent males, accustomed to dealing with greedy submissive females, expected to find housewives and fan-dancers. Instead they've found women ready to defend their honour and freedom with the last drop of their blood.

Sonia Butseva, who heard the communiqué of 16 October after a late shift at her factory, organised the other workers on her shift into a labour detachment to dig fortifications around the city. Olga Sapozhnikova and her workmates from the Trekhgorka mill were also mobilised into the labour front:

We were taken some kilometres out of Moscow. There was a very large crowd of us, and we were told to dig trenches. We were all very calm, but dazed, and couldn't take it. On the very first day we were machine-gunned by a Fritz who swooped right down on us. Eleven of the girls were killed, and four wounded.

Several thousand people, mainly women, led by teams of soldiers, dug huge seven-kilometre antitank ditches at the Naro–Fominsk defence line. Women from the Trekhgorka textile mill, directed by Nikolai Podvoiskii (one of the organisers of the storming of the Winter Palace in October 1917), dug another deep ditch in thick mud between the Moscow River and Kuntsevo. Shcherbakov and Pronin, inspecting an antitank ditch being dug in the Lenino district in the pouring rain, saw fifty wet figures slithering about in the mud at the bottom, and crawling down to ask who they were, found they were actors and workers of the Bolshoi Theatre – many of them in light coats and slippers. To the right and left of all the highways into town, women could be seen digging trenches, ditches and dugouts. For all the heroism of this massive labour, Stalin was sharply critical of its slow progress, and the Party was ordered to mobilise all available mechanical diggers and shovels and bring in a twenty-hour day.

On 17 October, all Communist Battalions and front-line soldiers were ordered to occupy the lines on the outskirts of the city. That evening, Shcherbakov addressed the panickers on the radio, firmly denying all rumours of surrender, which, he said, were spread by enemy agents:

Under attack by enemy forces, who broke through one of our defence lines, army divisions have gone to defend the lines nearest to Moscow. Moscow is threatened. But we will fight stubbornly, fiercely, to the last drop of our blood. Comrade Muscovites! Every one of us, no matter what his work or position, shall act like a soldier defending Moscow against the fascist invaders!

But perhaps it was his announcement that Stalin was in Moscow that made such a difference to people's morale. 'It now seemed certain that Moscow would not be lost,' said Olga Sapozhnikova.

Beside the deep crater outside the Kremlin made by the half-ton bomb that had fallen there in August was the entrance to the Kremlin's underground offices, leading off a long corridor like compartments in a train. That evening, Stalin summoned Zhukov. 'We all know the situation. Shall we defend Moscow?' 'We shall,' said Zhukov. Then Stalin dictated the orders for a state of siege to be proclaimed in Moscow and the outlying districts. 'All those who break the law will be immediately brought to justice by a court-of-war tribunal, and all provocateurs, spies and other enemy agents calling for the breaking of the law will be shot on the spot.'

After that he telephoned the commanders of all the eastern military districts of the Red Army (remembering all their names, recalled Zhukov, and only occasionally looking in his notebook), and ordered them to send to Moscow all available reinforcements. 'That man had nerves of iron,' wrote Zhukov later.

In October 1941, the battles around Moscow were fought in bitter cold and rain, carts and lorries were stranded in muddy roads, and soldiers heaved their supplies to the battlefield and went straight into the fighting. (Note the camera angle – the photographer did not take cover.)

Stalin's draconian but inevitable measures rallied flagging spirits. And his decision to stay had an electrifying effect, one that is still remembered by those who lived through those terrible days. 'By the 20th,' recalled Olga Sapozhnikova, 'the factory was open again. We all felt so much better, and were quite cheerful again after that.'

In the outskirts of Moscow, the last reserves of Home Guards and Communist Battalions threw themselves against the Germans, fighting, at devastating cost of life, with spades, pickaxes, petrol bombs and anything that came to hand. Cavalry regiments were assigned horses mobilised from the farms. Young, untrained and often unshod, these horses were generally used for transport rather than fighting. The men were equally exhausted. 'All the norms of sleep and rest were forgotten,' wrote General Belov, commander of the Ninth Cavalry Corps. 'People ate on the run, slept in snatches, however and wherever they could, and for days on end would have nowhere warm to go, even though the frosts by now were severe.'

The Battle of Moscow was the crucial hinge on which the outcome of the war turned. There were to be other turning points – at Stalingrad, and later at the Kursk salient – but this was to be the deepest crisis. Within it, no moment was more fateful than that of Stalin's decision about the question of personal evacuation. His decision to remain in the Kremlin had two consequences. It signified the Soviet leadership's determination to fight on to victory, and in this, Stalin's person became the symbolic focus of national unity. 'Stalin is with us!' became the popular rallying cry, and with it went another (from a poem by Surkov): 'Moscow is behind – there's nowhere left to retreat.'

More importantly, Stalin's presence in Moscow was crucial to the effective conduct of the war. Had the government been evacuated to distant provincial towns, the power of the state might have been dissipated, just as it was in France when the French government fled to Vichy in 1940. As it was, there was a unity of purpose between the people, fiercely determined to destroy the invaders, and a leadership which translated this into a war-winning political and military strategy. Surkov's 'A Soldier's Oath' concisely expressed this new mood of grim determination:

'Stalin has told me that the battle will be hard and bloody, but that victory will be mine. For my heart is burning with the tears of women and children. Hitler and his hordes will pay for those tears with their wolves' blood, for the avenger's hatred knows no mercy.'

'I shoot without missing,' said one soldier, 'for my bullet flies from my heart.'

Artists, poets and filmmakers celebrated and mourned the heroism and tragedy of those terrible days when Moscow's fate was decided, and visited the front to entertain, inspire and learn. Simonov's poems were immensely popular that winter, especially 'The Retreat from Smolensk':

And it seemed that outside every Russian village
Our grandfathers had risen from the dead
And were shielding us with outstretched arms
And praying for us, their godless grandchildren.
Russia, our homeland, what is it?
It is not Moscow houses, where we cheerfully lived.
It is rather these poor huts where our grandfathers laboured
And the Russian graves with their simple crosses . . .

Simonov, Surkov, Ehrenburg and other war correspondents gave poetry readings to front-line soldiers and on returning to the capital would write up

Aleksei Surkov (born 1899, of a peasant family). Wrote his first poems in 1918, about his experiences fighting in the Civil War. Went on to write numerous popular poems and songs, mainly about the Red Army (including his famous 'Song of the Red Army', written in the early 1930s). His war poems are contained in three anthologies: *December Outside Moscow* (1942), *Invasion* (1943), and *Russia the Punisher* (1944).

their experiences in powerful articles and poems. Bedny and Marshak continued to hand in their daily poems to artists who turned them into posters for the TASS windows on the Kuznetskii Most, and these were put on film and sent off to the front. Film, theatre and song-and-dance troupes streamed off from Moscow to entertain the soldiers. Anna P. took her portable film projector to the front, where, with scouts keeping an eye on the sky, she organised film shows for partisan and army groups in the rustling depths of forests or in villagers' huts. Art exhibitions were taken to the front at times of

Ilya Ehrenburg visiting the troops. Ehrenburg (born 1891, Kiev, of an engineer's family; died 1967 in Moscow) became a Bolshevik in 1908, and in that year emigrated under threat of prison to Paris, where he wrote his first poems. Returned to Russia in July 1917. From 1921 to 1924, worked as a journalist in Berlin, where he wrote his first novel, a philosophical satire published in 1922, called *The Strange Adventures of Julio Jurenito*. Returning to the Soviet Union, he worked as a journalist. From 1936 to 1939 he was an *Izvestiya* correspondent in Spain, and in 1937 published a poetry anthology called *What One Needs*. In 1940 he started writing his novel *The Fall of Paris*. His war journalism (mainly for the Red Army paper *Red Star*) was extremely popular, in the USSR and abroad.

lull, and artists like Aleksandr Deineki and Boris Polevoi left a vivid record of the battles around Moscow and the results of fascist brutality.

The twenty-two actors who made up the front-line branch of Moscow's Maly Theatre entertained soldiers with Novikov's play *Guilty without Guilt*. (Afterwards, they wondered whether this tearful drama had been the right choice, and found soldiers begging them for more comedies, saying, 'We've enough tragedy as it is!') Song-and-dance troupes from factories would go off with accordions and violins and play old wartime favourites like 'In the

Roman Karmen and Konstantin Simonov visiting the troops.

Roman Karmen (born 1906, Odessa) had filmed in Spain in 1939, and in China in 1941. During the war, he directed several famous Moscow Chronicle documentaries, including *The Rout of the Germans Outside Moscow* (1942), *Leningrad in Struggle* (1942) and *Berlin* (1945).

Konstantin Simonov (born 1915) started writing poems, mainly on war themes ('Conqueror', 1937, 'Kutuzov', 1939), and went on to write novels (*The Story of One Love*, 1940, *The Boy From Our Town*, 1941). He spent much of the war at the front, writing for *Red Star*, and these experiences produced his play *The Russian People* (performed in 1942), numerous popular poems (e.g. 'Kill Him!', 'Wait for Me', 'Do You Remember Alyosha'), and a number of novels, published after the war, including *Days and Nights* (1946) and the trilogy *The Living and the Dead*, which won the Stalin Prize. He was editor of the *Literary Gazette* in 1938 and 1950–54, and of *Novy Mir* 1946–50 and 1954–58.

Dugout', 'In the Forest at the Front' and 'Evening Raid', and a wealth of new popular songs were composed. There were classical front-line performances, too, of Tchaikovsky, Rimsky-Korsakov, Glière, Chopin and Dvořák.

Back in the capital after a week of fighting, a group of young volunteers met in a Moscow school building, where new divisions were being formed. Among them was a young conservatoire student (now an honoured musician in Azerbaijan) called Z. Bagirov. There he saw a grand piano, and with fingers stiffened by cold and exhaustion, he sat down to play a Chopin nocturne. As the others gathered silently behind his shoulder, he played on – Liszt, Beethoven, Chopin's Revolutionary Étude.

Never before had I played with such inspiration. There was a sudden crisis in my soul, and I wanted to convey these emotions to those standing behind me. When I'd finished I looked at the faces of my comrades, and felt their elation, as though I'd given them new courage. We talked of Beethoven and Chopin, and of concerts at the Bolshoi Zal, as though there were no war . . . Then we were assigned our regiments, and shaking off the memories, I put music behind me for a long time . . .

Yurii Ryzhakin, the actor and party organiser at Moscow's Vakhtangovo Theatre, had helped with the evacuation of old people and children from Moscow. In the hard days of October, he and the playwright Boris Voitekhov moved their beds into the theatre bookkeeper's office, where, with the director Nikolai Okhlopkov, they all worked on Voitekhov's new play *Salute to Arms*. The studio of the Moscow Chronicle was moved to the cellar of a building in Likhovo Street, and transformed into the headquarters for the filming of the Battle of Moscow.

Reduced teams of actors and directors at Moscow's theatres continued to produce new plays. Leonid Leonov's stirring drama *Invasion*, playing at the Maly Theatre's Moscow stage, showed familiar characters evolving in mortal battle, as the corrupt and aimless Fyodor is filled with love and warmth and finds his place in the world when his town is invaded.

'People must know that we've held out, that innumerable griefs haven't crushed our soul, that our spirit is alive,' Leonov told a correspondent of *Evening Moscow*. 'Let our ancestors say that our art was worthy of its great mission – the emancipation of the Soviet people.'

The factories came back to life. Workers remaining at the sites of the evacuated Podolsk mechanical factory restored the furnace that had been half destroyed by bombs, and started turning out grenades and trench stoves. Others used what machines remained to turn out armaments. Workers at the Kalinin and SAM factories produced rocket launchers and machine guns. Those at Moscow's car factory turned out some 1500 Shpagin machine pistols. The Vladimir Lenin, Red Proletarian, Fighter and Presnya machine-

'Evening Raid'

Music by Solovyov-Sedoi, words by A. Churkin

(two more verses)

Moscow's Dynamo factory and others did on-the-spot tank repairs.

building factories all made mines, shells and detonating fuses. Others turned out 'hedgehogs', spades and mess tins.

Half the workers from the Hammer and Sickle factory took rails and bars from the factory and went off to join the diggers. The rest used the remaining machinery, covered now in frost, to repair tanks. Workers at the Fighter, Red Metalworker and Dynamo factories repaired tanks too. When an exhausted tank arrived, with its full crew, for immediate repair, they would work around the clock, and as the mended tank slid out of the factory gates, an impromptu meeting would be held, with workers and crew members jumping onto the tank to bless it on its mission of destruction.

At the gates of Moscow the Germans had been more than ever convinced that the Soviet system was close to collapse and the Red Army played out. The truth was rather different. The Soviet Union had scarcely flexed its muscles. The *Wehrmacht* had compressed it like a giant spring. The recoil was the more shattering for being so unexpected. Confidence returned.

Within three weeks of the start of 'Typhoon', German divisions had broken through Moscow's first outer defence line, running from Kalinin to Kaluga, and were heaving themselves through thick mud towards the second, in places just some 43 miles from the capital. By then, Guderian's panzers had covered the 50 miles from Oryol to the city of Tula. But in Tula, the last gateway to Moscow, they were to be held up for over a month in a series of violent battles. And elsewhere Soviet troops were managing to hold back the German advance on the line from the Nara and Oka rivers and the Volga reservoir (east of Volokolamsk) to Aleksino. The immediate crisis at the front was receding.

What had happened to transform the situation in late October? Marshal Vasilevskii, head of a small group of general staff officers attached to GHQ in Moscow, later wrote:

In appraising the outcome of events in October it should be said that it was very unfavourable to us. The Soviet army had suffered severe losses. The enemy had advanced nearly 100 miles. But the aims of Operation Typhoon had not been achieved. One of von Bock's groupings had become hopelessly bogged down near Tula, another beyond Mozhaisk, and yet another in the upper reaches of the Volga. The staunchness and courage of the defenders of the Soviet capital stopped the Nazi hordes ... an enemy who enjoyed a numerical superiority in manpower and weapons ...

Leaving aside the failures of German planning, it is enough to quote General Blumentritt, chief of staff, German Fourth Army, to see what really went wrong:

When we reached Moscow, the mood of our commanders and troops sharply changed ... We discovered to our surprise and dismay that the defeated Russians had not ceased to exist as a military force, and the intensity of the battles increased every day ... All this came as a complete surprise to us. We could not believe that the situation had changed so radically after our decisive victories when, it seemed, the capital was almost in our hands. The troops recalled with indignation the bombastic announcements made in October by our Propaganda Ministry.

The Berlin correspondent of the *National Zeitung* was even more forthright. 'German troops advancing on Moscow realise that they're fighting for warm winter quarters and a roof to shelter them when the weather breaks up.'

'So now we know what animates the "heroes" of Volokolamsk and Naro-Fominsk,' wrote Ehrenburg:

they're flat-hunters, who have set out on a campaign in search of warm rooms. They have become modest. In the summer they were after estates. They each reckoned on a hundred acres of Russian land. The weather was fine. The s s men basked in the sun, gorged themselves and dreamed fondly of summer houses, verandas and hammocks.

Now they're no longer thinking of land, and the corporals have become very chilly. But they shan't enter Moscow! The wild beasts shan't warm themselves in our houses. Let them hibernate in snowdrifts. There's only one lodging for them, and that's in the frozen earth!

Confidence returned, and on the evening of 6 November 1941, the Moscow Soviet held its usual eve-of-Revolution anniversary celebration. This year, however, it was held not in the Soviet Building but in the marbled halls of the ornate Mayakovskii underground station. Many members were absent at the front. The atmosphere was eerie and depressing. But the brightly lit station was packed with delegates from soviet, party and trade-union organisations, who waited for Stalin to arrive. A train drew up quietly at the platform and he alighted.

The *Blitzkrieg* had already failed, he said. Hitler had failed to win Britain's support, and now Britain, America and the Soviet Union were in the same camp. 'The coalition between these countries is a very real thing [loud applause] which will continue to grow in the common cause of liberation.' The Germans had hoped that the Soviet regime would collapse and the USSR fall to pieces. 'Instead the Soviet rear is more solid than ever. Any other country, having lost as much as we have, would have collapsed.' Their supplies were constantly threatened by partisans, 'while ours are constantly supported by the rear, with manpower and ammunition.' He then concluded a catalogue of Nazi atrocities in Russia by appealing to Russian national pride:

The Germans want a war of extermination against the great Russian nation – the nation of Plekhanov and Lenin, of Belinskii and Chernyshevskii, of Pushkin and Tolstoy, of Gorkii and Chekhov, of Glinka and Tchaikovsky, of Sechyonov and Pavlov, of Suvorov and Kutuzov! Very well then, if they want a war of extermination they shall have it! [Loud cheers.] Our task now is to destroy every German, to the very last man, who has come to occupy our country. Death to the German invaders! [Stormy applause.]

The Russians had the advantage of fighting a just war, he concluded. And the defence of Moscow showed that in the fire of the Great Patriotic War new soldiers were forged. The speech ended on the usual note: 'Long live the Red Army and Navy! Long live our glorious country! Our cause is just! Victory will be ours!' (Stormy applause.) His speech was followed by a concert.

The next day, in an event which transformed the movement of troops into a political act of profound symbolic importance, Stalin reviewed the Red Army from Lenin's mausoleum in the traditional 7 November celebration of the Great October Socialist Revolution.

The Germans had planned to take Moscow in time to hold a victory parade on 7 November, the fourteenth anniversary of the Bolshevik Revolution. But Stalin ordered the anniversary celebrations to be held as usual in Red Square, and stood on the granite platform of Lenin's mausoleum to address the troops, who marched straight off to the front, in some places just 40 miles outside the capital.

Red Square was particularly solemn and terrible that day. Moscow had had its first snowstorm the night before, and the Kremlin and Lenin's mausoleum were covered in a thin layer of fresh snow, driven by piercing gusts of icy wind. The skies were dotted with barrage balloons and patrolled by fighter planes, the streets were littered with antitank obstacles, and German and Russian guns could be heard booming less than 40 miles away, as Moscow waited for the inevitable second offensive. All the way from Manezh Square, skirting the Historical Museum and filling Red Square stood thousands of troops, experienced soldiers and ragged volunteers, many just back from the front, many on their way there. Behind them were rows of tanks, old T-26s, as well as many of the new T-34s.

Stalin started by recalling the early days of the revolution, when foreign interventionists had overrun three quarters of the country and the Bolsheviks had no food, no equipment, no army, no allies.

Yet we organised the Red Army, and turned the country into a military camp . . . Our position is far better than it was twenty-three years ago. We are richer in industry, food and raw materials. We now have allies . . . We have a wonderful army and a wonderful navy . . . We have no serious shortages of food and equipment. Can anyone

doubt that we can and must defeat the Germans? Comrades, Red Army and Navy men, officers and political workers, men and women partisans! The whole world is looking on you as the power capable of destroying the German robber hordes! The enslaved peoples of Europe are looking upon you as their liberators. May you be inspired in war by the spirit of our heroic ancestors – Aleksander Nevskii, Dmitrii Donskoi, Minin and Pozharskii, Aleksander Suvorov, Mikhail Kutuzov!

The soldiers on parade then marched straight off to the front.

Stalin's order to hold the traditional revolutionary parade was an inspiring challenge to the Nazi hordes outside Moscow, and his speech, identifying as it did Soviet Russia with Holy Russia, had an immense impact. The poet Vera Inber, half-dead from cold and hunger in Leningrad, heard it on the radio in her dark room, amidst the din of sirens, guns and bombs, and 'everything merged for us as one great, shining consolation'.

And in an article for *Red Star* on 7 November, Ehrenburg stressed the world significance of Moscow, whose fight had buried the *Blitzkrieg* for ever and exploded the 'invincibility' of Hitler's army for all to see:

Today the whole world looks towards Moscow. People are talking of Moscow in Narvik and Melbourne. The telegraph wires of the world keep repeating the word

Moscow. Moscow isn't just a city, it has become the hope of the world ... Yet Moscow has remained a Russian city. Each one of its streets hold a memory for us. All our life and history is in its jumbled plan, in the mingling of old houses with new skyscrapers. By day, Moscow lives an ordinary industrious life. Only the crunch of glass and the stern look in people's eyes are reminders of this terrible autumn. By night, Moscow is blacked out. Yet this dark night-wedded Moscow remains a beacon for tortured humanity ... 'Death to our enemies!' is Moscow's cry. 'Glory to our allies, glory to the free peoples!' Moscow is fighting for itself, for Russia, and for you, distant friends, for humanity and for the whole world.

Indeed such was Stalin's confidence in Moscow that the general staff was summoned back, plus some VIPs and government departments.

The failure of the October offensive caused consternation in the German leadership. The front-line generals proposed to go on the defensive. Hitler would have none of it. The assault must be resumed, and for this purpose two large mobile forces were to be put together, mainly from troops stripped out of the Germans' stalled and depleted lines. These were to attack at Klin and Solnechnogorsk, north of Moscow, and at Tula and Kashira to the south, and thus complete the rout of the Red Army and the encirclement of Moscow.

Meanwhile Stalin continued his efforts for a treaty of alliance with Britain, which would prevent Britain from seeking a separate peace with Germany. Stalin wrote to Churchill of a 'lack of mutual trust' which was inevitable when no agreement existed on war aims, postwar plans and mutual military assistance, but Churchill refused to commit himself either to 'no separate peace' or to the Soviet borders of 1941, and wanted the Soviet Union to retreat behind its 1939 borders, so that victory would actually reduce the USSR's territory. Indeed, so obtuse was Churchill in these written exchanges with Stalin that Cripps felt too compromised to continue as British ambassador, and resigned. The foreign secretary, Anthony Eden, then offered to visit Moscow 'in a few weeks' to head off the crisis, but told Cripps that nothing could be settled with the Russians yet 'because the British position has to be squared with the Americans'.

On 22 November 1941, Churchill decided to conciliate Stalin with a telegram which read:

Our intention is to fight the war, in alliance with you and in constant consultation with you, to the utmost of our strength and however long it lasts, and when the war is won, as I am sure it will be, we expect that Soviet Russia, Great Britain and the USA will meet at the council table of victory as the three principal partners ...

Meanwhile, in preparation for Eden's visit, the British cabinet discussed with the Americans Soviet calls for a commitment not to negotiate unilaterally with the Germans and Stalin's request for talks about the postwar

In late November, Nazi soldiers broke into Klin, 60 miles northwest of Moscow, where they looted Tchaikovsky's estate museum.

settlement. Both of these demands Churchill emphatically ruled out – as did the Americans.

Churchill wrote to Eden:

No one can foresee how the balance of power will lie or where the winning armies will stand at the end of the war. It seems probable, however, that the United States and the British Empire will be the most powerfully armed economic bloc the world has ever seen, and that the Soviet Union will need our aid . . .

On 15–16 November, the Germans resumed the attack on Moscow, via Klin, Istra and Tula, looting, destroying and burning as they went, leaving charred forests and razed settlements in their wake. Only three houses were left standing in Istra, where they also blew up the famous New Jerusalem monastery. Tchaikovsky's house at Klin, near Moscow, was turned from a museum into a motorcycle repair station. Yasnaya Polyana, Tolstoy's family estate, was turned into a barracks, and priceless books, furniture and relics were burned in its heating stoves.

Just two miles from Yasnaya Polyana lay the ancient city of Tula, 100 miles south of Moscow. This great armaments centre and railway link to the Urals was a prize in itself, and the last barrier to Moscow. Guderian had failed to take it in his first attempt at the end of October. It was in late November, at the start of Hitler's second and final attempt to take Moscow, that his panzers again tried to encircle the city from the northwest, and were once again beaten back.

In the last week of October, remnants of the Soviet 50th Army, driven like chaff in a hurricane, had careered into Tula, where they were salvaged by the city's hastily improvised Defence Committee under its secretary, Vasilii Zhavoronkov. This committee was responsible for rationing, evacuation, civil defence, Red Cross work and casualty clearance. All citizens between seventeen and fifty-five were mobilised to dig defences, and underground partisan cells were organised in case the city should fall. The retreating Red Army units were re-equipped from the city's own arms factories, and disposed along new 'final lines' outside the city. On the perimeter of the munitions plants stood untrained Home Guards and Tank Destroyer Battalions, mobilised in record time and pitifully armed with Molotov cocktails and hand grenades. Zhavoronkov, working as if possessed, was everywhere, but most often in the trenches scratched out of the frozen earth by his untrained troops.

The panzers were beaten off – often by workers using mortars and hand grenades they had forged themselves. Tula became the southern bastion of the Western Front and the graveyard of Guderian's vaunted Second Panzer Army, and the Germans were forced further east, where their offensive finally stalled in a biting agony of frozen men and machines. Zhavoronkov was awarded the title Hero of the Soviet Union for his part in Tula's defence. Zhukov later wrote, in the stiff language of military protocol, 'All the units defending Tula fought with superior fortitude ... Its people contributed greatly to the Germans' defeat in the Battle of Moscow . . .' North of Moscow it was another story. By the last two weeks of November, the panzers had clawed their way into the outer suburbs of the capital, and the Kremlin was just 19 miles away.

As the Germans resumed their attack on the capital, thousands of cattle, sheep and tractors were driven out of the farms outside Moscow and through the centre of the city, to be evacuated to the east.

In the bloody battles of those weeks, countless Russians sacrificed their lives in circumstances of extraordinary heroism. Many such cases were picked up by correspondents who were there, and turned into legends of exemplary heroism and courage. Like the famous story of twenty-eight men from General Panfilov's Guards division, most of them very young, who tackled fifty enemy tanks at Dubosekovo Halt, on the Volokolamsk Highway, with little more than Molotov cocktails and rifles, and held them back until reinforcements arrived. The story was first reported by A. Krivitskii in *Red Star* on 28 November.

'Not a step back!' said Political Instructor Klochkov, as the tanks advanced. And at that critical moment the heroes, though only a handful, were not alone. With them were the heroes of old, who refused to submit to foreign invaders. Our ranks were thinning, but even in that moment when death tried to close the heroes' eyes for ever, they continued to strike back at the enemy. They fought on till none of the twenty-eight were left. They died, but they didn't let the enemy through. Our regiment came in the nick of time, and the enemy tank force got no further. Their voices ring out to us now, calling forth an undying echo in our hearts: 'We've laid our lives on the altar of the Motherland. Don't weep over our bodies, grit your teeth and be strong.'

The 'twenty-eight Panfilov's men' gave new meaning to the slogan 'One man against each tank'.

But perhaps the most moving and enduring story of personal heroism (first written up in *Pravda* by Pyotr Lidov) was that of an eighteen-year-old partisan called Zoya Kosmodemyanskaya, tortured and publicly executed by the Nazis in early December 1941 for blowing up a German munitions dump at Petrishchevo.

In June 1941, Zoya Kosmodemyanskaya was living with her widowed mother and younger brother in Aleksandrovskii Prospect, near the gardens of the Timiryazev Agricultural Academy. She was in the tenth form of School No. 201, in the October district of Moscow, where she was a model student, a Komsomol activist, and organiser of literature classes for housewives. She was also an idealist, copying into her diary whole pages from *War and Peace*, quotes from Chekhov ('Everything must be beautiful in a man – his face, his clothes, his soul, his thoughts') and Chernyshevskii ('Better die than kiss without love').

When war broke out she joined the Labour Front, working in a factory with her brother as a wood-turner. But her heart wasn't in it, and as the Germans drew nearer to Moscow she longed for active service. One day in October, she left the house and applied for active service in a sabotage unit behind enemy lines. 'Don't worry,' she said to her mother as she left, 'I'll either come back a hero or die a hero,' and choosing herself a new name, Tanya, she set off with a group of other young volunteers to the forested area between Mozhaisk and Moscow, deep in the German rear.

They were constantly on the move, scouting for guerrillas and the army, cutting telephone wires, blowing up bridges and harassing German transport convoys by night, and lying low in the forests and dozing by day.

When she learned that the Germans had settled in the little village of Petrishchevo, she determined to disturb their rest, and set off with matches and petrol to destroy their ammunition dump there. Just as she was lighting the match, some German soldiers grabbed her from behind, marched her off to a cottage, and there stripped and tortured her, till even some of the soldiers were sick. But she refused to tell them who she was or where she came from. All that night she was marched up and down half-naked in the snow, but still she refused to speak.

The next morning, frostbitten, covered in blood and half-dead, she was led to the gallows, with a placard saying 'Partisan' around her neck. While the Germans fiddled with their cameras trying to get a good angle, she shouted to the villagers ordered to attend, 'Comrades! Why do you look so glum? Show more courage! Fight, kill the Germans, burn them, hunt them down like rats!'

The soldiers hit her with their rifles and tightened the noose.

'I'm not afraid to die, comrades! It's happiness to die for your people! There are 200 million of us. They can't hang us all! My death will be avenged!'

On New Year's Eve, a crowd of drunken Nazis pulled her off the gallows, stabbed and hacked her body and left it in the square all day. That night, local people risked death by taking away her mutilated corpse and digging a grave in the frozen earth to bury it.

The story of Zoya Kosmodemyanskaya flew from village to village. Soldiers wrote verses about her. Her very name inspired courage. She was posthumously awarded the title of Hero of the Soviet Union, and she remains to this day a Soviet national hero, the inspiration still for poems, novels, films and paintings.

There were other young (often terribly young) partisan men and women who became national heroes in the Battle of Moscow; the graves of sixteen-year-old Shura Chekalin, hanged by the Germans near Tula, and of twenty-two-year-old Liza Chaikina, hanged by the Germans near Kalinin, have also become national shrines. But for all these reported examples, there were countless other, unreported cases of endurance and courage that winter.

Partisan heroism was the subject of songs, poems and plays. Sleeping by day in forests and swamps, by night they were constantly on the move, walking incredible distances, avoiding roads and carrying heavy equipment. There were few doctors, no hospitals, and, until December, no supplies from the outside world. But there were other stories too – of handfuls of brave Russians, outnumbered five times, who gave their lives fighting hand to hand in the snow, and of villagers who preferred death to submitting to Nazi rule.

The German advance continued, until calling up their last reserves, the Germans had fought their way to within 20 miles of the capital. By the end of November, the Nazis were approaching Kashira in the southeast, and had broken through to Klin and Istra, 15 miles west of the capital. From here the Germans said they 'could look at Moscow through a pair of good field glasses'. But this was the nearest to Moscow they ever got.

The fighting was bitter, and Russian losses were heavy. Snow and frosts

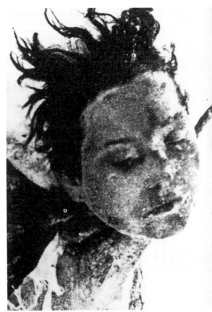

Zoya Kosmodemyanskaya, an eighteen-year-old tortured and hanged by the Nazis near Moscow, was one of the first partisan heroes of the war.

swept the earth, wet from the autumn rains, and hardened it like rock, stiffening the soldiers' coats and boots, and bringing an epidemic of frostbite. Gun barrels were white with frost, hands were inflamed, inhaling the air felt like breathing blocks of ice. 'Both sides were strained to the uttermost,' wrote General Konstantin Rokossovskii. His 16th Army, already bled white and 'still bleeding from countless wounds, clung desperately to every inch of the ground, resisting the enemy with dogged tenacity, retreating a step and coming back again, gradually sapping the enemy's strength'.

On 2 December, Germany's allies were called to Berlin to celebrate Hitler's announcement of the capture of Moscow, and the editors of Berlin's papers were told to leave a blank space in forthcoming issues. The stories were never filed. Hitler decided it wasn't worth appearing before his allies for nothing, so they had to make do instead with the former wine merchant Ribbentrop, who declared, 'The Russian is dull, cruel and bloodthirsty. The ideas of progress, beauty and family life are unknown to him.'

The Germans got no nearer to Moscow. At Kashiva, Klin and Istra they were stopped and forced to assume the defensive. And it was here, at the beginning of December 1941, when the fighting was particularly fierce, that the balance of the war began to change.

In a last desperate throw, the Germans sent in assault divisions of the

Military training continued for civilians, many of whom joined Home Guard and Red Army formations at the front.

Fourth Army to the Central Front. Advancing up to 15 miles towards Naro-Fominsk, they broke into the last defensive rings before Moscow. There, on 5 December, they were annihilated by Golubev's 43rd Army. By now the *Ostheer* had lost another 155,000 officers and men and almost all its remaining tanks.

In these battles, the Germans' plight seemed no less desperate than that of the Red Army soldiers, many of whom were the walking wounded from previous engagements. Commanders had had to plead, wheedle and cajole reinforcements out of Stalin in tiny packets – a dozen rifles here, a handful of mortars there, or a few fresh troops – when, as in the retreat from Klin, the alternative was catastrophe. The supremo had become a quartermaster, entering everything into his notebook with a blue pencil.

No Soviet soldier, no commander – not even Zhukov – who fought in the defensive battle, knew of the massive reserves accumulated by the *Stavka* in secret. The Germans suspected nothing; they failed to take Moscow, but were convinced the Red Army now had no reserves for a counteroffensive.

Throughout November, since Richard Sorge, the Soviet agent in Tokyo, told Stalin that the Japanese would move south against the Anglo-Americans, the *Stavka* had been shifting troops from the formidable, 750,000-strong Far Eastern Army to the Moscow front. By 1 December, the balance of forces had changed. The Germans and their allies still had over 5 million men in the field, one million more than the grievously mauled Red Army. But the *Stavka* reserve now had new stocks of materiel. Ammunition was desperately scarce, and remained so throughout the Soviet counteroffensive. But the Russians now had more tanks and aircraft than the Germans, and as many guns. The T-34s were beginning to be available in greater numbers. The outstanding tank of World War II, the T-34 could outrun and outshoot Hitler's panzers.

By early December, the German advance was spluttering out. Once again they blamed the weather. This time it was the frost, and it is true that the lowest air temperature in the Moscow region was 18 degrees Celsius below zero, while the average was minus 6 degrees. The weather was the same for both sides, of course, and fascist troops sat in warm requisitioned houses, firing from the windows, while the Russians were forced to sleep out in the snow for days on end. But the Germans were not so warmly clothed, and now the once proud *Wehrmacht* dreamed only of fur hats and strong boots.

'How the German soldiers freezing in the fields of Russia must envy their compatriots in Africa!' wrote Ehrenburg.

The Russian winter was a surprise for the Prussian tourists. When they send them into Russia they tell them 'Heil Hitler!', and instead of wool or fur, they give them a warm Hitler speech. As for 'diet', they prefer to feed their troops on victorious communiqués and military marches . . . Now they're running to Moscow like frozen men rushing to the fire . . . They're ready to risk death for a pair of felt boots or a woman's warm jacket. And that makes them doubly dangerous . . .

Later in December, the temperature fell to minus 31 at its lowest; the mean was 14.6 below. At this point, the Red Army counterattacked. Hitler's generals wanted to retreat, but the Führer saved the situation by ordering them to stand and fight. From this, Hitler concluded that neither the judgement nor the backbone of his general staff could henceforth be relied on. Thirty-five generals were dismissed, including Brauschitz and von Bock, and from then on Hitler rejected the word 'retreat'.

The British now had every reason to support the Soviet Union. The defence of Moscow, said Hewlett Johnson, the dean of Canterbury, was the defence of London, and the failure of Hitler's *Blitzkrieg* in the east had removed the danger of German invasion.

'I cannot tell you how relieved I am to learn daily of your remarkable

The British foreign secretary, Anthony Eden, visiting the newly liberated village of
Klin on 17 December, during his visit to Moscow for talks with Molotov and Stalin.

victories,' Churchill cabled Stalin in mid-December. 'I have never felt so
confident about the outcome of the war.'

So it was that on 15 December 1941, as the Germans were being driven out
of Klin, Eden and Cadogan finally arrived in Moscow. But by then, as the
Germans sustained their first defeats since the outbreak of the war, the
military situation had already transformed the background to their talks. The
international prestige of the Soviet Union had begun inexorably to rise, as had
Communist Party membership in Britain, and Communists were playing the
leading role in resistance struggles in the occupied countries. The Japanese
attack at Pearl Harbor the previous week had given the Americans new
reason to be allies with the USSR.

Eden's first meeting with Stalin and Molotov immediately threw up the
question of the postwar settlement, in a discussion about the fate of the Baltic
states, the remnants of whose reactionary governments were now installed in
London. Stalin asked Eden if he wanted the British government to appear to
be seeking the partition of the Soviet Union, which would be 'surprising and

astonishing'. 'Such an attitude is, in essence, the same as Chamberlain's government took.' Eden offered assurances that he would get the matter settled, but Stalin went on, as though not hearing him, 'I had thought that the Atlantic Charter was aimed against those nations which are trying to establish world domination. Things now look as if it is aimed against the Soviet Union.'

The next day, Eden was taken to Klin, an area only just cleared of the Germans. Back in Moscow, Eden warmly congratulated the Soviet leaders on the Red Army's brilliant victory. But in his memoirs, he recorded his shock, not at the evidence of Nazi atrocities and the unspeakable suffering of the Russians under German occupation, but at the enormous quantities of abandoned and damaged German equipment littering the battlefields. If Hitler were defeated, Eden concluded to his diary, the Russians would be far deeper into Europe at the end of the war than before, with alarming consequences for 'British interests'.

As Eden flew back to London, Churchill was leaving for a conference in Washington, which was to result in the setting-up of an Anglo-American Combined Chiefs of Staff. In the words of the US official historian, no such arrangements were to be made with the Soviet Union, since 'in effect two separate wars were being fought'.

The Soviet counteroffensive was finally to liberate an area of about 60,000 miles, containing some sixty towns, 11,000 villages and 5 million people. But within just a few weeks, Soviet troops had thrown the Germans back many miles across a very wide front. The retreat threatened to become a rout. The *Ostheer* seemed haunted by the ghosts of Napoleon's doomed *Grande Armée*; the memoirs of the Napoleonic general Caulaincourt appeared on the desk of Field Marshal von Kluge. By the end of December, people in Moscow were beginning to dream that war might be over by spring.

6

Reconstruction

On 22 December 1941, the winter solstice, Ehrenburg wrote:

The sun is set for summer, the winter is set for frost and the war is set for victory. We have not lived in vain through this painful autumn. We have learned to defeat the Germans. They've begun to meet their match. The conquerors of Paris are scuttling out of Levny. The 'heroes' of Thermopylae are losing their trousers at Aleksino.

From the occupation of Kalinin on 16 December to the capture of Mozhaisk on 10 January, the Russians were fighting for every village, every river, every road, in one great battle of an extraordinary bitterness and intensity, waged in heavy snow and exceptionally cold temperatures of minus 20–25 degrees.

By the end of December, the Red Army had advanced nearly everywhere between 20 and 40 miles, and had liberated Kalinin, Tula, Yelets and Istra, where all that remained was smoke-blackened chimneys. Kaluga was recaptured, and Volokolamsk, where the bodies of seven men and a woman swung from a gallows on the main square. When Russian troops recaptured Mozhaisk after three months' German occupation, they found houses burned, wells poisoned and everything mined. Mozhaisk, which was to have been the Nazis' last stopping place before Red Square, had become a symbol of Moscow's resistance, and its recapture had an immensely cheering effect. In a forest nearby, an inscription scored on a birch tree by a Russian soldier read, 'They set out for Moscow, and they found a grave.'

By the end of that year, the invincible German army was plodding through snowdrifts to the west, and the world was treated to the heart-warming spectacle of Germans in full and disorderly retreat, leaving thousands of tanks, guns and vehicles abandoned in the snow.

For most people in the Allied countries, particularly Britain, Russia was now the one bright spot in a bleak and depressing winter, and the Battle of Moscow continued to be front-page news in the British papers long after the Russian advance had stopped. If there was still any chance of winning the war, the feeling was that it would be thanks to the Russians.

Volokolamsk, 50 miles west of Moscow, liberated late December 1941. The
Germans broke through on 16 October. In twenty days' heavy fighting, Soviet
troops under Generals Rokossovskii and Panfilov held enemy forces three times
their number and killed 8500, before finally driving them out.

America's State Department, however, which continued to make policy
out of its traditional hostility to the Soviet Union, still recommended with-
holding recognition of the USSR's 1941 borders, and generally took such an
anti-Soviet line that the British again became alarmed at what Eden said 'may
be the end of any prospect of fruitful cooperation with a Soviet government in
our mutual interests'. He gave Halifax what was for him the painful
instruction to intercede with Roosevelt on behalf of their Soviet ally, and
Halifax was forced to tell the State Department that their attitude would

confirm Stalin's suspicion that he can expect no real consideration for Russian
interests . . . that we wish Russia to continue fighting for British and American ends;
and that we would not mind seeing Russia and Germany mutually exhaust each other.
This would make impossible any fruitful collaboration . . .

As demands for more Allied participation became increasingly insistent,
political leaders were sometimes forced to give expression to the popular
mood, which even Cadogan had to admit was 'enthusiastically pro-Russian'.

Top: Volokolamsk victims.

Bottom: Mozhaisk, liberated on 10 January 1942. Survivors of the Nazi
occupation welcoming soldiers of the Red Army.

'Words fail me,' Churchill wrote to Stalin on 11 February 1942, 'to express our admiration at the brilliant successes of your armies.' And Roosevelt, writing to Stalin two months later, said, 'The American people are thrilled by the magnificent fighting of your armed forces.'

The Germans' retreat from Moscow almost looked set to become a Napoleonic one, and *Pravda*'s front pages began to carry dramatic headlines of victory, with pictures of twisted enemy guns, vehicles blanketed in snow, and Germans, hands held high in surrender. Thus was born the new comic figure, the 'winter Fritz', icicles at the end of his nose, wrapped in stolen peasant blankets and women's coats and shawls.

'Happy New Year!' wrote Ehrenburg on 1 January 1942.

One year's different from another. Some years people build new roads, write novels or discover serums, newborn babies smile and old people die. Other years are hard to live through and impossible to forget. Such is 1941. On 1 January, Hitler said: 'This will be the year of our final victory.' At that time, having conquered half Europe, the maniac's head was reeling with visions of the whole world on its knees before him, the jungles of India transformed into a Munich beer hall, German women dropping their offspring on the Russian steppes and barbed-wire concentration camps from the North Pole to the South. But 1941 was not the year of Hitler's final victory, it was the year of his final defeat. December saw German soldiers, grey with hoarfrost, who'd forgotten all about their 'crusade' and 'racial characteristics', and preferred warm women's jackets to Iron Crosses . . .

Along the highways into Moscow, strewn with the shattered metal of the retreating German army, army sledges creaked, lorries, tractors and traction engines roared, signallers galloped past on hoarfrosted horses, machine-gunners skied along in white overalls, and frozen artillery moved in both directions. Through the mist, steam and snow could be seen burning fires, around which huddled half-frozen sappers, lorry drivers with snowbound lorries and crowds of women, children and old people who had trekked from their villages in which not a house had been left standing. Further towards Moscow could be seen the antitank ditches, barricades and wooden posts that still encircled the city, and exhausted women mending the roads.

In Moscow itself, an endless convoy of trucks moved through the city towards the Leningrad, Mozhaisk and Serpukhov highways. Although by December the bombing had been petering out, the capital was still blacked out, buildings were sandbagged, windows were taped, and militia men and women patrolled the streets. Everywhere in the city, teams of people were working to repair the bomb damage: the opera house had been hit by a one-ton bomb and was under repair; the windows of Moscow University were boarded up, its pale-blue stucco façade wrecked by a land mine, which

Moscow, winter 1941–42. The front had receded, but people were still cold and
hungry, the bombing continued and the dragon's-teeth barricades were still up.

had also half destroyed the adjacent building of the Manezh, the old riding
school.

Even though more than half Moscow's 4 million citizens were now out of
town, the streets, trams and shops were packed. But most looked haggard and
pale. The central heating was still off, and in houses and offices, people
shivered around small oil- and wood-burning stoves (the famous *burzhuiki*).
Medical supplies were running short, and teeth had to be pulled without
anaesthetics. A few impractical luxuries could be bought in the big department stores for prodigious prices, but nothing useful. The chemists and the
sandbagged food shops, with their dusty cardboard displays of hams, cheeses
and sausages, were empty. People went hungry, and there was endless talk of
rations and ration cards. What food reserves there were in the provinces had
been either looted by the Germans or sent to the front, and although bread
rations remained constant, at between one and one and a half pounds a day,
there was little else to eat. Vegetables were not to be had, and sugar, fats, milk
and tobacco were all scarce. Food prices went up – a pound of potatoes sold

for 20 rubles, a lump of sugar for 10 rubles, and profiteering cigarette owners would charge passers-by two roubles for one puff. The food shortages were hardest for the children, who were always hungry and suffered from ever-lasting colds and temperatures. Older people remembered the rationing of the Civil War, when the bread ration was just an eighth of a pound a day.

Thousands of Muscovites were killed or missing at the front, Moscow's Home Guards had been wiped out, and every day, communiqués brought news of more deaths. Some 15,000 towns and villages around Moscow had been destroyed. In Volokolamsk, Istra, Kalinin – in all the areas under enemy occupation – the Germans had robbed, burned, looted, raped, shot and tortured. And in their retreat, their 'torch-bearers' had blown up or burned to the ground every building, destroying thousands of schools, hospitals, kin-dergartens, creches, canteens and dwellings, leaving hundreds of thousands of people in the depths of winter without a home, so that Red Army soldiers were fighting to liberate mounds of rubble and ruin, of which little remained of the old wooden houses but their smoke-blackened chimneys.

From the districts around the capital, where millions still existed under German occupation, came stories of tragedy and heroism. But Moscow itself, through its own superhuman efforts and organisation, had been saved, and now there was a new sense of confidence, a feeling of pride at what had been endured, and a new attachment to Moscow as the fortress on which Hitler's hordes had been smashed. People were urged to mobilise all their inner resources, and not to allow the war to disrupt the life of the city. Factory workers were exhorted to increase output, with promises of free meals for good workers and double pay for overtime.

In the factories, Moscow's raw labour recruits were joined by young people who had been driven out of the surrounding villages into Moscow. Teenagers who had done firewatching on roofs during the bombing now toiled away, and in the breaks played. Workers lived on their nerves, and their fatigue was particularly evident on Mondays, when output was lowest. By Wednesday, they would get into their stride, but by Friday the exhaustion was again telling. Yet they worked on. Housewives and grandmothers laboured at their workbenches making munitions, and in their spare time collected clothing and food for 'adopted' villages.

One lunchtime, women of the Trekhgorka textile mill heard a talk in their canteen from Marina Alekseevna, a collective farmer from Manikhino, near Istra. When the Germans came, everyone had fled to the forests, and there they had stayed, in the depths of winter and with nothing to eat, for three weeks, during which two children died and two women gave birth to babies who died soon afterwards. Then guns were heard, the Red Army arrived, and

they returned to their village. 'But just think, comrades,' she ended, 'of our dear houses, only ashes now remain.' Women ran forward with clothes and adopted her village.

Three women called Ovchinnikova, Trutneva and Shcharova, from Moscow's Red Hero factory, adopted orphans from the liberated villages, and urged other women in Moscow to follow their example. In April, Elena Ovchinnikova helped to organise a meeting on the Defence of Children Against Fascist Barbarism, where she spoke of her adopted three-year-old daughter, whose parents had been killed by the Nazis.

When I first met my Nadya she could hardly see, her legs and hands were swollen with frostbite and her head was a mass of sores. At first when she saw me she'd whisper 'Mama!' She cried all the time, and screamed in her sleep, 'The strange men have killed my dad and put him in a hole in the ground!' But now when I come home from work my Nadya comes running to me, crying, 'My mama's home! My mama's home!' and I and my four girls have come to love her as our own. I'll bring up Nadya however hard it may be, and I'm sure thousands of other women will gladly do what we at the Red Hero are doing!

Children like fourteen-year-old 'Uncle Sasha' stood in for absent adults at the factories.

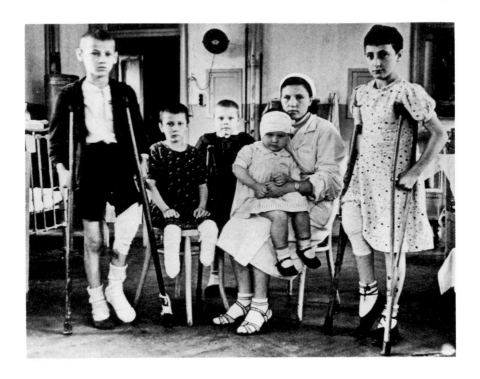

The meeting ended with an appeal to women in England (later published) to collect food, clothes and medical supplies for Russian orphans. Thirty-six orphans were adopted by women at the Red Hero, twenty-nine by women of the Moscow War plant, fifteen by the Novy Put collective farm, and soon Moscow families were applying to orphanages around the Soviet Union for permission to adopt.

As new teachers were trained to replace those at the front, and new textbooks published, younger children returned to school, most of them still in shifts and in new buildings, where they were urged as a patriotic duty to work hard, 'so the Red Army will be proud of you!' In their spare time they did hospital visiting and collected old saucepans and irons for tanks and munitions, or worked for small amounts of money in the school workshops, making tin mugs, gun parts and packing-cases for the munitions factories, rainproof clothes for soldiers at the front and slippers and bedlinen for hospitals. No one liked using children in this way, but there was no choice. 'Before the war, we brought up children rather differently, paying much attention to their spiritual development,' said one teacher. 'But this cruel war forces us to mobilise all the country's resources – even the immature power and abilities of our children.'

There were far more heartbreaking sights of suffering and curtailed

childhood in Moscow's orphanages and at the Vladimir children's hospital, in the north of the city, now crowded with starving, orphaned and injured babies and children evacuated from the liberated areas. Some had suffered injuries that would leave them cripples for life, while those mutilated by shelling and fire posed insuperable problems of plastic surgery. And there were countless others, infant witnesses and victims of Nazi torture, who would for the rest of their lives suffer the aftereffects in serious psychological injuries and speech defects.

Every day, as new casualties were flown into the capital from the front, scores of disabled servicemen were released from Moscow's hospitals to start the long struggle to rebuild their shattered lives and families. Special shops and restaurants opened for returning battle victims. And a new Soviet-appointed commission, responsible for their re-employment and rehabilitation, urged greater public sensitivity towards those leaving hospital, and called on women volunteers to shop and clean for unmarried invalids, 'not as a charity, but as a duty – for these men will be our new leaders!'

In the devastated towns and villages around Moscow, where families were living in freezing dugouts and cellars in the depths of winter, a massive reconstruction programme was launched hard on the heels of the retreating enemy by Moscow's regional and city soviets. Large numbers of Moscow's factory workers – including several thousand young women from the Stalin machine-building factory – were sent off to the wrecked and flooded mines of the Moscow Coal Basin, and there learned to hew coal, drive locomotives and operate hoists and hewing machines. By the end of 1942, thousands of women were working in Moscow's mines, and four of the largest pits had women managers, two of them in their early twenties. Meanwhile, Moscow's builders hastily designed standardised wooden buildings which could be put up quickly under winter conditions, workers were mobilised to cut timber in the forests around Moscow, and teams of carpenters left for the villages to start building. By the end of the year, 20,000 new flats for servicemen and their families had been built, plus some 400 schools, kindergartens and creches, and 25 canteens for delicate children.

In many occupied villages, where German troops had destroyed bath-houses and forced several families to live in one room, there were epidemics of typhoid fever, scarlet fever and measles. In Moscow, millions of rubles were spent to launch a massive public-health campaign, and people were mobilised to sweep streets and courtyards and ensure the uninterrupted functioning of public baths. Three groups of actors, two composed of children aged eight to fourteen, the other of some of the capital's best adult actors, set up the new Moscow Theatre of Hygiene Agitation, travelling around the liberated areas and the capital's hospitals, theatres and parks with sketches and playlets spreading information about anti-epidemic precautions and first aid.

A mass of paintings were produced (many of them bad) of ransacked villages and flaming German tanks lighting up the snow. TASS's inexhaustible artists and poets found yet more targets for their satire in the 'winter Fritz'. The Moscow Chronicle produced its first film of the Moscow battles, *The Defeat of the Germans outside Moscow*. And hundreds of poems and songs by soldiers and poets at the front poignantly expressed the experiences of the past few months.

Deep in the forests around Moscow one night, in the lull between fighting, the composer Kabalevskii, who was serving in a partisan detachment with the poet Dolmatovskii, hurriedly wrote the music for a song. Dolmatovskii scribbled down some words while an accordionist sketched in the harmonies, and the others gathered round to sing, 'in a whisper', since the Germans were so close.

Blue mists surround our forest, our travelling home.
Sing a song, partisans, so our friends can hear!
Let the stars in the sky shine bright,
We cannot guess our fate.
Why so sad, Olya? Are you dreaming of Kiev?

'My Moscow'

Music by I. Dunaevskii, words by M. Lisyanskii

March tempo

I—'ve se——en a lot of the wo——rld Lived in dug—outs and trench—es and forests I've been bur——ie——d twice a—li——ve———— Left my loved ones far be————hind———— — — But where—ev——— er ——— I have trav—elled These words ——————— fill me with pride My be—lo———ve ——————————d capital! My——— gold—en —— Mos————cow!

Don't be sad, we'll be there soon.
We'll warm our hearts by the Dniepr,
We'll avenge the enemy for our blood and grief.
Not for nothing we're called 'the Avengers'.
Now we sing in a whisper, so the enemy cannot hear.

'The Song of the Avengers' became one of the most popular of the partisan songs, and was given its triumphant first public performance that summer in Moscow's Hall of Columns.

After the battle of Istra, Aleksei Surkov, the 'soldiers' poet', had written a short love poem to his wife, filled with the pain of parting:

It's hard for me to reach you
Between us – snow on snow
You are far, far away
But death is four feet off . . .

He forgot all about it until February 1942, when a soldier called Listov arrived at the *Red Army Pravda* offices in search of material for a song. Then Surkov dug out his poem to his wife and gave it to Listov, who returned a few days later with his guitar and sang 'In the Dugout', whose simplicity and candour made it one of the most popular songs of the war.

Quantities of doggerel verses and songs were turned out that winter to celebrate the Moscow victory, and Moscow's Composers' Union building swarmed with front-line theatre and folk-song groups making deals with composers in an apparently inexhaustible search for new material. Cabaret and gypsy songwriters now turned their hand to soldiers' songs, at which some became quite talented and others very rich. (Alexander Werth tells the story of one second-rate songwriter who came to Moscow and in five weeks had sold enough songs to front-line ensembles to make a clear profit of 35,000 rubles.)

Some poets and writers anguished over this mass of new songs about soldiers going into sacred battle singing about their beloved. 'What is the point of all these verses?' a young poet called Gribachev wrote from the front to Ehrenburg. 'Is it possible that no bold authoritative voice will ring out in opposition to the vulgarity which – like mud on the soldiers' boots – looks as though it will stick to us as we march on to the very day of victory?'

Perhaps many finer poetic feelings were coarsened. Yet, as Ehrenburg recalled, people never failed to be moved by stories of self-sacrifice at the front. And the trash didn't bother him anyway, as all the old thoughts, doubts and inner themes were pushed into the background by the daily pressure of writing articles and giving talks.

Ehrenburg's talks at the front were especially popular, and soldiers and

A lull at the front.

partisans would eagerly swop food and guns for spare clippings of his articles and stories. But all Moscow's writers – Simonov, Korneichuk, Petrov, Svetlov, Aligher, Fadeev, Katayev, Lidin, Surkov and many others – now lived and breathed with the front, raising morale with their talks to barrage-balloon crews and anti-aircraft teams, to soldiers and pilots at the aero-dromes, hospitals and fronts.

The more serious traditions of Soviet literature found their home in a new four-page weekly paper, *Literature and Art*, whose first issue appeared on 1 January 1942 under the editorship of Aleksander Fadeev, secretary of the Moscow branch of the Writers' Union. It wasn't the easiest time to open a new paper. Its offices moved three times that year – from the Artists' Union building on Tsvetnoi Boulevard to Stanislavskii Street, then to the Central Theatre Library Building on Pushkin Street – and its small editorial board would huddle around the unheated rooms in their padded jackets, writing often in gloves. But the offices were always warmed by crowds of writers, arriving from the front to hand in material and share news. Sometimes the editorial board would meet at Fadeev's flat on Komsomol Street, where writers would read out their latest work, and it was there that Fadeev read the first chapter of his new novel *Young Guard*, about a group of young partisans in the town of Krasnodon.

Since writers were on secondary rations, they often went short of food, and could be seen with their families at the Central Art Workers' Club sharing one meal between three or four people. But spirits were generally high at the Moscow Writers' Club, as writers, most of them in army uniform, arrived straight from the front, now a few hours away, to consume vodka and pickled mushrooms, and discuss their experiences in battle. 'Before,' said Ehrenburg, 'we had met to discuss literary movements and trends. Now the only movement discussed was that to the west, and the only trend – victory.'

By the middle of January, German resistance was stiffening, and as the Russian counteroffensive advanced, the line of the Soviet front doubled. Thousands of Russian lives were lost in the mighty tank battles to recapture Vyazma, and by the end of January the Russians had failed to recapture Gzhatsk. In March the thaw set in, which further reduced Russian mobility. Supply lines were breaking down, Russian troops were exhausted, and the Moscow counteroffensive, which had raised such high hopes, was petering out, bringing with it an aching sense of disappointment. The Germans dug in till spring. They had failed to take Moscow, but it was clear that they were far from finished. Nonetheless, the Russian army had decisively driven the Germans from the capital. The Germans' failure to take Moscow and Leningrad had created a new undercurrent of hope, and the Battle of Moscow helped to sustain people through the anguish of the following year.

After the ordeals of winter, Moscow greeted the spring with joy. In May, a little snow still lay on the ground and the fields outside the city were a sea of mud, but the streets were clean. Although the last bombs had been dropped on Moscow in March, there was no certainty that air raids wouldn't start again. But the city's air defences were said to be stronger now than ever, and the skies hummed day and night with invisible air patrols, while antitank gunners still stood vigil on the roofs.

Early in the morning, young women would march singing down the streets on their way to military exercises. And as the night shifts poured out of the factories, leaving behind those who were doing a second shift, women with brushes and buckets would appear to paste up posters advertising the week's plays, lectures and film shows. During the lunch hour, in the side streets, parks and squares, people of all ages would emerge from the offices and factories to be put through rifle drill by fellow workers back from the front.

There were so few children left in Moscow now that people smiled at them with a special affection as they played. 'I think people never looked with such hungry tenderness at children as in the war,' said Ehrenburg. 'They looked, and they couldn't look their fill. Perhaps it was because everybody wanted a glimpse of the future, and no one had any certainty of lasting to see even the next day.'

War games were the only games most children knew now – although these always consisted in firing at an invisible enemy and storming barricades, never hand-to-hand fighting, since no child ever wanted to be a German.

At night, the roads were lit by feeble lights invisible from the air. From the factories came the dull whir of machines, and from the sky the drone of invisible planes.

While the snow was still on the ground, Moscow was already thinking about the spring sowing. In the surrounding areas and the Moscow Coal Basin, young labour recruits salvaged what they could of the devastated crops, then hitched tractors to car engines and prepared to sow tomatoes, potatoes and cabbages. In Moscow, it became a patriotic duty and a matter of sheer necessity ('Every blow with the spade is a blow against Hitler!') to augment destroyed food supplies. Soviets and unions urged people to dig allotments in courtyards, squares, factory yards and patches of waste land, and grow their own vegetables. Many factories set up their own allotments and produced their own gardening tools, and as the evenings grew longer, thousands of people could be seen after the day shift ended walking down the streets, spades in their hands, to dig, sow and weed. A hundred children from the Moscow Pioneers' Club organised themselves into gardening brigades, elected their own board of management, and were given their own plot of land. The Young Naturalists' Association was given a large plot of land by the Timiryazev Agricultural Academy, whose members they consulted on the latest methods of growing berries and vegetables. (They even managed to grow Indian corn – a rare delicacy in Moscow – which they took to the hospitals for the soldiers.) Even the writer Ovady Savich, who had always been convinced that 'bread rolls grow on trees', was eventually persuaded by the Writers' Union to 'remember Tolstoy' and dig for victory.

People also started keeping hens. The Moscow zoo contacted amateur poultry farms on the city's outskirts and in summer-holiday suburbs, which were turned into emergency breeding stations for the best strains of fowl. The breeders, in return for free veterinary service and advice, then handed over a proportion of the eggs and chicks to the zoo, which distributed them to people taking up the hobby for the first time in Moscow. Some went in for poultry-keeping in a big way, and a war invalid, Major Kozharinov, who had fought with distinction at the front, had crowds of poultry fanciers visiting his house to inspect his Leghorns.

*

Hitler's Directive 41, drawn up in the spring of 1942, announced plans to liquidate Russian forces in the Crimea, smash Voronezh, open the way to central and southeast Russia and Stalingrad, destroy Stalingrad, and then turn south to the oil-rich areas of the Caucasus and bring Turkey in on the side of the Axis. On 8 May, Field Marshal Manstein's 11th Army launched a massive air attack on the defenders of the Kerch peninsula. On 18 May, the Soviet communiqués were referring to 'important successes in the direction of Kharkov'. A week later, the Germans announced that three Soviet armies had been rounded up south of Kharkov, and on 7 June, the Germans started their final assault on Sevastopol, whose defenders fought on in circumstances of extraordinary horror and heroism. On 10 June, the Germans launched a major offensive on the southern front, focusing on Voronezh, the Don, Stalingrad and Transcaucasia. On 20 June, Kerch fell, and Manstein could concentrate his 11th Army for the decisive attack on Sevastopol.

Moscow was still very near the front line. The Germans had dug in at Rzhev, Vyazma and Gzhatsk, and no one could be sure that they would not start another all-out attack on the capital. But Moscow was by now ringed with so many artillery units that the feeling was that the Germans would never dare strike again. Now all eyes were fixed on the bloody battles unfolding in the eastern Crimea and the western Ukraine. And the worse the news from the front, the more urgent became the cry for a full-scale Anglo-American landing in France, which indeed for many Russians now seemed literally a matter of life and death.

As the Germans accumulated enormous reserves on the Eastern Front for their massive and, they no doubt hoped, final offensive, Stalin resumed his interrogation of the Allies' intentions, particularly on the Second Front issue. The published correspondence between Stalin, Churchill and Roosevelt at this time paints a sorry picture of Churchill's prevarications. To Stalin's insistent questioning of British intentions with respect to their own previous commitments, Churchill replied with a string of alibis for British inaction. The British were playing their old game of deep war, passive war. They had already been waging what Churchill called 'total war' against Germany for over two years, yet were still in no position to undertake any real offensive action against the Axis. Meanwhile in Britain, popular pressure for a Second Front was becoming more insistent, and a famous *Daily Mirror* headline read, 'Russia Bleeds while Britain Blancoes!'

The Americans, however, were now assuming a more amenable attitude, at least publicly. 'We want to help you in the destruction of Hitler's armies and materiel more than we are doing now,' wrote Roosevelt to Stalin. And to Churchill, 'Your people and mine demand the establishment of a front to draw off pressure on the Russians. And these peoples are wise enough to see

Kerch, occupied in the autumn of 1941 by the Germans. In December, 40,000
Soviet troops landed on the Kerch peninsula, and held the Germans back from
Sevastopol until May, when they were wiped out in the first Soviet disaster in the
Crimea. Soon after the Nazis had entered the town, the bodies of several thousand
Jews were found buried in trenches outside the town.

that the Russians are today killing more Germans and destroying more
equipment than you and I put together.'

As Joseph Davies, former US envoy in Moscow, put it that June, as the
Germans were advancing into the Caucasus:

The Soviet people are fighting for their own liberties, but it cannot be denied that they
are also fighting for the homes and liberties of all the free men on Earth – ourselves not
least. To the Red Army which stands at the ramparts of our civilisation, to the Soviet
Government and the Soviet people, we owe a measureless debt. The least that a proud
and self-respecting American manhood can do is to repay that debt.

The US chiefs of staff actually produced a plan for a major landing in
northern Europe for 1943, but this was soon shuffled aside. Writing of events

on the Eastern Front in the summer of 1942, the official *British History of the War* admitted that the Soviet army was engaging the bulk of the enemy's strength, 'which might otherwise have been used to overwhelm the British position in the Middle East, move through Spain to Morocco, or renew an attempt at invasion'. Thus did Britain acknowledge its debt to Russia.

Moscow still feared that the Western Allies might conclude a separate deal with Germany, which would leave them isolated. London and Washington, for their part, although happy to enter commitments of a positive but vague nature in order to avoid a public row over the second front, would not accept the USSR's 1941 borders, and preferred to back the 'London Poles'. On 20 May 1942, Molotov flew to London, where he hoped to take advantage of the current of popular pro-Soviet sentiment to press the British into treaty commitments which would help to prevent any backsliding later on.

In London, Molotov discussed with Churchill the Soviet–British treaty of alliance which had been proposed during the Eden visit, and agreed to forgo a decision on the crucial Polish question in exchange for a clause providing for that alliance to extend for twenty years. He went on to argue the case for a Second Front, plausibly demonstrating how it might be possible to beat Germany in 1943, or even 1942, if the Western powers could draw off forty or more German divisions from the Eastern Front. Churchill responded with various promises but no practical commitments.

A few days later, Molotov flew to Washington, where Roosevelt was more amenable to his arguments and followed up his written undertakings to Stalin with an apparently specific commitment to the Second Front. He went on to propose a postwar settlement based on a scheme for world disarmament that would exclude the USA, the USSR, Britain and possibly China, who would impose peace on the rest of mankind – and 'if any nation menaces the peace, it can be bombed'. What stood in the way of this Pax Americana (based as it was on the assumption that three of the four powers would be debilitated by the end of the war) was not even the fact that the Soviet Union was too resilient to become dependent on the US and Britain, but the simple truth, evident during the war itself, that while the Anglo-Americans could not hope to prevail if the Soviet Union was defeated, the Soviet Union could, and largely did, destroy Hitler single-handed.

In Moscow, the news that Churchill and Molotov had pledged their governments to twenty years of friendship raised high hopes that Russia would survive the war into a new era of peaceful coexistence with the West. But of far more impelling interest was the announcement, printed in full in all the Soviet and Western papers, of the agreement signed on 11 June by Britain, the United States and Russia on 'a landing on the continent of Europe in August or September 1942'.

A mass of pro-Alliance posters appeared in Moscow, including one of three lightning darts, representing the British, Soviet and American flags, striking a toadlike Hitler green with fear. There was even a popular new tinned Spam-like product called Second Front. A number of British films showing that summer in Moscow, like *London Doesn't Surrender, Women of England, The Defence of London Against Raids* and *Great Britain in Wartime*, attracted huge crowds, and their shots of British tanks and long-range Halifax bombers, shown moving off the assembly line for shipment to Russia, had pilots and tank drivers in the audience itching to get their hands on the new equipment of which they'd heard so much.

There were talks on Dickens, a new translation of *Oliver Twist* appeared, and the Moscow Children's Publishing House produced new editions of *Bleak House* and *David Copperfield*. Shakespeare became extremely popular. The Stanislavskii–Nemirovich Danchenko Theatre put on a new ballet version of *The Merry Wives of Windsor*, and his plays were performed at the fronts and the rear. *Othello* was especially popular for its dramatic refutation of fascism's disgusting race theories. It was performed in Tadjik at the Moscow festival of Tadjik art that summer, and the Moscow Shakespeare Society put on a production from which excerpts were taken to the fronts and army hospitals, along with scenes from *Cymbeline* and the famous soliloquy from *Henry V*. The Annual Shakespeare Conference opened in Moscow that summer with an address on Shakespeare's humanism by Professor Morozov, Russia's leading Shakespeare scholar, who concluded that Shakespeare's humanistic treatment of his women characters highlighted the heroic qualities of women revealed by war.

In Moscow's Hall of Columns that May, there was a large women's meeting. There were women artists, writers and scientists, women soldiers and pilots, women with sunburnt faces and bullet-riddled army coats who had built ditches, worked on at the factories while bombs fell, or carried soldiers to safety under fire. The mother of Zoya Kosmodemyanskaya presided, while Vera Prohkorova, an engineer turned partisan scout, spoke of killing Nazis in the forests, an engineer and oilworker called Agalareva, from Azerbaijan, spoke of women manning and managing whole oilfields in the east, and an elderly teacher called Fyodoronkina, heroine of the defence of Sevastopol, spoke of building forts and shelters while her four sons were away at the front. And all vowed to make 1942 the year of Hitler's final defeat.

On 3 July 1942, after eight months of relentless bombardment, Sevastopol fell, at appalling loss of Russian civilian lives, and there were rumours of a new German offensive on Moscow from the south. On 19 July, the important industrial city of Voroshilovgrad fell. By the end of July, the Germans were

The defenders of Sevastopol. By October 1941, the Germans had overrun all of
the Crimean peninsula except the great naval port of Sevastopol, which held out
under incessant bombing until 3 July 1942. The city moved underground, and
people built homes, schools, hospitals and factories in cellars and caves.

making rapid advances in the Caucasus and, in heavy fighting around a loop
in the river Don known as the 'Don bend', were advancing to Stalingrad. As
soldiers returned to Moscow with alarming reports of confusion and retreat,
a mood of despair swept the capital.

'Liberty or death!' wrote Ehrenburg.

There are hard times in the life of nations and the life of every person. We must be able
to look the truth in the face. Our country is in peril. The Germans sit in their air-raid
shelters with British bombers circling overhead, discussing who's to hold shares in
Magnitogorsk or Yusovka, and dreaming of a German trust to exploit the Baku
oilfields. They want to wipe out our intelligentsia. Russia is centuries old. We cherish
her history, her culture, her glory. The Soviet state is twenty-three years old. We
cherish its youth, its brotherhood and freedom.

On 28 July, Novocherkassk and Rostov were announced lost, amid
rumours (never officially denied) that officers had lost their heads and

Russian units had panicked and fled. The next day, Stalin delivered his 'not a step back' speech, whose frankness was somehow less appalling than optimism, and the despair, reaching its head, settled into a more sober confidence. Many old commanders from the Civil War days, like Budyonny and Voroshilov, were demoted, younger officers were promoted, and three new military orders were created for officers – the Nevskii, the Suvorov and the Kutuzov – recalling three ancestral Russian warriors who had driven off the Teutonic Knights and the Napoleonic invaders.

Meanwhile the writer Aleksei Korneichuk, allowed two months off his regular war writing, started work on his play *The Front*, which harshly criticised the older generals whose bungling inefficiency in battle had so tragically undermined the heroism of their troops.

The Rostov catastrophe and Stalin's speech marked a psychological turning point in the war, a feeling that from now on things could only get better. As a *Red Star* correspondent put it to Ehrenburg, 'A father tells his children, "We are ruined, now we must learn to live differently." '

Although Russian troops at the Don bend were at last beginning to slow down the German advance, the Germans had already overrun nearly all the surrounding countryside, and the war communiqués, with a new and cruel candour, now began to talk of Germans striking into the heart of Russia. That August, as the battle on the approaches to Stalingrad reached its height, Alexander Werth, then in Moscow, described the mood there as charged with an extraordinary tenderness for Russia in its hour of mortal danger.

It was in August that Shostakovich's famous Seventh Symphony, written in an inspired frenzy in Leningrad under bombing, siege and famine, was first performed in Moscow's Hall of Columns, its first movement, depicting the German advance, rising to a relentless war theme of overwhelmingly dramatic power. Literature and music expressed the same warmth and love of Russia as in the Battle of Moscow, but now there was a new and poignant hatred for the Germans, which was no longer tempered with scorn. There was Sholokhov's essay-story in *Pravda*, 'The School of Hate', about a Russian prisoner tortured and humiliated by his German captors. There was Aleksei Tolstoy's appeal 'Kill the Beast':

The only emotion possible at this time, the only passion with which people must burn, is hatred for the enemy. You love your wife and child? Then turn this love inside out so that it hurts and oozes with blood . . . Friend, comrade, dear companion at the front and in the rear! If this hate cools, then stroke the warm head of your child – and you will realise that you cannot get accustomed to hate. Let rage burn in you like a constant pain, as though you saw a German tightening on the throat of your child . . .

There was Surkov's poem 'I Hate', published in *Red Star*, which concluded:

My heart is hard as stone
My griefs and memories are countless
With these hands of mine
I have lifted the corpses of little children
I hate the Germans, for those hours of sleepless grief
I hate them, because in one year my hair has turned white . . .
My house has been defiled by Prussians,
Their laughter dims my reason,
And with these hands of mine
I will strangle every one of them.

There was Simonov's poem 'Kill Him', also published in *Red Star*:

. . . Kill a German, so that he, not you, shall lie in the ground
Kill him, so that the tears shall flow in his house, not yours . . .

And there was his play *The Russian People*, which was published in *Pravda* and performed in theatres up and down the Soviet Union. Its bewildered Russian characters, fighting against the inhuman Nazi occupiers, carried an immense emotional appeal, and on its opening night at the Moscow Arts Theatre that summer, Alexander Werth recalled many in the audience weeping, and when the curtain fell on the last words of the third act, 'See how the Russians go to their death,' there was a complete silence.

And then there was Ehrenburg, whose caustic, witty articles did so much to sustain Russian morale that summer:

One can bear anything – plague, hunger and death – but one cannot bear the Germans. One cannot bear those fish-eyed oafs snorting at everything Russian. We cannot live as long as those grey slugs are alive. Today there are no books, today there are no stars in the sky, today there is only one thought: 'Kill the Germans.' Kill them and dig them into the earth . . . Let us not speak, let us not be indignant, let us kill. If you do not kill the German, he will kill you. And if you have killed one German, then kill another . . .

As the Germans advanced inexorably north, south, east and west, and raced through the open spaces of the Don country, the summer campaign reached its great climax, and in Moscow's streets and parks, the banners promising 'Victory in 1942' were now replaced by ones announcing 'Stalin says not a step back'.

On 12 August, as Russians were retreating from the north Caucasus and the Germans were advancing on Stalingrad, Churchill paid his first visit to Moscow, along with Averell Harriman and a large military delegation. As is

Left: Aleksei Tolstoy (born 1882, of a noble family, died 1945) wrote his first lyrical poems in the 1890s, and went to the front as a journalist in the 1914–18 war. Emigrated to Paris in 1919, where he wrote his science-fiction work *Aelita* (1922), and returned in 1923 to the Soviet Union, where he wrote several more novels. His best-known novel, *Road to Calvary*, about people caught up in the Civil War, was written during the 1930s and completed on 22 June 1941.

Right: Dmitrii Shostakovich (1906–75). Apart from seven symphonies (his tragic Eighth was first performed in 1943), Shostakovich had already written two operas, *The Nose* (1928) and *Lady Macbeth of Mtsensk* (1932), three ballets, *The Golden Age* (1930), *Bolt* (1931) and *Bright Stream*, three film scores and numerous works for piano and orchestra.

clear from his memoirs, it was not a visit Churchill relished making, and his first duty was to stand to attention while the military band at Moscow's Central Airport played the 'Internationale'. That evening, he met Stalin for the first time, in his office at the Kremlin. There was 'simply no limit', he said, to his joy at being in the heroic city of Moscow. His agitation was obvious.

Winston Churchill's visit to Moscow, 12–15 August 1942.

Stalin, who had sized him up in a sidelong glance when he entered, was less effusive.

After inviting everyone to sit down at the end of the long table near his desk, Stalin started by summarising the position on the fronts. The Germans had gathered an enormous fist of armour and infantry in the south, he said, and were now breaking through Soviet lines and racing towards Stalingrad, which 'we are determined to hold'. 'Hitler has pumped all he can out of Europe . . .' he went on. 'The Red Army is now preparing to launch a major attack north of Moscow to draw Nazi forces away from the southern fronts . . .' As he listened to all this, Churchill's massive head settled deeper into his shoulders. He knew what was coming next.

He then made a speech describing in detail the growing concentration of British and American forces in Britain, emphasising his fears for the success of any Allied attack in Normandy, and mentioning, almost in passing, that preparations for such an attack would be completed 'in the following year'. At this, Stalin rounded on him. People who could not take risks do not win wars, he said, and he reproached the British for being afraid of the Germans – an insult Churchill never forgot. During the bitter exchange that followed,

Stalin repeatedly emphasised to Churchill his disagreement with the prime minister's positions, while Churchill agitatedly doodled a drawing of a large crocodile, its jaws opening to engulf the British Isles.

'Look,' he said, 'I want to attack the soft underbelly of this crocodile, Hitler Europe.' He then proposed to Stalin a 'Second Front' involving the landing that October of twelve British and American divisions in French North Africa, entering Europe via the Adriatic and through the Balkans. Operation Torch would be 'the best Second Front in 1942, and the only large-scale operation possible', he said. What he did not say was that such an approach would also insulate the Mediterranean basin and the Middle East against Soviet influence, and would help prevent countries like Yugoslavia, Greece and Bulgaria from turning their resistance struggles into socialist revolutions. Even in their common struggle, Churchill could not disguise his nostalgia for the old *cordon sanitaire* against Bolshevik Russia.

Harriman mentioned Roosevelt's support for 'Torch'. But Stalin was unmoved. Nothing would make him agree to change the original plan, which called for an Allied landing in 1942.

Their discussion continued late into the night. The following evening, Stalin entertained his guests for dinner in the Kremlin's Katherine Hall. The general secretary was in a good mood – not so the British prime minister, who puffed agitatedly at his cigar and resorted frequently to the cognac bottle. But toasts were drunk and the evening livened up, and on 18 August, after the visitors had returned home, a joint communiqué was issued which read:

... Both governments are determined to carry on this just war of liberation with all their power and energy until the complete destruction of Hitlerism ... has been achieved. The discussions ... have reaffirmed the close friendship and understanding between the Soviet Union, Great Britain and the United States ...

Nonetheless, Churchill's visit to Moscow had spelled the end of the Anglo-Soviet honeymoon, and throughout the summer and autumn of 1942, as relations between the Soviet Union and their Anglo-American allies deteriorated, the pro-Alliance posters disappeared, and talk of a 'Second Front not later than . . .' (the date varied) was tempered by a new sense of unease about British and American motives. Yet hope was not completely lost.

That September, cinema producers and actors, most of them in army uniform, gathered in Moscow's House of Architecture, amid stills from Vidor's *Citadel*, Ford's *Grapes of Wrath* and Disney's *Snow White*, for a conference on British and American cinema. Roman Karmen, from the Moscow Film Chronicle, spoke on American and British war newsreels, the popular actress Zoya Fyodorova on American film stars, and the veteran filmmaker Aleksander Dovzhenko on Charlie Chaplin, actor, filmmaker and supporter of the Second Front: 'Master and friend, Chaplin, your demand for the immediate opening of a Second Front is the expression of the common sense of the British and American people.'

There were few young men left in Moscow now, and almost none in civilian clothes. The military training of civilians continued, and detachments of armed men were seen marching down the streets. Some 100,000 to 200,000 people, mostly girls and women, had been sent out of the capital to cut timber and peat for the winter. Children, despite their meagre rations, looked better than they had done that winter, but most of the younger ones had been sent off after the end of the summer term to children's homes for the summer, while the older ones had been mobilised to help bring in the harvest around Moscow.

There was a peculiar chaos to Moscow that summer, with its strange camouflage, its shop signs which no longer meant anything, its austerity, its bread queues, and its festivities in the midst of toil and tragedy. In theatres and factories, front-line groups with names like the Happy Raiders, strained and exhausted after hundreds of performances at the battlefields, would bring a whiff of the front with high-spirited song-and-dance shows. At Moscow's aerodromes, chess tournaments would be held in between aerial combats and chess masters would lecture on the game and recreate games of past tournaments. Moscow's circuses were now performing without animals, but people crowded in for shows in which the 'winter Fritz' was the new star.

In the Izmailovskii Park, war had thinned the crowds, and the parachute tower was closed, but on Sundays the giant merry-go-round still attracted long queues, with calls of 'Red Army soldiers first, please!' On the dance floor around the bandstand, soldiers and officers on leave (greatly outnumbered by women) danced to the band's renderings of 'The Lambeth Walk' and 'Goodnight, Sweetheart', which competed with the loudspeakers. Nearby was a large pavilion containing the twisted metal and dented fuselage of several downed Junkers and Heinkel bombers, cannons and machine guns.

In the Hermitage Park, the restaurants and cafés were closed now, except for a pavilion distributing milk in paper cups for small children. But two theatres were still open, one performing a three-act comedy called *Long Ago*, based on the life of Nadezhda Durova, the 'Maiden Horsewoman', the first woman to fight Napoleon.

Korneichuk's *The Front* opened simultaneously, amid immense publicity, at three of Moscow's theatres, the Moscow Arts, the Maly and the Moscow. No reviews had been allowed to appear when its first instalment appeared in *Pravda*, so that people could freely assess its damning criticisms of the old

From July 1942, Soviet troops had been fighting at terrible cost to liberate the ancient city of Rzhev, 60 miles west of Moscow, and to divert German forces from Stalingrad. Thousands of Rzhev's inhabitants were shot, tortured, starved or deported by the occupying Nazis, who destroyed in their retreat most of the town's buildings and all its churches.

'pre-Rostov' warhorses, and now discussions raged as to the various interpretations of the old General Gorlov and the youthful, soldierly Ognev.

By September, Moscow's hospitals were crowded with soldiers flown in from the massive and heartbreaking battles raging near Rzhev, just 60 miles away. And on 5 September, amid rumours of a renewed German advance on Moscow, there was a sudden unexpected daylight bombing raid on the capital. Few people bothered even to go to the shelters, and no planes got through. All thoughts in Moscow were now of Stalingrad, whose loss meant inevitable German victory in Russia, England and the world.

On 3 September, the Nazis broke through the Volga, south of Stalingrad, and on the 13th, under the eyes of the world, the all-out attack began. By the 24th, most of Stalingrad was in German hands, but from September 1942 until February the following year the defenders stubbornly fought on, under a

Stalingrad. The Germans assembled large land and air forces for their offensive
against Stalingrad, which began on 23 August 1942 with a bombing 'terror raid'
which killed 40,000, injured thousands, and left others to crawl to shelter in caves
and sewers across the Volga. Over the next three months, the city was pulverised
by 24-hour bombing raids and tank assaults. The Germans had the advantage of
numerous roads and extensive space for manoeuvre, whereas Soviet troops' only
route to the city was the ferry across the Volga. Barges carried reserves and
ammunition. By 4 September, the Germans had reached the Volga on the south
side of Stalingrad, and on 13 September, the all-out attack started. Ten days later,
most of the city centre was in German hands, and the battle for the city began, with
hand-to-hand fighting of unparalleled ferocity, for every staircase, rooftop and
garden, which changed hands again and again. The Russians held on to positions
in ruins made by German bombs, tanks and shells. The German onslaught began
to falter, and by mid-November, the Soviet counteroffensive had started.

hell of bombing, shelling and machine-gun fire. The battle was the great turning point of World War II, prefiguring Hitler's final defeat.

In October, the Soviet Union was in even greater danger than it had been during the Battle of Moscow. Anglo-Soviet relations had deteriorated, and the Battle of Stalingrad was going very badly. Yet the feeling now was that Stalingrad wouldn't fall, and people found a new and bitter determination not to be beaten – when they'd already given so much for victory.

By the second half of 1942, Soviet war industry was producing more than Germany did in the whole year: 22,000 fighter aircraft, 25,000 tanks and self-propelled guns, 128,000 field guns and 230,000 mortars. And this despite the fact that German forces occupied an area inhabited by 80 million Soviet people, nearly half the population, where 60 per cent of the country's steel and nearly half its food had been produced. Despite all the difficulties, the balance of forces was slowly and irrevocably swinging to the Russians. The Eastern Front was the hinge of the war: in the year of El Alamein, 96 per cent of all German casualties were in the east – and that was during a period of German advance, before the Battle of Stalingrad reached its shattering climax.

In Moscow, by now in the deep rear, people were looking at their city, so solid and confident, and recalling those agonising weeks a year ago, when the Germans were on the outskirts. The usual 6 November eve-of-Revolution anniversary celebrations, although on a smaller scale than the previous year, were held secretly 'somewhere in Moscow' in a mood of optimism.

'It will soon be our turn to rejoice!' said Stalin in his radio broadcast that night. He then spoke of the Germans' Moscow offensive, emphasising that their main objective was not the 'drive for oil', but to outflank Moscow from the east by the end of that year; this was why they had concentrated their armies in Oryol and Stalingrad, rather than in the south. Then came praise for the Big Three alliance, 'which, from the standpoint of human and material resources, has the unquestionable advantage over the enemy'. Had there been a Second Front, Rostov, the Donbas, Kharkov, Kursk and Oryol would have been saved, and the Leningrad blockade lifted.

Now what is needed is the ability to mobilise these resources, and the will to do this properly. Yes, there will be a second front, sooner or later, and not just because we want it, but because the Allies need it no less than we. Comrades, we are fighting a war of liberation, not alone, but with our Allies. Long live the victory of the Anglo-Soviet-American Fighting Alliance! [Applause.] Death to the German fascist invaders!

The twenty-fifth anniversary of the Revolution was an ordinary working day, not marked by any special parades or Red Square demonstrations. But red flags flew on all the public buildings, Red Square was decorated with banners, and the façade of the Bolshoi was adorned with portraits of Marx, Engels, Lenin and Stalin.

On 19 November, the Russians started their counteroffensive at Stalingrad, and three days later came the stupendous news that over 300,000 Germans had been encircled. Even the British military mission in Moscow was now talking of this as the start of something much bigger, and the signal for a new Russian drive all the way to Kharkov. A week later, the Germans tried to break out of the encirclement, but failed. After long delays caused by transport difficulties and partisan harassment, a large German strike force was assembled at Kotelnikovo, south of the Don bend, and on 12 December struck out for Stalingrad. Russian reinforcements were rushed across the snow-covered steppes. By the 24th they had hurled the Germans back to the Aksai River, and by the 29th, as the Russian blows became heavier, the Germans were in full retreat from Kotelnikovo, where they had started from.

7

The Turning Point

While the Russians were driving back the German army across the snow-swept steppes of Stalingrad, Moscow was suffering its second freezing winter of the war. By then, the temperature in the capital had dropped to 15 degrees of frost, and deep snow lay on the streets. The mines of the Moscow Coal Basin were still not producing enough for the city's heating to be turned on, the timber gathered that summer could heat only a few buildings and hospitals, and people worked in freezing factories and huddled in their beds under mounds of clothes.

But people still packed the unheated opera houses for cheerful perform-ances of Rossini and Mozart, shivered in concert halls through poetry recitals, or listened to Gilels or Sofronitskii, fingers stiffened by cold, play Rachmani-nov or Scriabin. (There were no encores – the pianists couldn't bear any more.) On 1 December 1942, Chistyakov, Kondratiev and other chess masters returned from the front to attend the National Chess Tournament, which opened as usual in the Great Hall of Soviets, and over the next month players solemnly crouched in the icy hall over their boards. (The winner was Ivan Smyslov, then a 22-year-old student at Moscow's Aviation Institute.)

By the end of December, the Germans within the 'Stalingrad pocket' had been encircled and had lost all hope of rescue. From the city itself, the famous Stalingrad journalist Ivan Grossman wrote:

Those Germans who in September broke into houses, danced to the loud music of mouth organs, drove about at night with their headlights full on, and, in broad daylight, brought up their shells in lorries – these Germans are now hiding among the city's stone ruins. There, like savages grown over with wool, they sit in their stone caves, gnawing at a horse's bone . . . There, in the dark cold ruins of the city they have destroyed, they will meet with vengeance; they will meet it under the cruel stars of the Russian night . . .

By 4 January 1943, their retreat from the Caucasus had started, and Russian troops on the Don front, under generals Rokossovskii and Voronov, were preparing for the final onslaught. On 8 January, an ultimatum was issued to Paulus's Sixth Army, rejection of which would mean that 'the Red Army and Airforce will be compelled to wipe out the surrounded German troops . . . for whose annihilation you will be responsible.'

The ultimatum was rejected, and at 8am on 10 January, the Russians attacked. It took three days to encircle German troops in the 250-mile radius of the Western pocket, and the advance became even more rapid over the days that followed. By 17 January, the Russians had captured nearly half the 'Stalingrad cauldron', and another ultimatum was issued to the German generals. Again it was rejected. By 22 January, when the final Russian assault started, the Germans were retreating or being killed off rather than left to the Russians. By 31 January, the Russians were closing in on central Stalingrad from all sides, and von Paulus, von Seydlitz and Schlommer were ready to negotiate. Two days later, the Germans had capitulated at Stalingrad, and troops were surrendering en masse.

The news in Moscow of the Stalingrad victory brought a wave of elation and feelings of joy and national pride which overwhelmed all others. Now, with Stalingrad pointing to even greater victories to come, it seemed that the Soviet Union would win its battle for survival. Ehrenburg wrote:

Could our young ten years ago have thought of a Schieffen plan, of tanks and pincer movements? We lived for other things then. The Germans have discipline, technical training and accuracy. But where are those pork-butchers and brewers when it comes to Russian talent, inventiveness, breadth of mind and heart? War is a hard, terrible business, but it is profoundly human. Victory depends on the heart . . .

For all the rejoicing in Moscow that February, people had now put all thoughts of peace out of their minds for a long time to come. A new, wartime way of life was evolving, and the new year of 1943, the year of hard victories and 'deep war', opened with a new slogan: 'Toughen up!'

Physical fitness and preparedness became an almost fanatical preoccupation. The military training of civilians intensified, with exercises now often carried out at the double, and day and night, young factory workers thronged the factory yards, rifles on their shoulders, or marched down the streets, coats belted army fashion. School and factory sports clubs organised skiing lessons to train people to ski long distances with the minimum expenditure of energy. New ski bases were set up on the city's outskirts, and people would spend any spare time during weekends and after work at the Moscow Young Pioneers' Stadium ski run practising their runs and jumps.

All children in elementary and middle education now had military training as part of their school curriculum, with new examinations in military subjects which had to be passed before they could move up to the next class. For younger children this meant physical education, simple military games and

Moscow ski detachment in training.

the elementary rules of military life. For boys of twelve to fourteen, there was military instruction equivalent to basic Red Army training, and for boys of fifteen to seventeen, there was a complete military preparatory course in tactical theory, weapons training, shooting and bayonet practice. Perhaps it was a sign of confidence in future victory that for girls the new rules were limited to nursing training and instructions in switchboard operation.

New teams of factory workers set off in the depths of winter to restore and work the pits of the Moscow Coal Basin. But as more evacuees returned from the east, more people moved to the capital from the surrounding villages, and the continuing influx of invalids and orphans meant that yet more apartment buildings had to be requisitioned for hospitals and children's homes, housing became increasingly crowded. But finding premises was the least of the problems. The reminders of that terrible year around Moscow were everywhere to be seen, and there was still immense suffering and sacrifice in store as the price of victory.

One old apartment mansion was converted into a sanatorium for seventy-five children, aged three to seven, from the occupied areas around Moscow, whose parents had been killed by the Germans or herded off as slaves to Germany. Every child there had suffered enduring traumas that required the most sensitive and devoted care. Nina, aged three, whose mother had been sent off to Germany, had been hidden in a dugout by a neighbour with four other children until the Germans were driven out of Yudino, and she could be brought to Moscow. Six-year-old Vova, who had lived through the German occupation of Istra, had lost his mother when she jumped to her death out of the window of a school which the Germans had turned into a brothel. Four-year-old Yurik, who had been saved by Red Army soldiers from a blazing house, couldn't be left alone, was terrified of matches, and wept constantly for his mother.

Everyone in Moscow suffered. Buildings were cold, people toiled and grumbled, food was short (sugar sold for 1500 rubles a pound on the black market). But amidst the ruins of the old life, a new one was slowly being built. Moscow's theatres returned from the east to triumphal openings at their old buildings. Moscow's Higher Education and Theatrical institutes created two new chairs, of Russian music and Russian theatre. And a new 10-mile extension to the Moscow underground was opened, its grey and pink marbled halls decorated with mosaics of legendary Russian warriors.

After Stalingrad, Hitler was desperate to regain his prestige and repay the Russians for their spectacular victory, and looking around for a suitable place to attack, he decided on the 'Kursk salient', a strip of land between Oryol and Belgorod. That spring, thirty-eight German tank, infantry and motorised divisions were assembled, reinforced by powerful new Tiger tanks and Ferdinand self-propelled guns, and officers swore that within three days they would have wiped out the massive Russian troop concentrations around the salient and captured the town of Kursk itself. The assault was delayed by bad weather, which held up reinforcements, and it was summer by the time the Germans had concentrated their forces. Meanwhile, the Red Army, under generals Zhukov and Vassilevskii, had brought up an enormous quantity of tanks, planes and men.

On 5 July, when the German offensive began, the atmosphere in Moscow was extremely tense, and *Red Star*'s editorial that day soared to new heights of patriotic intensity:

Our fathers and forefathers made every sacrifice to save their Russia, their homeland. Our people will never forget Minin and Pozharskii, Suvorov and Kutuzov, and the Russian Partisans of 1812. We are proud to think that the blood of our glorious ancestors is flowing in our veins, and we shall be worthy of them.

Yet within just one hour the German attack had been checked by a massive Soviet artillery volley, and by the end of that first day, the news from the war was of 203 shot-down enemy planes and 586 destroyed tanks. It was those 586 tanks, Werth recalls, that captured people's imagination. 'There'd never been anything like it in one day. The feeling produced was like that in London at the height of the Battle of Britain, when it was announced that 280 German planes had been shot down in one day.'

The Battle of Kursk, 5–15 July 1943.

The vast tank and air battles that raged in the heart of Russia over the next eight days (involving some 6000 tanks and 4000 planes) were of a ferocity unparalleled in modern warfare. Yet from the start it was clear that the *Wehrmacht* had thrown in tremendous forces and were suffering unprecedented losses, and there was not very much anxiety in Moscow after the first day. The Germans dug trenches, tank pits and dugouts, and on 12 July, the Red Army went over to the attack and started smashing through the enemy defences. By then, bewildered German prisoners were being driven off the battlefield, and the Red Army was ready to continue its advance north and south to Oryol and Belgorod. Two weeks later, the Red Army received orders to wipe out the German offensive launched the previous summer, and to recapture all the territory seized by the Germans since 5 July.

On the morning of 5 August, Levitan's voice came as sweet music to Moscow's ears: 'Today the troops of the Bryansk, Western and Central fronts recaptured, after bitter fighting, the city of Oryol. Today also the troops of the Steppe and Voronezh fronts broke the enemy's resistance and recaptured the town of Belgorod.'

Victory salvo in Moscow for the liberation of Oryol and Belgorod, August 1943.

Then followed words which, with slight variations, were to be repeated over 300 times in that 'era of victory salvoes' before Russia's final victory over Germany.

Tonight, at 2400 hours, the capital of our country, Moscow, will salute the valiant troops that liberated Oryol and Belgorod with twelve artillery salvoes from 120 guns. I express my thanks to all the troops who took part in the offensive . . . Eternal glory to the heroes who fell in the struggle for the freedom of our country. Death to the German invaders.

The Supreme Commander in Chief of the Soviet Union,

Marshal of the Soviet Union

STALIN

Kharkov was recaptured, then Taganrog, then Glukhov, the Donbas, Mariupol, Novorossisk, Smolensk . . . And night after night, Moscow's streets and squares were filled with people as the skies blazed with rockets, searchlights striped the clouds, and the salvoes rang out for new victories. Yet still people waited, agonisingly, for Victory itself.

*

By now the Allies had recognised the centrality of the German–Soviet front, and the Western leaders were under urgent popular pressure to discuss with the Soviet Union the postwar settlement and general measures to shorten the war. And since neither Stalin nor Molotov, his first deputy, could leave the Soviet capital, Eden and Cordell Hull, Roosevelt's elderly, austere secretary of state, travelled to Moscow on 18 October 1943 for a conference of Allied foreign ministers.

At their first meeting in the Kremlin, they discussed the terms of the surrender of the hostile states, and this led on to the postwar future of Germany, for which the US delegation had brought proposals for its dismemberment and denazification. Next they discussed the text of an Allied declaration on German atrocities, providing for the punishment of war criminals and their extradition to the countries in which their crimes had been committed. (This declaration, signed by Stalin, Roosevelt and Churchill, became the basis for the Nuremberg war-crimes trials.) Next for discussion was the Declaration on General Security, which was published at the end of the conference. It reaffirmed that hostilities would continue without separate peace negotiations, and provided for the continued cooperation of the three powers after the war. Cordell Hull pressed the USSR to start hostilities with Japan, which Stalin assured him would be done after the Germans had been routed. Eden cabled to Churchill, 'The Russians really want to establish good relations with the United States and Great Britain, on a footing of permanent friendship, and they have done their best to meet British and American views.'

But the underlying tensions between the Western powers and the Soviet Union still remained. One night, the conferees attended a gala performance at the newly reopened Bolshoi of *Ivan Susanin*. Sitting in a special box, draped with the flags of the three nations, Eden turned to Molotov during the ball scene at the Polish king's palace, and said, 'Look what nice people these Poles are – it's simply a pleasure to be friends with them!' Eden's remark, an obvious reference to the 'London Poles', brought a frown to Molotov's face. 'In real life things are more complicated,' he said icily. Later in the opera, when Susanin was being murdered by the Poles, Molotov turned to Eden, 'You see, our relations with the Poles have had their awkward moments. As for us, we want good relations – with an independent and friendly Poland.' After a while, Eden replied, 'I understand you. But you must understand us too. After all, it was because of Poland that we entered this war.'

Despite these tensions, the conference did serve to deepen Allied unity, and although Stalin felt constrained by the situation at the front not to leave Russia for another meeting until the spring of 1944, Hull insisted on the importance of meeting again to further wartime cooperation between the three powers 'now, at the present time. The situation calls for it, and if no such meeting is held there will be profound disappointment among all the Allied peoples.'

At the end of the conference, Stalin gave a dinner for his guests in the Kremlin. Along the vast front the Red Army was pouring over the Dniepr and streaming westward; Russia's allies had swept Italy, Hitler's main ally, out of the war. There was good reason to feel elation – which indeed seemed to glitter from the chandeliered magnificence of the Katherine Hall, crowded with Soviet officers whose chests, blazoned with medals, testified to their achievements in battle. It was an evening of toasts and speeches. Hull spoke of 'these two great nations', the Soviet Union and America, saying, 'It is important to assure that trust, understanding and friendship develop between them in a collective spirit,' and Stalin filled his glass with sweet Georgian wine to toast this friendship. An American officer, General Deane, caught Stalin's eye and proposed a toast to the day when the armies of Great Britain and the United States met the Red Army in Germany. Stalin rose from his place and, going to Deane, clinked glasses with him and clapped him on the shoulder.

When it was already past midnight, Stalin took his guests to a screening room for a showing of the prewar film *Days at Volochaevka*, about the liberation of Siberia from Japanese interventionists after the 1917 Revolution. In that war, the invading Japanese armies were among the cruellest – and the last to leave. Even before that, in 1904, Japan (with Britain's support) had attacked Russia, destroyed most of its fleet, and imposed humiliating peace terms. And in 1939 the Japanese armies had invaded Manchuria, whence they launched a series of raids on the Soviet Union's eastern borders. This culminated with an invasion (backed by Hitler) of the Mongolian People's Republic – where Zhukov's tank and air strategy decisively beat them back at the river Khalkin-Gol.

Cordell Hull took the point at once and, as soon as the film was over, turned to his host, saying, 'Now I see, Marshal Stalin, that you have accounts to settle with the Japanese, which you will undoubtedly present in good time. I understand you and am confident of success.'

The communiqué at the end of the Moscow conference, on 30 October, emphasised the close cooperation between the Allies not only over the conduct of wartime operations, but in the period of reconstruction after war ended. This emphasis on political and military unity was designed first and foremost to impress the Axis leadership with the hopelessness of their position. But to the millions whose lives had been disrupted or blighted twice in a generation the promise of a healthy international order and a genuine, permanent peace had a profound appeal. And what had made this unity possible at all was the great, and in the West largely unanticipated, feats of

Soviet arms. And it was the certainty of victory in the foreseeable future which had transformed the atmosphere of suspicion and distrust between the Allies.

The victories of the summer of 1943 produced intense diplomatic activity in the Allied capitals. Crucial decisions were looming, each of the Big Three had its own ideas about the postwar dispensation, but Soviet intentions were 'the great enigma' which Roosevelt decided would have to be unravelled in a private meeting with Stalin, to which Churchill would not be invited. Roosevelt and Cordell Hull shared a vision of what Hull called 'a movement for international cooperation', which they promoted with missionary zeal.

They envisaged a postwar world in which the victorious alliance would be transformed into a permanent international structure, the United Nations, with many of the functions of a world government and its own armed forces on call to 'stamp on any bar-room skunks', as Hull put it, who might rise up, like Hitler and Mussolini, to challenge the peace.

In the future, frontiers would not corral mankind but ensure the genuine self-determination of individuals and peoples. This apocalyptic vision drew public expressions of support from Whitehall, but in private Churchill was contemptuous, regarding Roosevelt as 'a charming country gentleman', an innocent abroad ('He'll end up in Stalin's pocket,' said the chief of the Imperial General Staff). Britain was weak, and dependent on US support; Churchill was forced to endure Roosevelt's moralising and to behave 'like a courtier' according to Alexander Cadogan, his top Foreign Office aide. 'I feel like a donkey squashed between the Russian bear and the American buffalo,' Churchill complained. The British were unable to alter this situation; moreover, circumstances compelled them to take sides. The Americans could be patronised. ('Extraordinary people,' Cadogan said to his wife. 'Quite charming, and kind to an unimaginable degree, in some ways rather like ourselves.') But the Russians only inspired fear and loathing. The Americans were a threat to the British Empire, determined to undermine it – but the Russians were the enemies of civilisation itself.

Churchill meant to show the Americans that defending the British Empire was also defending capitalism; whatever disagreements the British might have with their 'American cousins', common interests bound them together in a world which victory would not make safe. Churchill was already obsessed with the nightmare of a stricken Europe cowed by a rampant Red Army, while postwar America retreated into isolationism, abandoning wicked Europe to its fate, as it had in 1919.

Churchill never forgot that betrayal, or the shock he had felt at the fall of the tsars which overnight made his world an Edwardian anachronism. The situation was more dangerous still in 1943. In their hour of danger the British had had to take Bolshevik Russia for an ally. What Roosevelt called the 'skill, courage, sacrifices and ceaseless effort' of the Red Army, which Churchill too praised, caused heart-searching in Downing Street. Soviet victories opened up vistas of the restoration of British global power in the wake of Axis collapse. Egypt and Suez, Arab oil and the great sea lanes to India and the Far East – all these now fell into a power vacuum which small British forces could fill; it was tempting to picture Anglo-American forces advancing through the Balkans to the very borders of Soviet Asia, sealing off Asia and Africa from communism and keeping the Soviet navy out of warm waters. Yet these prospects went along with the menace of immense and unexpected Soviet power; the Red Army, unlike most others, prospered on a diet of perpetual battle. And this wasn't all: the British had agents in every resistance movement and knew a strong tide to the Left was running throughout occupied Europe. Even the British people, Churchill grudgingly told Stalin, 'have grown pinker', which the Soviet leader joked was 'a sign of returning health'. In France and Italy, there was no doubt that the Communists would emerge after liberation as the strongest political parties, backed by popular social movements with definite programmes and the credibility to carry them through. In Greece and the Balkans, Churchill could see no way to prevent the Communists from taking power as soon as the Germans left. Only determined efforts by the Anglo-Americans to restore prewar governments and crush Communist-led resistance movements could prevent the Russians from dominating all Europe and much else besides.

The British were already sponsoring discredited prewar regimes in Poland, Albania, Yugoslavia and Greece (where British troops eventually crushed the Greek resistance more effectively and bloodily than had the Germans). But across eastern, central and western Europe, the tide was running against them. The same problem existed elsewhere. When the question of India was raised, the angst in the British cabinet became palpable. The Americans not only disapproved of the British Raj, they supported Gandhi's Congress Party. Roosevelt suggested to Churchill that the Atlantic Charter's provisions on self-determination applied as much to India under British occupation as they did to German-occupied Europe, and reproved him for '400 years of acquisitiveness'. But India remained at the heart of British policy. It was not just the pivot of the Empire, it was a key link in the chain of international capitalism; if India could not be held, what power on earth could stop the triumphant march of Bolshevism?

When Hitler attacked the Soviet Union in 1941, leaving Britain safe from invasion, fifty British divisions were sent to India. Molotov was quick to see what was afoot, and accused the British of bad faith. While Russian blood flowed, British spokesmen – Eden, Halifax, even the 'left-wing' Moscow ambassador, Stafford Cripps – could produce only weasel words to justify the failure to open a second front. Nor did the British intend to help in the war against Japan; the Raj garrison was reinforced to suppress rebellion in India. It was clear to the US and Soviet governments that British war policy was being conducted at their expense; one result was that they were drawing closer together, as was evident during Cordell Hull's Moscow visit. Churchill was appalled to hear from Eden that Hull had asked for a private meeting between Stalin and Roosevelt, from which Churchill would be excluded. One purpose of such a meeting would be to discuss plans for the postwar United Nations – and its role in dismantling the great colonial empires. These considerations produced near panic in the British government. They touched the deepest chords of sentimental imperialism, which seemed to resonate equally in Tory and Labour hearts. Seizing on Goebbels's suggestion that an 'iron curtain' divided off Bolshevism from civilisation, Churchill now cut through the Gordian knot and evolved a strategy to carry the British and Americans forward together into the postwar era.

The Soviet Union and its 'sphere of influence' would have to be sealed behind a modernised *cordon sanitaire*, this time with a stringent ideological mobilisation of the Western peoples, which meant portraying the Soviet Union as a diabolical aggressor bent on world domination. The British needed a stick to beat the Soviet Union with, and one was to hand: Poland. A year before, in the dark days of 1942, Eden's talks in Moscow for a British–Soviet treaty of alliance nearly foundered on Britain's refusal to recognise the Soviet Union's 1941 borders. Churchill expected the Soviet Union first to beat Germany, then to surrender western Byelorussia and part of the Ukraine to Poland. This was obviously unrealistic – no country expects victory in war to leave it reduced in extent. Nor could Churchill argue that the 1941 border was a Soviet land grab, since it had first been suggested by Lord Curzon in 1919 – on the grounds of self-determination: more than half the population in the disputed territories was Russian, not Polish. Thus the dispute about Poland which lay at the heart of wartime conflict and suspicion was deliberately nurtured by the British (and later by the Americans under Truman, who brought about a sea change in US policy). Here was an issue over which the Soviets could not compromise. For Poland's disastrous prewar policy had led straight to the abyss of a war which was to swallow 50 million lives.

Poland was one arm of Churchill's Iron Curtain strategy; the other was the campaign to open a Second Front in the Balkans rather than France. The British knew there was a danger this approach would leave the Red Army master of Germany if the Hitler state should suddenly collapse; so they agreed with the US joint chiefs a contingency plan for massive airdrops of troops into central Germany, to accept their surrender before the Russians arrived.

These manoeuvrings set the stage for the Tehran meeting in the autumn of 1943, which Churchill insisted on attending. The Western Allies held a pre-meeting with Chiang Kai-Shek in Cairo, breaking off from the endless argument about India, Burma and the second front to make sightseeing trips to the Sphinx and the Great Pyramid.

The Tehran conference began on 28 November 1943; Roosevelt flew there from Cairo in his personal plane, *Sacred Cow*. It detoured over the Holy Land, and as the plane circled low over Bethlehem his senior aides and advisers crowded around the cabin windows to get a view. Cameras clicked; the plane wheeled in a slow arc northward, followed by the escort fighters circling invisibly three miles above. In Palestine, they were the only evidence of conflict. To the north, west and east, more than 40 million soldiers were fighting on five main fronts. While *Sacred Cow* meandered on over Jerusalem, Jericho and the river Jordan, the tourists on board continued to argue about decisions facing them at Tehran.

The Soviet delegation of Stalin, Molotov and Defence Commissar Kliment Voroshilov had left snowbound Moscow a few days before. Their special train was a mobile *Stavka* headquarters with dining car, conference rooms, press-corps carriage and radio and cipher equipment to maintain contact with the fronts.

Tehran was a modern-looking city built in what looked to Elliott Roosevelt, the president's son, like a dust bowl at the foot of a mountain range. Its broad avenues and the fine buildings that came with oil revenues barely hid a dusty Middle Eastern world of raw smells, noisy bazaars, minarets, veiled women and the sharp contradictions of a still-feudal society. The merchants had grown fat on the war; Russians who came for the conference, hastily shedding their winter furs for Tehran's autumnal warmth, were staggered by the wealth and diversity of the bazaar; goods came from all corners of the earth and found a market among rich war-exiles. Elliott Roosevelt wrote of the fantastic prices in Tehran, where a bag of flour cost more than the average Iranian's annual wage, a pack of cigarettes was five dollars, a Swiss watch $1500 and a radio set $8000. Here anything and most people could be bought.

Amid the glitter was poverty and squalor: the city had electric power but no sanitation so dysentery was epidemic. One night Roosevelt was stricken with stomach cramps, causing panic among his Soviet hosts, who feared poison; he recovered within hours. But the danger from Hitler's assassins was real; Iran was a neutral country on the edge of war, with a German business community which sheltered *Abwehr* agents, Gestapo men and Himmler's feared *Sonderkommandos* who were infesting the city. Hitler had got wind of the meeting and had detailed Otto Skorzeny, Mussolini's liberator, to kill Churchill and Stalin and take Roosevelt hostage. Soviet and British intelligence learned of the plots festering in the city, and at the last moment it was decided to accommodate Roosevelt inside the large and defensible Soviet embassy compound, which adjoined the British mission. The area was cordoned off by huge N K V D security men with guns bulging under civilian gaberdines.

This arrangement prevented the three leaders risking car journeys through the city, but added to the hothouse atmosphere of the conference. While Allied agents scoured Tehran, uncovering a secret base in a Turkish communal cemetery and apprehending German agents riding camels and disguised as nomadic tribesmen, the Big Three meeting developed into a bitter feud between the British and Russians rivalling the secret-service wars outside the compound.

Before the first plenary session Stalin and Roosevelt had a private meeting, to the anguish of Churchill who, ominous precedent, had to wait in the anteroom of history while his senior colleagues met in the intimacy of their uniquely shared power. Valentin Berezhkov, Stalin's interpreter, was present and described the scene: Stalin, in the white uniform of a Red Army marshal, sat at the end of a sofa next to Roosevelt's armchair, talking in his low voice and looking quizzically at the president when he suggested dispensing with a formal agenda. Roosevelt was in good humour, determined to get on with 'U.J.' (Uncle Joe), who paused for a long moment to select a cigarette from an open box of Herzegovina Flor before agreeing to an informal discussion.

Roosevelt asked the Soviet leader about the situation at the front.

'The main thing is that our forces recently lost Zhitomir, a vital railway junction,' Stalin said, adding that they were in danger of losing Kiev again as well. This gloom was a tactic to put pressure on the Western Allies over the second front. The Red Army's relentless advance had continued after the victory at Kursk in July, engulfing German armies whole, sweeping through the southern steppes, over the Caucasus mountains, across the Dniepr and deep into the Ukraine – an unstoppable mass of men and steel that in four months had destroyed half the German army in the east.

Roosevelt indulged Stalin by saying, 'I would like to divert some 30 or 40 German divisions away from the Soviet–German front,' adding that they would not leave Tehran without settling the second-front issue.

They decided to do business; a degree of trust grew between the New York lawyer and the son of Georgian serfs, but in any case Roosevelt's main concern was to maintain unity between the Allies, and that meant trying to look at the world through Kremlin eyes. He sought agreement with Soviet Russia about the postwar world and put this goal above the 'special relationship' with the British. Later, talking with his son Elliott, he said of Stalin,

Tehran 1943: the postwar world makes its first appearance. Eden eavesdrops
while Harriman and Stalin discuss the shape of things to come. Stalin's interpreter,
Valentin Berezhkov, stands to attention (centre); Kliment Voroshilov (right) stands
at ease. The British felt excluded at Tehran, where the future superpowers decided
on the Second Front and discussed the future of India.

'He gets things done, that man. He really keeps his eye on the ball he's aiming
at. It's a pleasure working with him. There's nothing devious. He outlines the
subject he wants discussed, and sticks with it. He's got a kind of massive
rumble, talks quietly, deliberately, seems very confident, very sure of himself,
moves slowly – altogether quite impressive, I'd say.' Elliott Roosevelt added
his own observation of Stalin, which was not untypical of contemporary
accounts:

Shorter than average . . . I realised something else about him: that his quiet, deep,
measured voice and his short stature notwithstanding, he had a tremendously
dynamic quality; inside him there seemed to be great reserves of patience and
assurance. Beside him, his Foreign Commissar, Molotov, was grey and colourless . . .
Listening to Stalin's quiet words, watching his quick, flashing smile, I sensed the
determination that is in his name: Steel.

The two leaders discussed the fate of India. Roosevelt spoke of the need for a new approach to the colonial countries' quest for independence. He wanted to free the world market to the dollar and all-conquering American capital; Stalin wanted to renew the wave of revolution-making which had broken out among the submerged colonial masses after the First World War.

'India is Churchill's sore spot,' Stalin said.

'In the end the British will have to do something about India,' Roosevelt replied. 'I hope to discuss this in more detail with you, bearing in mind that it is easier to solve this question for people removed from the Indian issue than for those directly involved in it.'

Decolonisation; the postwar order; the creation of a United Nations, with its array of proto-governmental institutions for safeguarding the health and welfare of mankind; the problem of what to do with Germany after the victory; the issues raised by Soviet participation in the war with Japan – all was in suspense while the conference nearly foundered at the first plenary session on the question of the Second Front. Churchill doggedly deflected attempts to discuss the timing of 'Overlord'. 'Whenever the PM argued for our invasion through the Balkans,' Roosevelt told his son, 'it was quite obvious to everyone in the room what he really meant. That he was above all else anxious to knife up into central Europe, in order to keep the Red Army out of Austria and Rumania, even Hungary if possible. Stalin knew it, I knew it, everybody knew it . . .'

Stalin reproached Churchill, denounced him, even teased him. 'I can't understand you at all; in 1919 you were so keen to fight and now you don't seem to be at all! What happened? Is it advancing age? How many divisions do you have in contact with the enemy? What is happening to all those 2 million men you have in India?'

'Don't know what this meeting will produce,' Cadogan wrote to his wife. 'PM and President ought to have got together before meeting Russians. But that, through a series of mischances, has not happened. [Eden said] things had gone pretty badly . . .' Cadogan was acutely aware of how marginal the British had become at Tehran. He spent his days skulking in the garden of the British embassy or visiting curio shops ('Full of rubbish!'). The meeting seemed to serve no purpose. 'Great ones woolly and bibulous,' he told his diary. 'Nothing for me to do but hang about.'

The dispute over the Second Front came to a head during a plenary session halfway through the conference. Stalin as usual abandoned diplomatic niceties and told Churchill with brutal frankness what he thought of the British position. He would take no other subject on the agenda until the date of 'Overlord' (the operation to open a Second Front in France) and the crucial appointment of its supreme commander were categorically decided.

Churchill was evasive but finally immovable. He did not want a Second Front. Claiming concern for 'Russian interests', he proposed operations in the Mediterranean, which could be mounted 'without delay', although they would perhaps result in 'delays to "Overlord"'. Churchill's cynicism astounded the Americans and angered the Soviet delegation.

Before speaking, Churchill would rise to his feet, pushing away his chair to leave room for his bulky frame, which rocked back and forth as if to emphasise his words. Placing his cigar on the ashtray before him, with his hands in the side pockets of his RAF jacket (he abandoned his pinstripe suit on first seeing Stalin wearing uniform), Churchill's lips would move in the pauses for translation as though he were rehearsing the lines of a script. He spoke at length on the choice between 'Overlord' and operations in the Mediterranean, raising his arms theatrically and ending, 'There is our dilemma. In order to decide which way to choose we should like to hear the view of Marshal Stalin, because we are delighted and inspired by the military experience of our Russian allies. The next problem I want to speak of,' he continued, without waiting to hear Stalin's views, 'is political rather than military . . . I have in mind the Balkans . . .'

Churchill was playing a stalling game, but the pressures on him were growing. The American and even the British general staff had come round to 'Overlord'. The president told his son:

Our chiefs of staff are convinced of one thing. The way to kill most Germans, with the least loss of American soldiers, is to mount one great big invasion and then slam 'em with everything we've got. It makes sense to me; it makes sense to the Red Army people. That's that. It's the quickest way to win the war. That's all . . . I see no reason for putting the lives of American soldiers in jeopardy in order to protect real or fancied British interests . . .

Stalin denounced the hypocritical talk of 'serving our Russian friends' by attacking in the Balkans now rather than in France later. 'It would appear from the prime minister's words that the Russians *want* the British to be idle,' he said.

Churchill suggested delegating the discussion to a 'military committee of experts'. Stalin instantly rejected this obvious time-wasting device (while making a note of the tactic, which Soviet negotiators subsequently made frequent use of), and asked bluntly, 'Do the British believe in "Overlord", or do they speak of it only to reassure the Russians?' Suddenly he jumped to his feet; there was an instant hush as, turning to Molotov and Voroshilov, he said, 'Come on! We're wasting our time here. We've got plenty to do at the front.'

Roosevelt had called the participants at Tehran 'members of a new family' that had gathered 'for one purpose, for the purpose of winning the war as soon as possible'. That is what public opinion would assume; Roosevelt was under intense pressure to coordinate plans for the war in Europe and, closer to home for many GIs' parents, in the Pacific. It would have been a military and political catastrophe if the first news of the conference was its collapse. Stalin had hinted that the Red Army was 'tired'; when, he enquired, would the West honour its repeated promises?

The spectre of a separate peace haunted each of the Allies; if that was the result of Churchill's intransigence, the British government would probably fall. The British Tommy in Africa, Italy and the 'forgotten armies' of Burma and India wanted the Second Front and Britain to be seen playing its part. Neither would the average GI, or his family back home, accept a split in the alliance. People wanted an end to the war and its continual dangers, privations, boredom and grief, and its separated families for whose children father was a photograph; an end to the dislocation of everyday life and the conscription of all need, desire, hope and ambition.

Churchill had said, 'The story of the human race is War.' However it was not liking for war which led him to prolong it, but the notion that victory at the price of the empire he was given in trust would be no victory at all. Churchill stared at his papers in silence; he had nothing more to say.

Molotov and Voroshilov, stunned by Stalin's outburst, didn't gather their papers, and the president took advantage of the pause to say, 'We are very hungry now, so I propose that we adjourn to attend the dinner given for us today by Marshal Stalin.'

Though nothing was settled, at least there was no longer any disguising the problem that had to be dealt with. The atmosphere of intrigue changed to one of expectancy. That evening a terrible row broke out during the dinner. Stalin taunted Churchill mercilessly, saying, 'Just because we Russians are simple people, it is a mistake to think we are blind and cannot see what is before our eyes.' As usual, an abundance of food was accompanied by endless toasts (Elliott Roosevelt said, 'The only way we talked was through a toast'), and they reflected the mood. Thus a Soviet delegate toasted 'future lend-lease deliveries arriving on time'. Stalin commented that future peace would only be assured when the German officer cadre was eliminated, and raised his glass to the summary execution of 'at least 50,000 of such war criminals'.

Churchill's anger boiled over at this. Denouncing Stalin as little better than a mass murderer, the outraged British leader stumbled to his feet and delivered an impromptu speech on the principles of 'British justice', which did not allow a person to be charged retrospectively with a crime which when committed was not on the statute book (a principle which would have made the Nuremberg trials impossible). Roosevelt, trying to defuse the situation, suggested 'a compromise' – shooting only 49,000 German officers. Churchill stalked from the room; Stalin and Elliott Roosevelt had to entice him back. His outrage was synthetic; less than a month before the British had agreed a convention on war crimes during the Moscow meeting between the foreign ministers. But the row let Churchill ventilate his anger at being out-manoeuvred over the Second Front issue.

The next morning Stalin met the Western leaders for luncheon; Roosevelt was cheerful, almost jubilant. Churchill looked gloomy and harassed. The president solemnly announced the decision, made that morning by the Western Allies, to carry out Operation Overlord in May 1944. At last it had come! Some of the Soviet delegates could barely keep from applauding; Stalin, his complexion paler than usual, murmured only, 'I am satisfied with this decision.'

The conference ended two days later, with much business done. After Churchill's capitulation, the atmosphere became euphoric. A cake with sixty-nine candles was produced to celebrate Churchill's birthday, and he was persuaded to drink a toast to the proletarian masses; Stalin toasted the Conservative Party. A more solemn event was the presentation by the British premier of the Sword of Stalingrad. The boardroom was filled with men: an honour guard of Red Army officers and British Tommies. The Red Army guard, carbines angled across their chests, watched, silent but not entirely expressionless, as their leader took from Churchill the sword (a gift from George VI) and, raising it aloft, kissed the hilts. Stalin passed it to Roosevelt, who drew the 50-inch blade from its elaborate gilded scabbard, saying, 'Truly, they had hearts of steel.' Elliott Roosevelt later said, 'From an Empire, a King had dispatched by his Tory Prime Minister a gift forged by craftsmen who, in their skill, were themselves aristocrats, working an aristocratic and medieval trade. Now the gift was given to the son of a shoe-cobbler, a Bolshevik, leader of a dictatorship of the proletariat . . .' Cadogan, more laconic, recorded, 'PM made a short speech,' adding that as Stalin handed the sword to Voroshilov, the latter dropped it on his toe.

On 2 December the conference broke up. Snow had fallen in the mountains and Roosevelt was anxious to get away before conditions worsened. In the final rush there was no time to draft and type up a communiqué properly. Scraps of paper were hurriedly circulated and the end result was a crumpled sheet signed – in pencil – 'Roosevelt. Stalin. Churchill.'

This was the famous Tehran Declaration. 'We express our determination,' it said, 'that our nations shall work together in war and in the peace that is to follow.' Calling for the United Nations 'to banish the scourge and terror of war for many generations', the declaration said:

We have surveyed the problems of the future. We shall seek the cooperation, and the active participation of all nations, large and small, whose peoples in heart and mind are dedicated, as our own peoples, to the elimination of tyranny and slavery, oppression and intolerance . . . No power on earth can prevent our destroying the German armies by land, their U-boats by sea, their planes from the air . . . We look forward to the day when all the peoples of the world may live free lives . . . We came here with hope and determination. We leave here, friends in fact, in spirit and in purpose.

The Soviet delegation left Tehran that afternoon to make the four-day train journey back to Moscow. They made one extended stop, at Stalingrad, where the generalissimo took his small party on a guided tour of the fire-blackened ruins. On the outskirts a new city of tents had sprung up in the snow. Thousands of former inhabitants had returned and rebuilding work had already begun.

8

The Road to Victory

In the new year of 1944, the mood among Muscovites was one of exultation as they surveyed the past year's fighting. The initiative had passed to the Allies at Kursk, El Alamein, Tunis and in the battle of the Atlantic, down whose sea lanes came a growing flood of war supplies. Italy was out of the war. At Tehran the second front had been decided. On 18 January 1944, the siege of Leningrad, in which 600,000 had died, was raised. On 27 January, hundreds of guns in Moscow and Leningrad saluted the city's defenders. The spring offensive gathered pace, 100,000 Germans were wiped out in one huge battle at Korsun-Shevchenkovsky, and by the end of March the Ukraine was cleared west of the Dniepr.

By 26 March, Soviet forces had reached the Rumanian frontier. In April and May, German defences in the Crimea collapsed; Sevastopol, which had taken the Germans 250 days to capture, fell in five days of hard fighting. Odessa was liberated on 10 April. A week later the Germans moved to occupy their ally Hungary when she tried to leave the war. The fascist camp was disintegrating, and Muscovites day by day observed the front serpentining west through the thickets of arrows on *Pravda*'s maps. Moscow was now hundreds of miles in the rear.

In Moscow on 20 March bands, bunting and thousands of people greeted the first Red Arrow Express since 1941, which arrived from Leningrad crowded with dignitaries and journalists. Football began again and a capacity crowd watched a Spartak vs Torpedo match. The thirteenth USSR chess championships opened in April in the Hall of Columns, and at the Udarnik, Metropol and Kolizei cinemas the British colour film *Mowgli* was being shown, while the Zarya was running a prewar Soviet feature, *Mashenka*. In May, as Mosfilm returned from its wartime home at Alma Ata ('Soviet Hollywood'), twenty Moscow cinemas prepared for the film event of 1944: the simultaneous premiere of Sergei Eisenstein's *Ivan the Terrible*. Not all films were on patriotic themes – Mikhail Shapiro made *Christmas Eve*, a film version of Tchaikovsky's opera, and the most popular film in Moscow that May was *The Swineherd and the Shepherd*, a romantic comedy about life on a Daghestan collective farm.

Korsun-Shevchenkovskii: German prisoners after the battle.

But the war dominated the film industry like everything else (the film-makers even funded their own tank brigade, the *Kinorabotnik*). Sometimes film stars were caught up in the fighting; when Olga Rayevska performed for the troops, she found herself carrying the wounded under fire as the Germans counterattacked. Soviet war films released in 1943–44 included *Kutozov*, *Front* and *Two Fighting Men*, which were shown abroad, as were documentaries about the battle of Oryol–Kursk and the siege of Stalingrad (where the cameraman Valentin Orlyankin had hurled grenades while filming German attackers). Soviet newsreel crews were always in the thick of the action, and many were killed. Boris Sher took his camera on a bombing mission, and when the Sturmovik's radio operator/gunner was killed Sher took over the gun, shot down the attacking plane and then filmed it crashing. Sher was famous for his newsreel coups, filming von Paulus's interrogation after the surrender at Stalingrad, and taking his crew behind German lines to film the partisans in action. In July, President Kalinin awarded honours to newsreel crews at a ceremony in the Kremlin. Maria Sukhova, the first Soviet newsreel camerawoman, was not present to receive her Lenin Prize – the former tea lady in film studio A930 was filming partisan operations deep in the German rear and, a few days later, was killed by a sniper's bullet.

The Red Army's spring campaign had pierced German defences to a depth of 250 miles and Hitler brought up forty fresh divisions from the Western Front to plug the gaps; but the Germans still held vast tracts of Soviet territory behind a 1300-mile front which stretched from the Arctic to the Black Sea. Hitler hoped to wear down the Red Army, knowing that each new offensive meant rebuilding reserves and mobilising, training, equipping and deploying whole new armies across ever extending supply lines in the logistic nightmare of a razed countryside. Since attack was more costly than defence, yet required a numerical superiority to succeed, the German high command thought that in time the Red Army would, must, run out of steam.

Moscow, the communications hub of the Soviet Union, was deeply involved in the vast campaign to resupply the fronts. Its railway stations were always crowded with soldiers going to join their units, or on leave. At the Byelorusskii terminus the station depot had a storeroom full of musical instruments, and impromptu concerts were held in a waiting room decorated with the flags of the three Allies above the words 'Long Live the Victory of the Anglo-Soviet-American Alliance!' A huge map of Europe showed the latest position at the fronts. At the station was a cinema which often screened films from Allied countries, such as the British film *In Which We Serve.*

Despite the optimism in Moscow, Hitler still hoped to stave off defeat for several years, till the conflicts simmering beneath the 'unholy alliance' of capitalist countries and the Soviet Union exploded.

On 5 May Field Marshal Keitel, Hitler's chief of staff, reported to the Führer that, despite the devastating losses of spring 1944, 'the situation on the Eastern Front has stabilised. There is no cause for alarm, because the Russians will not be in a position to launch an offensive in the near future . . . they will most probably concentrate their forces on the southern sector of the front. They are now unable to make several major thrusts simultaneously.'

The same calculation – that the Soviet–German war might subside into a battle of attrition, bleeding both sides white and leaving the Anglo-Americans masters in Europe – had lain behind Churchill's procrastination over the Second Front. But the noose round the Axis was growing tighter. On 4 June the liberation of Rome was announced, and on 6 June came the long-awaited news that the Second Front had been opened.

When first reports of the Allied Normandy landings reached the capital at 12.45 on 6 June 1944, crowds appeared around the loudspeakers in the streets, cars screeched up on the kerbs, trams stopped and passengers alighted, as people shook hands, hugged and kissed and congratulated one another. Moscow went shopping for maps of France and western Europe, and in one bookshop a queue sang 'We'll hang out our washing on the Siegfried Line'. On 8 June, dozens of war correspondents attending a euphoric meeting of the Moscow Writers' Club discussed new postings in western Europe instead of 'the international situation'. Stalin cabled Churchill to say 'Overlord is a source of joy to us all', and promised a summer offensive 'in keeping with the Tehran agreement'.

That weekend, tens of thousands of cheerful Muscovites poured into the parks and gardens newly opened for the summer. Music lovers in the Izmailovskii Park lounged under trees in the warm sunshine listening to a concert over the loudspeakers, and strollers enjoyed the 50,000 lilac, acacia and currant bushes planted in the previous year by schoolchildren (Active Park Volunteers); but the conversation was all of the Second Front and victory.

Crowded cinemas cheered the first newsreels of the landings. Other news items were more ironically greeted. On 8 June the Presidium of the Supreme Soviet adopted a decree 'On mothers of large families and motherhood care': the aim was to raise the peacetime birth rate to compensate for war losses, but it came to be criticised for reinforcing the 'double burden' on women of domestic and wage labour. With it went a new title, Heroine Mother, for mothers of more than ten children, and an Order of Motherhood Glory. 'Without women there is no love,' wrote *Pravda*, 'without the mother there is neither poet nor hero.' Special family allowances were given to mothers of large families, and new benefits were established for unmarried mothers. More than 90 per cent of young men aged between 18 and 21 when the war started had been killed, the peacetime lives of millions of women were going to be affected as a result, and the new rules anticipated the possible increase in the number of single-parent families.

That same week the papers reported the recommissioning of more than 10,000 miles of railway lines and over 2500 stations. Not publicised were orders issued to partisans to begin the 'Battle of the Rails' – the destruction of German-controlled lines in preparation for Operation Bagration, designed finally to clear Germans from Soviet territory.

In the occupied Ukraine and Byelorussia, the Germans had murdered 2 million people – half the population. They had destroyed every school, library, hospital, museum and theatre; thousands of towns and villages and tens of thousands of dwellings had gone; only the concentration camps had flourished. The village of Masyukovshchina had been turned into a camp, where 80,000 prisoners of war and civilians died. In the Minsk ghetto, the Germans had killed 90,000 Soviet Jews. They starved people, hunted them with dogs, hanged and burned them alive, drowned them in rivers, buried them in ravines and antitank ditches. Some 374,000 young men and women had been sold as slaves to German housewives, farmers and factory owners (the proceeds going either to Himmler's s s or Rosenberg's Administration of the Occupied Lands); they were exported to Germany and most never came back. 'The soil shall burn under the invaders' feet!' was one partisan slogan, and after three bitter years the moment of revenge was near.

Reconstruction would have to wait, but plans for the refurbishing of devastated towns and cities were far advanced. In Moscow the Academy of Architecture had drawn up plans for simple-to-make prefabs, using novel materials like compressed, heat-treated gypsum bricks, dyed different pastel shades on each side so that the new houses would be predecorated inside and out. They were a far cry from the wooden lean-tos hastily improvised in the early stages of the war, and plans were laid to build them in huge numbers to rehouse tens of thousands of people living in dugouts or forest clearings behind German lines.

In the spring of 1944, Hitler's eastern empire was a strip along the western Soviet borders 200–300 miles wide except for a huge bulge taking in Byelorussia and the western Ukraine. The German high command expected a Soviet offensive to begin south of the bulge, where the shortest route over passable terrain led to the Vistula and Poland. Further north were the Pripet Marshes – hundreds of miles of forest wilderness and intractable bog, defended by von Busch's Army Group Centre; facing them a concealed Soviet army 2.5 million strong waited to begin 'Bagration'.

By 10 June, preparations were complete; to get across marshes the *Wehrmacht* had found impassable and left undefended, the soldiers learned the Byelorussian peasant skill of making 'bog shoes' shaped like snowshoes and woven from birch twigs. Brushwood tracks were laid to support heavy equipment; they made sledges for machine guns and built boats and rafts; tanks were sealed tight with oiled tow so they could plough through the swamps. Log corduroys were laid up to two metres deep, but the noisy job of securing them was left till the softening-up bombardment began, to avoid raising German suspicions; men drilled constantly, following 'creeping' barrages, crossing water barriers – before reaching Poland they would meet hundreds of streams and dykes and twelve major rivers including the Dniestr, Vistula, Narew, Bug, Pripet, Berezina, Drut, Dvina and the mighty Neman.

They built miles of road – lorries brought up tens of thousands of tons of gravel and sand – and created huge dummy airfields and tank parks to fool the Germans.

They hauled up 320 heavy guns to every mile of front; enormous reserves of ammunition, petrol and food were accumulated; 100 trainloads of supplies arrived each day at the front; 294,000 hospital beds were made ready. A fleet of 12,000 lorries transported fuel and supplies to the front from the railheads. Nothing was left to improvisation, as it had been in the past. Operations were coordinated with the partisan formations for whom this was to be the last operation behind enemy lines; in the front-line districts Smersh ('Death to Spies') and army counterintelligence agents were everywhere, suppressing enemy scouts and spies; complete radio silence was preserved.

The high command knew of all German movements, plans and intentions, intercepting and decoding orders before they were even delivered. Every night Russian scouts in speckled camouflage units made their way behind enemy lines to take prisoners; reconnaissance planes flew constantly overhead, but Soviet air defences denied the skies to the Luftwaffe. Even so, many Soviet preparations were made under cover of darkness.

On 23 June Operation Bagration began with a massive series of explosions behind German lines as the partisans blew up dumps, railway lines, telephone exchanges and power plants, paralysing the German rear. The Red Army had only a slight overall superiority in numbers, but concentrated its forces on the lines of attack to achieve crushing surprise. The four armies at Vitebsk-Orsha, Mogilev and Bobruisk burst forward at 6am. The onslaught began with a terrifying roar from the Katyusha rocket mortars; a dense screen of smoke dust, clods of soil and smashed logs filled the air over the German lines. For two hours shells from 36,000 guns poured on observation posts, command centres, assembly areas, living quarters and forward lines. At 8.30 Pe-20 bombers and Ilyushin-2 ground-attack planes swept over enemy lines covering them with bombs and rockets, fusillades of cannon and machine-gun fire. The first wave of tanks and infantry moved against the German lines.

After two days the first Baltic front had reached the Dvina and troops crossed it on logs, barrels, bundles of twigs, empty drums, whatever came to hand, to meet units of the third Byelorussian front on the far bank and trap 60,000 enemy troops in the ancient town of Vitebsk, where fierce street fighting began as the Germans fought for every house and cellar.

Next day salvoes were fired in Moscow to salute the freeing of Vitebsk. The town was in ruins, not a street, office, school or factory remained standing; of the inhabitants, 50,000 had been shot, hanged or drowned by the Nazis in the western Dvina and a further 20,000 sold off as slaves and sent to Germany; no one was left to greet the liberators.

During the occupation the Germans had not had everything their own way; the partisans executed scores of minor Nazis as well as a regional commissioner, Ludwig Erenleiter, a gendarme, Karl Kahll, and, in September 1943, even the general commissioner for Byelorussia, Wilhelm Kube. Now, in their

Soviet troops find a way through the marshes during Operation Bagration.

Battle of the Rails, the partisans had destroyed more than 5000 trains carrying troops and supplies in the enemy rear, blown up 1001 bridges, 73 aircraft and 397 German tanks.

Mogilev was liberated on 27 June 1944; the next day, 600 miles to the north, troops of the Karelian front took Petrozavodsk, releasing 20,000 Soviet citizens from a concentration camp there.

Also on 28 June, Wilhelm Kube's successor, General Kurt von Gottberg, abruptly closed down a conference of Nazi collaborators being held in Minsk. The 1039 'delegates', including Dmitrii Kasmovich and others who had guided the *Sonderkommandos* to their victims and so made possible the Nazis' reign of terror in Byelorussia, had just elected Radislav Ostrovskii president of 'free' Byelorussia. His first task in office was to plead with the SS for a special train to take the collaborators to Germany. They left Minsk that same afternoon; General Reinhard Gehlen, head of Hitler's secret service in Russia, decreed they should be evacuated in preference even to wounded German soldiers. The core of Nazi Germany's and, later, NATO's Soviet spy system, they were a bargaining counter with the Western Allies; Gehlen meant to trade them to the Americans, in exchange for his own freedom. At least 400 of the 1039 later found their way to the United States and most eventually became American citizens. Today Ostrovskii lies buried in the cemetery of St Euphrosynia in a small town near Washington DC. On a mound behind the church is a monument whose inscription reads, 'Glory to those who fought for the freedom and independence of Byelorussia,' and above it flies the white-red-white Byelorussian flag and the Stars and Stripes. Between them is an iron circle enclosing a double-barred cross: the symbol of Hitler's Byelorussian SS.

On 3 July 1944, Minsk was liberated and 100,000 Germans were taken prisoner. The capital of Byelorussia was now a city of smouldering, gutted ruins. The railway station was a heap of rubble, 323 out of 332 factories and enterprises were destroyed, the university campus, all higher educational establishments, 78 schools, the concert hall and theatre were razed. The streets were filled with piles of German helmets, gas masks, rifles, machine guns and other abandoned equipment. The few emaciated inhabitants re-maining (the Nazis had killed 120,000 citizens) emerged dressed in rags, weeping for joy, from the shadows of a three-year ordeal.

At 10pm that day Moscow fired a 24-salvo salute from 324 guns in honour of the liberators of Minsk. On 16 July, as Moscow marked the fortieth anniversary of the death of Anton Chekhov and the government announced that a Chekhov museum would be opened and Malaya Dmitrovka Street, where he had lived, would be named for him, the people of Minsk held a rally with a march past by 50,000 partisans, whose columns came from all over liberated Byelorussia to attend. They felt a combination of exultation, pride and grief – but most of all anger, for the sufferings of Hitler's most ill-used province still continued, and defeat did not lessen German barbarism. Word was already spreading through the front of new atrocities. The day after 'Bagration' began, the Germans had captured eighteen-year-old Yurii Smir-nov, a private in the 11th Guards Army; next day troops found his body nailed by the palms to a dugout wall and on the mess table was the unfinished record of an interrogation. How many tanks are there? No answer. Where are the tanks heading for? No answer. What is the composition of your regiment? No answer. The story was not unusual; those who questioned were not even Gestapo, just ordinary German infantrymen. Men of his company wrote to his mother, 'Maria Fyodorovna! . . . We who are Yurii's comrades-in-arms have sworn mercilessly and relentlessly to avenge your son's death. Each of us has pledged himself to fight for two: for himself and for Yurii . . .'

Some heroism aroused pity rather than anger. On the day of the Minsk parade, Maurice de Seynes, a pilot of the Free French Normandie fighter regiment, was blinded by a fire in the cockpit of his Yak fighter plane as he approached an airfield near Minsk; the controllers tried to guide him down

German prisoners of war parade through Moscow, 17 July 1944.

but, when it was clear this was impossible, ordered him to bail out. But Vladimir Belozub, his mechanic, was squashed without a parachute into the space behind the Frenchman's seat; de Seynes would not abandon him and finally the plane exploded in midair. *Red Army Pravda* said the tragedy showed the internationalism of the Free French, reflecting a feeling shared within the government that French honour had been redeemed by the loyalty and sacrifice of the Resistance. The Normandie squadron had fought alongside the Red Airforce since the darkest days of the war.

Two months later, in August 1944, the Soviet government argued strongly with the Western Allies that France should become a permanent member of the United Nations Security Council; in December de Gaulle visited Moscow to conclude a treaty of alliance and mutual assistance with the USSR. He said that in the past France had 'betrayed' Franco-Russian solidarity, which still remained necessary 'both from the standpoint of the German threat and of Anglo-Saxon hegemonic ambitions'.

On 17 July, the day after Minsk's victory celebration, 57,600 German prisoners taken during 'Bagration' were paraded through Moscow. Hitler

German mobile bone-grinding mill.

had promised them a different review in 1941. After spending the night encamped in the Moscow Hippodrome racecourse they shuffled their way down Leningrad Highway in the city centre, though Red Square itself was not to be defiled by the fascist footsoldiers. They were accompanied by sabre-bearing mounted guards; with impeccable military etiquette, the generals at their head were allowed to retain their side arms. Among them was Major-General Hamann, the Butcher of Bobruisk, and other war criminals. On his orders 19,000 civilians had been shot; special equipment in Hamann's corps baggage train was a mobile bone-crushing mill used to destroy the traces of his cremated victims. The Reich's soldiers shambled along with downcast eyes as though expecting abuse from the thousands of Muscovites lining the route, who for the most part looked on in silence.

In the shattering retreat through Byelorussia and the western Ukraine the Germans exchanged much space for a few weeks of time; Latvia and Lithuania were freed, the Red Army entered Poland, on 17 August the river Neman was crossed and the war carried on to German soil. Muscovites were becoming nonchalant about the stream of victories, celebrated in fusillades of artillery fire each night; many were more excited by the recommencement of horse racing at the Moscow Hippodrome. Huge crowds, including many off-duty soldiers, watched as the first race of the season was won by a three-year-old filly, Valencia, which had been evacuated from a Ukrainian stud farm in the first weeks of the war.

The Germans defending *Grossdeutschland* fought for every inch. There were still 235 *Wehrmacht* divisions on the Eastern Front: ten times the number faced by the British and Americans in France. The Red Army ground its way into eastern Poland, and before long a new kind of refugee appeared. Passing like groups of wraiths down the roads and railways of Europe, they were the survivors of the death camps. Maidanek was liberated and the remains of an estimated 1,380,000 murdered inmates uncovered. Only 800 Soviet prisoners had survived; they arrived in the Ukraine in two special trains and some were sent on to Moscow for treatment and rehabilitation.

A Polish–Soviet extraordinary commission set up to investigate German atrocities issued a communiqué listing some of the camps on Polish soil: Auschwitz, Treblinka, Sobibor, Chelm, Biala Podliaska and many more. There, people from every occupied country, the Jews, gypsies, anyone offending against what the Nazis termed 'racial hygiene', had been condemned to 'gas and fire'. A prisoner wrote, 'The furnaces howled like wolves all night, my ashes were turned over by a poker. But soaring in a whirl of smoke from Dachau pipes, I landed on the meadows, alive, unbroken.'

Gradually the story of the camps was published to a world which found the sadism of individual torturers and executioners easier to grasp than the true novelty of the Nazi achievement – they had made evil into an industrial process, managed by accountants. Wickedness on so vast and impersonal a scale was banal, even meaningless. But the revelation of the camps cast a pall over that summer of victories and made many ashamed to be human. The Red Army fought on, more implacable than ever.

In midsummer, when Soviet forces were deep into Poland and stopped to resupply, the underground Armia Krajowa, armed only with 4000 hand guns, began its quixotic, doomed uprising in Warsaw. In the same week Stanislaw Mikolajczyk, leader of the reactionary government in exile which sponsored the Armia Krajowa, came to Moscow from London for talks. At his first meeting with Stalin, Mikolajczyk boasted, 'Warsaw will be free any day now.'

'God grant that it be so,' Stalin replied. 'What kind of army is it – without artillery, tanks or air force? They do not have enough hand weapons . . . I hear that the Polish government instructed these units to chase the Germans out of Warsaw. I don't understand how they can do it. They don't have sufficient strength for that.'

On 2 October the rising collapsed, and a week later Churchill arrived, full of bitter reproaches, blaming Stalin for the loss of 200,000 Polish lives and the destruction of historic Warsaw, but silent about the still greater count of Red Army soldiers who died trying to relieve the city.

Churchill concealed his own share of responsibility for the disaster, in which the communist-led underground was also destroyed. His anguish was genuine, though; like Mikolajczyk, he had hoped to celebrate in Moscow a different outcome to the rising. Knowing the Red Army was too distant to liberate Warsaw before the autumn, Mikolajczyk had meant to expel the *Wehrmacht* by the unaided efforts of the Armia Krajowa, install the London Poles as the government of liberated Poland, and triumphantly await the belated arrival of the Red Army. Devastated Warsaw paid dearly for this piece of adventurism, which Churchill encouraged in the hopes of recreating the Polish buttress against Bolshevism.

The Red Army was moving beyond Soviet borders. In the Baltic states, Poland and the Balkans, Soviet forces had been greeted as liberators. Churchill, fearing Soviet influence in these countries in the aftermath of the war, had come to Moscow to see if the gains of the Red Army on the battlefield could be prised from Stalin at the conference table.

At their first Kremlin meeting Churchill offered Stalin a 'spheres of influence' deal, which would limit Soviet sway in postwar Europe regardless of which borders the Red Army crossed or where the final battle lines lay. Churchill spoke of giving '90 per cent influence to the Russians in Rumania, 90 per cent to the British in Greece, 50–50 in Yugoslavia' and so on, dividing up the destinies of millions in a manoeuvre which ignored the principle of self-determination enshrined in the Atlantic Charter.

While his words were translated, Churchill jotted down the percentages on a sheet of paper he handed to Stalin, who glanced at it, making no comment. Churchill was offering British help in gaining recognition for any Soviet 'conquests' in Europe, provided these did not exceed agreed limits. Embarrassed by Stalin's silence Churchill said, 'Might it not be thought rather cynical if it seemed we had disposed of these issues, so fateful to millions of people, in such an offhand manner? Let us burn the paper.' But there was to be no collusion. 'No, you keep it,' Stalin replied, and the British prime minister took it back; it was left to Churchill to dispose of the compromising document. Roosevelt, too, would have none of British scheming, and the percentages deal disappeared from the international agenda.

While the British and Soviet leaders were meeting, the hunting season had begun and Moscow's 30,000 hunters went out into the swamps and forests around the city in pursuit of martens, otters, elks and wolves. From the Dynamo factory club, one party bagged fourteen wolves in the first weekend; their numbers had grown during the war.

In the same week the Central Council for Trade Unions opened a sanatorium for expectant mothers, newly built in a beauty spot outside Moscow. A young telegraphist, Ekaterina Likhacheva, was one of the first arrivals; she was given a warm dressing gown labelled 'Best wishes to the Soviet people from the Canadian Society for Russian War Relief'.

Despite the confrontation over Poland, the Moscow meeting was judged a success; it paved the way for the last Big Three conference, at Yalta in February 1945. But before that, the Germans launched a powerful offensive on 16 December 1944. The Nazi onslaught began in the Ardennes, and soon a dire situation developed on the Western Front.

The German high command announced that 'the aim of this operation is to turn the tide of the war in the west, and possibly of the war as a whole'; they intended completely to smash the Allied Western Front, before turning again on the east.

The Allies were caught unawares. Panzers burst through American lines, prisoners were taken, a retreat began and the Germans captured hundreds of guns and vast quantities of supplies. The terrible memory of Dunkirk spread through the lines. In two days the attack split the US 12th Army in two; a gap of 60 miles opened in the Allied front. Despite counterattacks the situation worsened and on 31 December the Germans pressed on into Alsace; air strikes destroyed 800 Allied planes at forward bases and on 4 January 1945 the Germans launched an offensive north of Strasbourg. Soon they were back over the Rhine. They did not seem like a broken enemy, and Eisenhower and Montgomery, the Allied commanders, hurried to confer with Churchill. On 6 January, Churchill wired Stalin about the catastrophic situation on the front:

You know yourself . . . how very anxious the position is when a very broad front has to be defended after temporary loss of the initiative. It is General Eisenhower's great desire and need to know in outline what you plan to do, as this obviously affects all his and our major decisions . . . I shall be very grateful if you can tell me whether we can count on a major Russian offensive on the Vistula front, or elsewhere . . . I regard the matter as urgent . . .

Stalin replied the next day:

In view of our allies' position on the western front, GHQ have decided to complete our preparations at a rapid rate and, regardless of weather, to launch large-scale offensive operations along the entire central front. Rest assured we shall do all in our power to support our valiant allies . . .

Five days later the Soviet offensive began; along a swath of central Europe 300 miles wide, the Red Army pushed into the heart of Hitler Germany. A gigantic pincer crushed the Axis forces between the Vistula and Oder rivers. A

Soviet strike force 2,200,000 strong, equipped with 33,000 guns, 7000 tanks and 5000 combat planes, ground into dust the Germans' last defence line in the east.

To fill the breach Hitler rushed in twenty-nine divisions and four brigades, including the Sixth Panzer Army which, poised like an axe over the Americans, had been Eisenhower's biggest worry. Churchill said this act of Soviet solidarity was 'a fine deed', but he had no doubt that beginning their offensive early to help the Western Allies had made it 'very costly in loss of life'.

Hitler's aim in the Ardennes offensive was political. He imagined a discouraged Western public opinion, hating the war and still fearing the *Wehrmacht*, turning against the endless loss of life. Hitler was encouraged by the continuing secret talks between Nazi and Western diplomats – contrary to Allied agreements not to seek a separate peace. The future CIA boss, Allen Dulles, had met Hitler's emissary, Prince Hohenloe, in Geneva and reported enthusiastically to Washington on the prospects for turning the war into a crusade against communism. In Madrid the British ambassador, Sir Samuel Hoare (former home secretary in Neville Chamberlain's government), told General Franco that at least one British cabinet minister advocated peace with Germany and a general European front against Bolshevism. Churchill himself had visited Turkey in 1943 and suggested the possibility of a postwar anti-Soviet pact – knowing the Turks were German sympathisers and would be sure to alert Hitler to the divisions within the Allies.

But Hitler's schemes were soon overwhelmed by events – and by Roosevelt's unabated desire to continue the wartime collaboration with the Soviet Union in the period of postwar reconstruction. The missionary zeal for a powerful United Nations and a harmonious peace displayed by the president and his ailing secretary of state, Cordell Hull, was shared by few others in positions of power and influence in the West. But Roosevelt's unassailable moral authority was enough to stop the clandestine talks – once Stalin alerted him to the activities of his own maverick secret service.

The Ardennes offensive was the *Wehrmacht*'s last fling, and the Red Army's advance was now so rapid that, according to Elliott Roosevelt, when the Yalta conference opened on 4 February, the US and British military 'conjectured that the Russians had finally breached the German front in the East and the fascist state would collapse before the Conference ended'.

It was clear that the Soviet Union could end the war in Europe by itself. Zhukov's armies were less than 60 miles from Berlin. Eastern Prussia, the citadel of Junker militarism, was cut off; Poland and Czechoslovakia were cleared of Germans; Budapest was about to fall; and Nazi Germany had lost Silesia, a vital arms and raw-materials supplier. The Red Army was nearing the end of its mission, during which it inflicted three quarters of all German losses and liberated 200 million people in eleven European and two Asian countries, including Rumania, Norway, Hungary, Austria, Lithuania, Poland, Latvia, Czechoslovakia, Estonia, Bulgaria and Yugoslavia.

The Yalta conference began with the British prime minister lecturing Roosevelt on the Bolshevik menace in the Balkans, the Middle East, Asia and India – to little avail. Roosevelt felt that Churchill wanted to embroil the US in the defence of British imperialism, but he doggedly upheld the vision of a world without wars or empires.

Roosevelt was dying; Churchill sulked; platoons of Soviet waiters and British Royal Marines scurried to and fro in the gloomy chaos of the great Livadia Palace, which had been Hermann Göring's holiday home until the Germans were expelled from the Crimea only weeks before. Now it had to cater for the hordes of pressmen, soldiers, couriers, advisers, family members, hangers-on, bodyguards, cooks and personal physicians making up the entourage of the world's three most powerful men. (Charles Moran, Churchill's doctor, worried that 'Winston never talks of Hitler these days; he is always harping on the dangers of Communism. He dreams of the Red Army spreading like a cancer from one country to another; it has become an obsession . . .') There was no agenda, and most of the minutes of the previous meeting, in Tehran, were mislaid. (They were found some years later by another president, in a bedroom cupboard in the White House.) Roosevelt resisted to the last the cold-war blandishments of the State and War departments, ignoring their background briefings and holding informal meetings with Stalin and other Soviet leaders. His advisers anxiously created a roster of 'duty drinkers' so that some might remain sober enough to ensure the convivialities did not result in too much being 'given away' to the Russians.

The influence of the cold warriors was weakened by recent events: the public in the Western countries was well aware of the aid rendered by the Red Army during the Ardennes crisis, in response to pleas from the Western commanders, Eisenhower and Montgomery. In the prevailing climate, it was impossible for the West to continue insisting that the Soviet Union abandon its western provinces to Poland, and the issue which had festered at the heart of the alliance was settled. The Polish–Soviet frontier would for the most part follow the line proposed by Lord Curzon in 1919. Stalin clinched matters by declaring that his people would think him no Bolshevik if he went home with less than an English nobleman had once thought was rightfully Russian soil – which was good tactics and bad Marxism. Poland's western frontier would be the Oder–Neisse line, so that Poland stayed much the same size, but moved bodily westward.

To please the Americans and regain the Kurile Islands and southern Sakhalin (lost to Japan by the tsar in 1905), the Soviet Union agreed to enter the war in the Far East. The US hadn't yet tested the atomic bomb; later they regretted asking for Russian help.

Yalta had turned into a festival, a game with no losers – even the vanquished were told they had not been beaten but liberated from without, though their reprieve depended on future good behaviour. There was to be no vengeful peace to fuel future discontents in the manner of Versailles two decades before.

On 11 February the victors departed in glory to their respective capitals. In Washington, the ailing president told a triumphant Congress, 'The Conference was a turning point – I hope in our history and the history of the world . . . [it] ought to spell the end of the system of unilateral action, the exclusive alliances, the spheres of influence, the balances of power, and all the other expedients that have been tried for centuries . . .' Instead there would be 'a universal organisation in which all the peace-loving Nations will finally have a chance to join'.

For once, not all was vainglory. At Yalta, might had proved to be right. In the words of the Soviet historian Pavel Sevastyanov, it was 'a brilliant page over which time and altered circumstance has no power. No falsifiers can rewrite it.' The Allies reaffirmed the decision to offer the enemy no terms except unconditional surrender. This was not from an intention to impose a peace of retribution, since revenge puts victim and aggressor on the same moral level. By now public opinion in the Allied countries regarded fascism as a unique evil, with which civilised nations could not treat, and which must be extirpated at whatever cost. For the first time in modern diplomatic history the defeated powers were to lose, not merely possessions and territory, but the right to exist. Surviving Nazi leaders did not expect this, assuming to the last that the victors would afford them the normal courtesies and that their state would continue. But Yalta was unique: it set a moral standard above the nations, soon to be inscribed in the United Nations Charter, the foundation of modern international law. Punishing the war criminals and cleansing the world of fascist laws, ideas and institutions would mark a clean break with the progenitive politics of the 1930s, that remote and shabby era of national hypocrisy and the shameless indulging of fascist aggression.

Yalta's call for justice, issuing subversively from the lips of the mighty, also foretold the disappearance of the vast colonial empires which still enslaved hundreds of millions. Yalta set new tests of human, social and national rights against which progress might be measured.

The future which Roosevelt invoked to Congress required, as the Yalta Declaration said, 'continuing and growing cooperation and understanding among our three countries and among all the peace-loving nations'. This was the high ground Roosevelt and Stalin had staked out in settling the Polish and

Stalin, Churchill and (top right) Averell Harriman, Yalta, February 1945. The most convivial of the wartime Big Three conferences.

other long-standing questions. But in the West other, now dominant, forces were already shaping post-Roosevelt policy, and they regarded the Yalta decisions only as concessions extracted under duress. Roosevelt was increasingly remote from events, which no longer justified the rosy view of future collaboration he still portrayed to the Soviet leadership.

Outside the president's narrow circle, American political and military leaders were preparing for a postwar role based on domination in the West and a policy of *cordon sanitaire* in the East.

The balance of power had changed. The European nations, victors and defeated alike, were now only regional powers. A background paper for the Yalta conference, sent by the us War Department to the secretary of state, had said, 'The successful termination of the war will find a world profoundly changed in respect of relative national military strengths, a change more comparable indeed with that occasioned by the fall of Rome than with any other change occurring during the succeeding 1500 years.' The battle lines were already being drawn up.

As the Third Reich passed into history, its retinues of quislings and fifth columnists, poisoners and hangmen, sinister technicians and secret policemen fled west with their booty, many into the waiting arms of the Americans. A special us task force snatched Wernher von Braun, father of the ballistic missile, from the maw of Soviet and British armies, airlifting his entire design team with hundreds of tons of equipment, including rocket motors and missile mock-ups, to the Azores and then the United States.

Then, in the hour of victory, General Strong, head of the Western Allies' intelligence service, ordered the scouring of prisoner-of-war camps for Reinhard Gehlen. The head of the Nazi *Abwehr* spy service was found, and offered his us captors a deal to avoid prosecution as a war criminal. Within days Gehlen, his headquarters staff and a mountain of documents detailing German espionage in the Soviet Union were airlifted to an Office of Strategic Services camp in the United States. (The oss was a forerunner of the cia.) A year later Gehlen was back in Germany, working for his American patrons. He was to become the first head of West Germany's secret service, the *Bundesnachrichtendienst* (bnd). His teams of informers, who had given good service to Nazi extermination squads in Byelorussia, the Ukraine, and in all the Nazi-occupied territories, were infiltrated back into Eastern Europe, this time under us patronage. These were straws in the wind; there were many others.

The Cold War had begun even before the *Wehrmacht* had laid down its arms.

9

The Day War Ended

Throughout February and March 1945 the Red Army continued its relentless advance on Berlin. By 13 February, they had entered Budapest. By 29 March, they had crossed the Austrian frontier, and by the 30th, Zhukov and Rokossovskii's armies had taken Danzig and Gdynia. On 4 April, Malinovskii's troops captured Bratislava, the capital of Slovakia. By 13 April, the Russians were in Vienna, and by the 16th they were starting their final offensive on Berlin. On 23 April, Zhukov and Konev's troops broke through the city's defences, and on 2 May, after a week of ferocious street-to-street and house-to-house fighting, during which Hitler and Goebbels committed suicide, Berlin surrendered, and an anonymous Red Army soldier hoisted the Red Flag over the Reichstag.

Stalin, when people used to ask him when the war would end, had often joked, 'Don't worry, Levitan will tell you!' Now Moscow was hanging on Levitan's every pronouncement in a frenzy of impatience for news of the end. The sculptor Manizer was already working on sketches for his new victory monument, depicting the triumph of light over darkness. Igor Moiseev, director of the State Dance Ensemble, was rehearsing a Victory Day folk-music concert. And the ailing Sergei Prokofiev was 'secretly' and against doctor's orders composing in his mind an 'Ode to the End of War'. Even the inexhaustible 'Kukriniksy' trio, from the TASS poster workshop, were dreaming of the day when they could do their last drawings of Hitler and his hangers-on. 'We're so bored of drawing that dog's snout, with his damned moustache and his greasy tuft of hair.'

Ever since Monday 7 May, when General Jodl finally signed the document of Germany's surrender in Rheims, small groups of people had been gathering in Red Square in the drizzling rain waiting for Levitan to speak. At midnight, Keitel, Stumpf and Friedenburg met generals Spaatz, Tedder and Zhukov in Berlin, to sign the final act of unconditional German surrender, and by dusk on Tuesday groups of people in Moscow were reading in the evening papers the TASS dispatch from London with the full text of Dönitz's surrender broadcast to the German people. Germany's armies were surrendering now, but the Reich's death agony continued in heavy fighting with Soviet troops around Prague, and that morning, while Churchill in London was broadcasting the end of the war, Moscow Radio had been putting out a story about a bird and two rabbits for its usual 'Children's Hour' programme. That Tuesday evening there were two salvoes, one for Dresden and one for several Czech towns, and it was only at ten minutes past one on the morning of Wednesday 9 May that Levitan's voice finally brought news of the surrender in Berlin: 'Attention, this is Moscow. Germany has capitulated . . . This day, in honour of the victorious Great Patriotic War, is to be a national holiday, a festival of victory.' Then followed the 'Internationale' and the national anthems of Great Britain, France and the United States.

Suddenly the whole population of Moscow was on the streets, many still in their nightclothes or carrying children, dancing, praying, sobbing, laughing and shouting, 'Victory! Victory!' By early morning, a mass of people was sweeping through the broad streets, below the western walls of the Kremlin, past the university and the Lenin Library to the Moscow River, lining the embankments, packing Red Square each side of St Basil's Church, towards the Theatre Square, and into the dark streets of Chinatown. 'Never has Moscow seen such crowds,' wrote the *Manchester Guardian*,

and never before have the Soviet people shown their wholehearted appreciation of Allied help so freely and emphatically . . . It was enough to look like a foreigner to be kissed, hugged and generally feted. In Red Square, all foreign cars were stopped and their occupants dragged out, embraced, and even tossed in the air . . .

'The biggest turnout in history,' wrote *The Times*. 'A democratic crowd, of generals and soldiers, commissars and workers . . .'

At an impromptu meeting in the foyer of the Moscow Arts Theatre, Khmelev, the director, struggled for words to meet the occasion as he addressed the actors:

What immense joy is ours today! We've been waiting for this so long, but now that it's come, I can't find words to express what we feel. Last night, when the radio played victory marches, I saw a woman through the brightly lit window of a house, dancing and singing to herself . . . Yes, what a joy it is today to live in the Soviet Union!

At a meeting at the Kamerny Theatre, speeches from the director, Tairov, and the youngest actress, Nina Korneeva, were followed by a minute of mourning, then everyone sang the 'Anthem of the USSR'.

During those years of war, people had grown so used to toiling without holidays or time off that work had become for some a conditioned reflex. The artist Pavel Korin stayed on in his studio at the Tretyakov Gallery to finish his triptych on Dmitrii Donskoi. At the TASS poster workshop the 'Kukriniksy'

continued working as usual. But now the longed-for day had come when they could draw their last picture of Hitler – as a beast lying dead on the ground.

In Red Square, strangers danced and embraced, and soldiers were tossed in the air. 'It's over! It's over!' they shouted, laughing. In every street and square, poets, writers, dancers, jazz bands and folk groups performed for the crowds from makeshift stages on lorries. By evening, hundreds of bands and orchestras were playing in the parks and squares as people danced the night away.

That evening, Mrs Churchill (in Moscow to deliver Red Cross aid to Russia) spoke on Moscow Radio:

It is my firm belief that on the friendship and understanding of the British and Russian peoples depends the future of mankind . . . After all the sacrifices and sufferings of the Dark Valley through which we have marched together, we may also in loyal comradeship and sympathy walk in the sunshine of victorious peace . . .

And at 10pm Stalin spoke briefly:

My dear fellow countrymen and women. I am proud today to call you my comrades . . . The age-long struggle of the Slav nations for their existence and independence has ended in victory . . . Your courage has defeated the Nazis. The war is over . . . Now we shall build a Russia fit for heroes and heroines . . .

Then a gigantic salvo of 1000 guns thundered out, rockets blazed, and the skies were lit with the rays of coloured searchlights, which played on a huge red banner held by invisible cords from invisible balloons.

The *Manchester Guardian* called this day 'the greatest moment in this country's history since the Revolution', and it was an extraordinary day, a day in which people were drawn together by shared tenderness, pride and immeasurable grief. They had despaired, toiled, hated, mourned, and stood to the death at the gates of Moscow, Leningrad, Stalingrad, Kiev, wrote Ehrenburg. And now a new life was beginning. But that night, after the dancing had stopped and the rockets and songs had faded out, each person went home to mourn for those they had loved and lost. In the words of the poet Tvardovskii: 'To the thunder of guns, for the first time we bade farewell to all who had died in the war, the way the living say farewell to the dead.'

Welcome home, son.

Bibliography

P. Addison, *The Road to 1945. British Politics and the Second World War*, Cape, London, 1975.

M. Beloff, *The Foreign Policy of Soviet Russia, 1929–41* (2 vols), Royal Institute of Foreign Affairs, London, 1947.

General Belov, *Za Nami Moskva* (Moscow is behind us), Moscow, 1962.

Valentin Berezhkov, *History in the Making* (tr. D. Hagen and B. Jones), Progress, Moscow, 1982.

Earl of Birkenhead, *Halifax. The Life of Lord Halifax*, Hamish Hamilton, London, 1965.

A. Birse, *Memoirs of an Interpreter*, Michael Joseph, London, 1967.

O. B. Borisov, Y. V. Dubinin, I. N. Zemskov et al., *Modern Diplomacy of Capitalist Powers* (tr. not given), Pergamon, Oxford, 1983.

Sir Alexander Cadogan, *Diaries, 1938–45*, Cassell, London, 1971.

Erskine Caldwell, *Moscow Under Fire*, Hutchinson, London, 1942?

H. C. Cassidy, *Moscow Dateline (1941–3)*, Houghton Mifflin, Boston, 1943.

Winston S. Churchill, *The Hinge of Fate*, Bantam, New York, 1962.

W. P. and Zelda K. Coates, *A History of Anglo-Soviet Relations*, Lawrence and Wishart, London, 1944.

Correspondence Between the Chairman of the Council of Ministers of the USSR, the Presidents of the USA and Prime Minister of Great Britain During the Great Patriotic War of 1941–5 (2 vols), Progress, Moscow, 1957.

Joseph E. Davies, *Mission to Moscow*, Gollancz, London, 1942.

Walter Duranty, *The Kremlin and the People*, Hamish Hamilton, London, 1942.

Anthony Eden, *Memoirs* (3 vols), Cassell, London, 1960–65.

Ilya Ehrenburg and Konstantin Simonov, *V odnoi gazete* (In one newspaper) (their articles for *Red Star*), Novosti, Moscow, 1984.

Ilya Ehrenburg, *The War, 1941–45* (vol. 5 of *Men, Years, Life*), (tr. Tatiana Shebunina and Yvonne Kapp), MacGibbon & Kee, London, 1964.

John Erickson, *The Road to Berlin*, Grafton, London, 1985.

John Erickson, *The Road to Stalingrad*, Panther, London, 1985.

Herbert Feis, *Churchill, Roosevelt and Stalin*, Princeton University Press, New Jersey, 1957.

Gabriel Gorodetsky, *Stafford Cripps' Mission to Moscow*, Cambridge University Press, 1984.

Marshal A. A. Grechko, *Liberation Mission of the Soviet Armed Forces in the 2nd World War* (tr. David Fidlon), Progress, Moscow, 1979.

A. A. Gromyko et al. (eds.), *Soviet Peace Efforts on the Eve of World War II* (tr. not given), Progress, Moscow, 1976.

A. A. Gromyko and B. N. Ponomarev, *Soviet Foreign Policy* (vol. 1, 1917–45) (tr. not given), Progress, Moscow, 1981.

A. A. Gromyko, *Lenin and the Soviet Peace Policy* (tr. not given), Progress, Moscow, 1980.

J. M. A. Gwyer, *Grand Strategy* (vol. 3), HMSO, London, 1964.

A. Harriman and E. Abel, *Special Envoy to Churchill and Stalin, 1941–6*, Random House, New York, 1975.

Marilynn Giroux Hitchens, *Germany, Russia and the Balkans*, Columbia University Press, Boulder, Colorado, 1983.

G. Hilger and A. G. Meyer, *The Incompatible Allies. A History of German–Soviet Relations, 1918–41*, Macmillan, New York, 1953.

Maurice Hindus, *Mother Russia*, Collins, London, 1943.

Cordell Hull, *Memoirs* (2 vols), Hodder & Stoughton, London, 1948.

Ellen Jones, *Red Army and Society*, Allen & Unwin, London, 1985.

Philip Jordan, *Russian Glory*, Cresset Press, London, 1942.

S. S. Khromov et al., *Istoriya Moskvy. Kratkii Ocherk* (A brief history of Moscow), Nauka, Moscow, 1978.

I. K. Koblyakov, *USSR. For Peace, Against Aggression, 1933–41* (tr. not given), Progress, Moscow, 1976.

Viktor Koretskii, *Tovarishch Plakat* (Comrade poster), Plakat, Moscow, 1981.

Daniil Kraminov, *The Spring of 1945* (tr. Sergei Chulaki), Novosti, Moscow, 1985.

Evgeny Krieger, *From Moscow to the Prussian Frontier* (tr. not given), Hutchinson, London, 1945.

I. I. V. M. Krivonogova (ed.), *Moskva za nami* (Moscow is behind us), DOSAAF, Moscow, 1966.

Basil Liddell Hart (ed.), *The Soviet Army*, Weidenfeld & Nicolson, London, 1986.

John Loftus, *The Belarus Secret*, Penguin, London 1983.

Ivan Maisky, *Memoirs of a Soviet Ambassador, 1939–43* (tr. A. Rothstein), Hutchinson, London, 1967.

Charles Mee, *Meeting at Potsdam*, André Deutsch, London, 1975.

D. S. Morris, R. H. Haigh, A. R. Peters, *Molotov–Ribbentrop Pact No 6*, Sheffield City Polytechnic, Dept. of Political Studies, 1980.

D. S. Morris, R. H. Haigh, A. R. Peters, *Molotov–Ribbentrop Pact No 13*, Sheffield City Polytechnic, Dept. of Political Studies, 1980.

Narodnoe opolchenie Moskvy (Moscow's Home Guards), Moscow, 1961.

I. Ovsyany, *The Origins of the Second World War* (tr. Arkadii Illarionov), Novosti, Moscow, 1984.

B. Polevoi, *The Final Reckoning* (tr. Janet Butler and Doris Bradbury), Progress, Moscow, 1978.

Arthur U. Pope, *Maxim Litvinoff*, Secker & Warburg, London, 1943.

D. N. Pritt, *Light on Moscow. Soviet Policy Analysed*, Penguin, London, 1939.

D. N. Pritt, *Must the War Spread?*, Penguin, London, 1940.

Elliott Roosevelt, *As He Saw It*, Duell, Sloan & Pearce, New York, 1946.

Russians Tell the Story (war sketches from *Soviet War News*), Hutchinson, London, 1944.

Vladimir Sevruk (ed.), *Moscow–Stalingrad, 1941–2* (English editor, Bryan Bean), Progress, Moscow, 1974.

Henry Sigerist, *Medicine and Health in the Soviet Union*, Citadel Press, New York, 1947.

Vilnis Sipols, *Diplomatic Battles Before World War II* (tr. Lev Bobrov), Progress, Moscow, 1979.

Vilnis Sipols, *The Road to Great Victory: Soviet Diplomacy 1941–45* (tr. Lev Bobrov), Progress, Moscow, 1984.

E. Sokolova (ed.), *Bitva za Moskvu* (The Battle of Moscow), Moskovskii Rabochii, Moscow, 1966.

Soviet War News Weekly, London, 1942–5.

William Taubman, *Stalin's American Policy*, Norton, New York, 1982.

Tehran, Yalta and Potsdam Conferences, Progress, Moscow, 1969.

T. J. Uldrichs, *Diplomacy and Ideology*, Sage, New York, 1979.

Max Werner, *The Great Offensive* (tr. H. & R. Norden), Gollancz, London, 1943.

Alexander Werth, *Moscow 1941*, Hamish Hamilton, London, 1942.

Alexander Werth, *The Year of Stalingrad*, Hamish Hamilton, London, 1946.

Alexander Werth, *Russia at War*, Barrie and Rockliffe, London, 1964.

Joseph G. Whelan, *Soviet Diplomacy and Negotiating Behaviour*, Bowker, London, 1983.

G. K. Zhukov, *Vospominaniya i razmyshleniya* (3 vols) (Memories and reflections), Novosti, Moscow, 1974.

K. Zilliacus, *I Choose Peace*, Penguin, London, 1949.

Index